Support Coach

7 TARGET Reading Comprehension

Support Coach, Target: Reading Comprehension, First Edition, Grade 7
555NASE   ISBN-13: 978-1-62928-595-5

Triumph Learning® 136 Madison Avenue, 7th Floor, New York, NY 10016

Printed in the United States of America.   10 9 8 7 6 5 4 3 2 1

Contents

Fiction

Nonfiction

Tools

Graphic Organizers and Close Reading Worksheets

Lesson 1
Traditional Literature

Traditional literature is made up of stories that have been handed down from one generation to the next. The stories may contain animal characters who talk and act like humans, foolish people or animals who are taught important lessons, or explanations for natural events like earthquakes or lightning. Every civilization has its own form of traditional literature, and the stories can be broken down into specific categories. **Folktales** are timeless and placeless stories that can be reworked slightly to fit a specific culture's needs. They involve universal human desires, follies, and struggles, such as the vanity of kings or tall tales about fantastic characters. **Myths** tell legendary stories of heroes and gods, while **fables** teach a lesson, usually using animal characters who speak and behave like humans. What kind of story do you think this storyteller is telling?

Skills Focus

The Boy Who Dreamed Too Much

Draw and Support Inferences   Point of View

The Blue Jackal

Summarize   Figurative Language

Practice the Skill

Draw and Support Inferences

When you draw an **inference**, you figure out something the writer implies but does not state directly. You draw the inference by reading what the writer says, looking for clues in the text, and using your own knowledge of how things work and how people often behave. In other words, you come to understand something the author means to convey, even though he or she does not state it directly.

The clues you find while reading are the textual evidence that supports your inference. For instance, if a character frowns, you might infer that she is unhappy about something, although the text doesn't specifically say that she is. The frown is your clue—the textual evidence that supports your inference. Also, you know from your own experience that someone who is frowning is usually unhappy or upset. If you are reading a story or drama and a character enters the room laughing, you don't need the author to tell you that the character is happy. You can infer it for yourself.

These examples are fairly easy. Sometimes inferences can be much more subtle, and you may infer incorrectly at first. That's OK. Just keep reading and know that new information and plot events may make you infer something new.

Try It Read the paragraph below.

> The princess shivered as she hid in the small cave. She knew the huntsman and his dogs were close at hand. She could hear their baying grow louder and louder. As she waited to be discovered, she wept silently and despaired of ever seeing her family again.

> Discuss > **What can you infer about the scene? Why is the princess shivering? How is she feeling? Underline the textual evidence that supports your inference. Then, circle details that suggest *why* she is feeling the way she is. What is the reason?**

As you read, complete the Draw and Support Inferences Chart on page 279.

Practice the Skill

Narrative point of view is the way a story is told. Authors usually tell a story in the first or third person. In a story told from the **first-person** point of view, the narrator is a story character who tells what happens using the pronouns *I*, *me*, *us*, or *we*. When an author uses **third-person** point of view, the story is told by an outside narrator who uses the pronouns *he*, *she*, or *they* to describe events.

Point of view also refers to the attitudes, perspectives, and outlooks different characters have in a story. Each character has a unique point of view that the author has to carefully develop, and characters' perspectives very often change over the course of a story. By paying close attention to what characters say and do and how others react to them, you identify their particular points of view.

Try It Read the beginning of a short story.

> Kate threw her pom-poms angrily onto the bed. "Everybody leave me alone!" she roared, slamming her bedroom door. The first day of cheerleading tryouts had been miserable. Every bone in her body ached, and she could still hear the chattering and giggling of the older girls who knew they'd make the squad. *What's the point*, Kate fumed. *It's all a big popularity contest anyway, it's all rigged—*
>
> Her phone rang. Oh, no! It was Aunt Patty calling! She'd been a cheerleader and had encouraged Kate to try out for the squad, insisting that girls were judged solely for their talent. How could she tell Aunt Patty that she planned to quit the tryouts even if she made it to the next round?

> Discuss

From what point of view is the story being told? Circle words in the first paragraph that show you. What is Kate's outlook regarding cheerleading? What is Aunt Patty's? What do you imagine happening as this story continues that could change Kate's point of view? Keep in mind that her attitude could change for better or worse.

As you read, record your answers to questions about point of view and perspective on the Close Reading Worksheet on page 280.

Purpose for Reading
Read along with your teacher. Each time, read for a different purpose.

First Read — Focus on drawing and supporting inferences.

Second Read — Focus on analyzing point of view.

Third Read — Focus on evaluating the story critically.

The Boy Who Dreamed Too Much

What can you infer about how Fritz feels about chopping firewood? Underline textual evidence that supports your inference. Write your answer on the **Draw and Support Inferences Chart**.

From what point of view is the story told? How can you tell? Circle point-of-view clues in the first paragraph.

1   Outside a small, snow-covered village, a boy called Fritz lived with his mother. The boy's father had died years before, and now the family was **destitute**. Each day, Fritz looked with longing as the village children went to school while he chopped firewood and carried water for his mother, who took in sewing from the wealthy ladies in the village. She barely made enough money to buy eggs and flour for their bread, and she had to sew by firelight because candles were too expensive.

2   "Someday," said Fritz, "I will make enough money so that Mother can live a life of ease, and I will never have to chop wood or carry water. It will be a good life."

3   One winter's day while Fritz was in the woods, he heard a sound like a mewling cat coming from a small cave. He peeked in and discovered a lamb that had been abandoned by its mother. Fritz wrapped the lamb in his coat and carried it home to his mother.

4   "Can I keep it please, Mother? I'll take good care of it, and in the summer, I'll take it out to graze every day."

5   So, even though they barely had enough food for themselves, Fritz's mother said he could keep the lamb.

6   As the months went by, the weather got warmer and spring slowly arrived. The lamb thrived under Fritz's care and grew to be a healthy sheep. He became very fond of it. Each day it accompanied him as he searched the forest for firewood, and it slept in a shed behind the house at night.

7   The village children would see Fritz traveling around the woods with his sheep and tease him mercilessly.

8   "Look at Fritz! Not enough money to go to school, but he has a pet sheep!" and "Don't you know you should kill the sheep and let your mother make stew? Then you'd have something more to eat than dry bread!"

9   But Fritz ignored them and held his head high as he walked with his sheep behind him.

10 During the summer months, the days were long, and Fritz didn't have to spend hours gathering wood for his mother. This gave him **ample** time to wander the countryside with his sheep following. Some days, Fritz would sit in a sunny spot and daydream his favorite dreams—all about what he would do when he was wealthy.

11 "I know," he said to himself. "Next March, when it is shearing time, I'll take my sheep into town and sell the wool, and with that money, I'll buy a second sheep. Then, in a year, I'll have even more wool to sell. Soon Mother and I will be able to move into a nice house and hire servants to take care of us."

12 Through the summer, Fritz spent his days calculating how much wool his sheep had and how much money he would make when she was sheared, and then he planned how he would spend all of his money. Each day, he would inspect the sheep's wool, removing any sticks or twigs that could damage it.

13 On particularly nice afternoons, he would get so caught up in his planning and dreaming that he would lose track of the time, and he often returned home after the sun had set.

What can you infer from Fritz's special care of the sheep? <u>Underline</u> textual evidence that supports your inference, and record your answer on the **Draw and Support Inferences Chart**.

What is a quality that Fritz displays that is shared the world over and makes this a folktale?

From her scolding, what can you infer about what Fritz's mother is afraid of? Underline textual evidence that supports your inference. Record your answer on the **Draw and Support Inferences Chart**.

Why is the wool from other sheep so much less nice than that from Fritz's sheep?

14   "Oh, Fritz! You daydream too much," his mother scolded. "It is better to focus on what you have here and now rather than building imaginary castles in the sky. Are you taking proper care of your sheep?"

15   "Of course, Mother," replied Fritz. "I love my sheep and take great care of her. Once we get through the winter, I'll take her to town for shearing. I'll sell her wool and get enough to buy another sheep and something nice for you."

16   The winter slowly crept in, and as the days grew shorter, Fritz once again had to spend most of his time chopping wood to warm their cabin—but he kept himself warm with dreams of his coming riches.

17   As the months passed, the sheep's wool grew longer and thicker. Fritz inspected it every day for briars and was proud of how fluffy and clean the wool was, and he was sure that the wool would fetch a good price at market.

18   Soon enough, it was time to take the sheep to town for shearing. When Fritz arrived, the other men selling wool complimented him on the quality of his sheep's coat, saying it was the cleanest, softest wool they had ever seen. All of Fritz's hours of hard work **diligently** removing briars and twigs had paid off.

19   As Fritz predicted, the wool fetched enough money for him to pay a shepherd in advance for a lamb, which would be born in a few weeks. He also had money left over to buy his mother a warm shawl and some cake.

20   He walked home, his sheep still following, his head held high with pride.

21   "Look, Mother. I sold the sheep's wool and earned enough money to buy a lamb in a few weeks, and I got you a pretty shawl and cake for our dinner. Soon we will live in a big house, and I'll be the richest man in town."

What is Fritz's mother's point of view about life? How do her behavior and dialogue reveal her point of view about life? Circle words on this page that show the mother's point of view.

22   Fritz's mother was pleased, but she shook her head knowingly. "It is all well and good to have dreams, Fritz, but you must not forget to take care of what you have right now. People like us will never be rich, you know."

23   A few weeks later, when spring arrived, Fritz collected his new lamb from the shepherd. The village children laughed even harder when they saw Fritz being followed on his daily rounds by two sheep, but he kept his head held high.

24   During the summer months, Fritz turned the two sheep loose to graze in the fields, and he spent even more time dreaming of the riches their wool would bring him.

25   "Soon I will have a whole flock of sheep, and I will be able to hire someone to watch them for me."

26   Day after day, Fritz returned from the fields talking endlessly as he **regaled** his mother with details of how he was going to spend his future wealth. She just shook her head and went about her housekeeping, yet Fritz was so caught up reciting his grand plans that he didn't even notice that she wasn't listening.

27   One beautiful summer afternoon, after inspecting the sheeps' wool for twigs and briars as usual, Fritz fell to daydreaming about his coming wealth. The day was so nice and the sun so warm that Fritz soon fell asleep to dreams of a fine house and great piles of firewood— chopped by someone else, of course. The sheep grazed contentedly nearby. When he woke with a start, the sun had already set, so he quickly gathered the sheep and started for home.

28   As they walked through the forest, Fritz heard animals close by, breathing heavily and growling. He urged the sheep to walk faster, but the animals gained on them, and he finally saw that they were being followed by a pack of wolves.

What is the effect of the wolf attack on Fritz's point of view regarding his future?

Why is Fritz more successful with his chickens than he was with his sheep?

Identify

What universal lesson about life does this story teach?

29   Fritz turned and ran in terror, and the wolves dragged the sheep off into the bushes.

30   He staggered home, sobbing and crying in despair.

31   "Mother! I fell asleep, and we were overtaken by wolves in the forest, and they killed both of my sheep. My plans for riches are all gone!"

32   Fritz's mother shook her head, but she smiled. "I warned you this would happen. You were so busy dreaming about what you didn't have yet that you didn't take care of what you had."

33   Fritz learned his lesson.

34   The next spring, he used his few remaining cents to buy a chicken. It quickly started laying eggs, which he sold to women in the village, and soon, he earned enough money to buy more chickens. He took very good care of his flock, and they produced dozens of eggs each week for him to sell.

35   Fritz never again got caught up in daydreams about wealth and grand houses, but through careful work and saving, he was able to buy more food for himself and his mother and candles to light their house. They weren't rich, but they were happy.

Vocabulary: Context Clues

In your reading, you will often come across unfamiliar words. **Context clues** are hints within the sentence or paragraph that can help you understand the definition of an unknown word. One type of context clue is **synonym**. An author sometimes includes words that mean about the same thing as the unfamiliar word. Look at this example: "The dancers performed with élan, grace, and elegance." If you don't know what *élan* means, the words *grace* and *elegance* offer clues.

Try It Read the excerpt from the selection.

> The boy's father had died years before, and now the family was **destitute**. Each day, Fritz looked with longing as the village children went to school while he chopped firewood and carried water for his mother, who took in sewing from the wealthy ladies in the village. She barely made enough money to buys eggs and flour for their bread, and she had to sew by firelight because candles were too expensive.

Discuss **Look for words that could give you clues to what *destitute* means. What context clues provide information about the word?**

Read the sentences from the selection that contain the following words. Record the words in the selection that helped you determine the meaning of each word, and then use it in a new sentence.

1. **ample,** p. 9 _____

_____

2. **diligently,** p. 10 _____

_____

3. **regaled,** p. 11 _____

_____

Practice the Skill

When you **summarize** a story, you take the main ideas and most important details of the plot, characters, and setting and put them in your own words. A summary briefly retells what is in a story without changing any of the important details of the characters, setting, and plot. Similarly, a summary of a nonfiction selection should only retell the most important ideas, facts, or opinions the author has included.

Before you summarize a text, you should read the whole selection. Then think about the main message or theme of the story and all the important details and scenes that support it. A summary is shorter than the original story but should still include all the major details and plot points. It should not include minor details, such as a character's eye color, or any opinions, thoughts, or outside knowledge you may have about the ideas presented.

Try It Read the paragraph below.

> When the old king died, the residents of his kingdom mourned deeply. Some people cut their hair to express their grief. They had flourished under his rule, with everyone having enough to eat. But they knew that things would be different under the rule of the king's son. He was spoiled and impatient and loved fine things and had little interest in governing. Instead, he traveled about collecting fine silks and exotic animals. He was known to spend days on end trying to teach his parrots to talk. They all feared that he would not be a good leader.

> Discuss

What is the paragraph mainly about? What are the important supporting details? How would you summarize it in your own words? What would you leave out? Put a box around any details that aren't important enough to be included in a summary.

As you read, complete the Summarizing Chart on page 281.

Practice the Skill

Second Read Figurative Language

Using **figurative language** is a way for authors to describe something by comparing it to another thing. Comparisons made using figurative language are not meant to be taken literally. Two of the most common types of comparisons are simile and metaphor. A **simile** makes a comparison between two unlike things using the word *like* or *as*, such as *Her manicured nails glistened like wet ice cubes*. A **metaphor** compares two unlike things without using *like* or *as*; for example, *My love is a rose*. Similes and metaphors can be used in an exaggerated way for humorous effect: *The guy has a chin like an ironing board*.

Personification is another type of figurative language, in which an author assigns human attributes and characteristics to nonhuman things, often to aspects of the natural world; for example, *The mountain looked down at us, sneering at our pathetic efforts*. Mountains don't sneer, nor do they care at all about human efforts, but at times, it might feel to us as though they do. Personification can also be used for comedic effect. *When I command her to sit, my dog just rolls her eyes at me*.

Try It Read the paragraph below.

> The sun crept over the mountains like a ghost, illuminating the forest. Marilyn smiled as she watched the fawns graze next to their mothers, miniature versions of the adults. All around her the birdsong was a symphony. This was her favorite time of year, when everything seemed new and promising, like a rosebud about to open.

Discuss Look for examples of figurative language. Underline examples of personification. Box any metaphors, and circle any similes. Note that a complex figurative expression can be more than one type of comparison. Do you see an example here?

As you read, record your answers to questions about figurative language on the Close Reading Worksheet on page 282.

Purpose for Reading
Read along with your teacher. Each time, read for a different purpose.

First Read   Focus on summarizing.

Second Read   Focus on figurative language.

Third Read   Focus on evaluating the selection critically.

The Blue Jackal

What important details about the jackal's character on this page would you include in a summary? Record your summary on the **Summarizing Chart**.

Where does the author use personification on this page?

1   Near a small village in India was a jungle filled with all kinds of animals. They lived in fear of the mighty lion, who ruled over them all.

2   One of the animals in the jungle was a sneaky, lazy jackal named Kakudruma. Instead of hunting with the other members of his pack, Kakudruma preferred to slink into the village and steal food from the humans' gardens and homes and pick through their garbage piles.

3   He knew it was dangerous to go into the village, for if the humans caught him in their gardens, they would pelt him with rocks. Each time he went into the village, he also had to avoid the pack of dogs that lived there, for if they spotted him sneaking among the houses like a thief, they would attack and drive him from the village.

4   But Kakudruma was just too lazy to hunt for himself, and he loved human food too much, so he returned to the village again and again, willing to risk being caught. He especially loved baking day, when the women of the village set their breads and pies on the windowsills to cool. He would snatch a loaf and run into the jungle, hiding in the bushes while he gobbled it down.

5   All in all, Kakudruma was happy, for he had plenty of food, and he didn't have to spend tiresome hours hunting for prey.

6   One bright afternoon, while the rest of the jackals were out hunting together, Kakudruma strolled to the village. He was content—the sun was smiling down on the world, and it was baking day—but suddenly, the village dogs spotted him, started howling, and set off after him.

7   Terrified, Kakudruma darted into the nearest house, the house that belonged to the village cloth maker and was filled with tubs of brilliant dyes in every color of the rainbow.

8   In a panic, Kakudruma didn't look where he was going, and—*splash!*—he landed in a tub of blue dye. He climbed out of the tub, shook himself, and then looked in the cloth maker's mirror. To his surprise, his fur was as blue as the sky above.

On the **Summarizing Chart**, record a summary of what has happened in the story so far.

9   "Come out here, you **scoundrel**," barked the lead dog from outside. "We know you're in there!"

10   Kakudruma thought about what the dogs were likely to do to him, sighed, and slowly walked out of the house, for he knew they wouldn't go away until he came out.

There are two similies on this page. Underline them.

11   As he emerged, the village dogs stared at Kakudruma in shock. They had never seen such a brilliant blue creature before and, howling in fear, they turned and ran away.

How could Kakudruma's plan fail?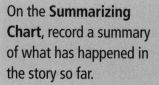

12   It took a moment for Kakudruma to realize what had happened, but when he did, he quickly came up with a plan.

13   "If the dogs didn't recognize me," he said to himself, "maybe no one else will either. I can go into the jungle and **profess** to be a king. I can make all the other animals serve me! I'll never have to hunt or steal my own food again."

14   With that, Kakudruma trotted off into the forest, his blue fur shining in the sun like a sapphire.

15   When Kakudruma reached the watering hole where all the animals gathered, the animals gasped in awe. He sat on top of a boulder, in a patch of sunlight, and did his best to look regal and commanding.

16   The lion, king of the beasts, stepped forward, asking, "Who are you, and why are you here?

17   "I have been sent by Lord Seepka's spirit to rule the jungle. You must all obey me and do exactly as I wish." Lord Seepka was an ancient king of the jungle, **revered** by all the animals.

18   The animals looked at each other in surprise.

The Blue Jackal   **17**

In a single sentence, explain what Kakudruma is afraid of and why. Record your summary on the **Summarizing Chart**.

Underline an example of personification on this page. What does it mean?

19   "But I have always been ruler of the jungle," said the lion, "and my father and my father's father and his father before him back to Lord Seepka's time. Why should we believe that you are the new ruler and that we must obey you?"

20   "Well, have you ever seen an animal like me before, Lion?" asked Kakudruma. "Look at my shining fur and brilliant color. Any fool can see that I have been sent by Lord Seepka to rule you. Furthermore, if you don't obey me, Lord Seepka said he'll be very angry and will destroy the jungle and all of you with it."

21   The trees in the jungle shook their branches in terror at this statement. There was a great stir and chattering among the animals. When they finally quieted down, the lion slowly bowed his head, and all the other animals did the same.

22   From that day on, the blue jackal lived a life of complete laziness, commanding the animals to hunt for him and steal food for him every day.

23   Only one thing worried Kakudruma. He feared that if the other jackals in the jungle saw him, they would recognize him despite his blue fur. If that happened, the animals would see who he truly was and drive him from the jungle.

24   Being lazy, Kakudruma got tired of ruling all of the animals by himself. He decided he needed help, so he made the lion his adviser and the tiger his chamberlain.[1] He named the wolf as the head of security and gave him one job only.

25   "You must keep all the jackals out of the jungle," said Kakudruma. "They have displeased Lord Seepka and my royal self, and they must be banned. If they come near the jungle, you must drive them away. If you don't, Lord Seepka will be angry."

26   And so the months passed. Kakudruma grew fat from all the food the other animals provided, and he became even more lazy than he had been before he crowned himself king. He spent most of his days napping in the sun outside his den while all the other animals hunted for him.

[1]**chamberlain** a chief or administrator in the household of a ruler

27　　In time, the other animals, especially the lion and tiger, grumbled about having to hunt for Kakudruma every day. "I am growing thin and weak, like a newborn kitten," growled the lion, "for after the king eats his fill, there's not enough left for us to eat."

28　　"But what can we do?" asked the tiger. "If we don't hunt for the king, he will tell Lord Seepka, who will be displeased."

29　　The wolf was the only animal who was happy because he spent his days patrolling the edge of the jungle, puffed up with pride at his important job of warding off any jackals who dared approach.

30　　One day, the jackals decided to stand up to the wolf and dared to enter the jungle, which looked as angry as the wolf himself.

31　　"You are not allowed here," snarled the wolf. "You must get back, and if you come in, the king will be displeased, and he will tell Lord Seepka you have disobeyed his orders, and Lord Seepka will destroy the jungle and all the animals in it."

32　　"Please let us come back," begged the lead jackal. "We miss living in our snug dens, and we miss all of our friends."

33　　The wolf bared his fangs, growled, and snapped at the jackals. In fear and confusion, the jackals all began to howl together, making a frightful noise, because there is nothing jackals like more than howling together.

34　　Kakudruma, sitting in front of his den with the lion and tiger, heard the **commotion** and got up to listen, and when he heard the howling, Kakudruma couldn't help himself—he joined in the chorus of howling, just like a regular jackal.

35　　The lion and tiger stared in shock. The howling revealed to them that Kakudruma was actually a jackal. All of the animals in the jungle were furious at Kakudruma for tricking them.

Summarize the important plot points on this page. Record your answer on the **Summarizing Chart**.

Underline the simile in paragraph 27. What does it mean?

The Blue Jackal　19

In your own words, provide a brief summary of "The Blue Jackal" in the box at the bottom of your **Summarizing Chart**.

<u>Underline</u> the metaphor in paragraph 40. What does it mean? ✎

Why did the jackal's trick anger the other animals so much? ✎

Identify

Identify the things in and about this story that make it a fable. ✎

36   The wolf, followed by the pack of jackals, came running to investigate. When he realized that he had been duped along with all the other animals, the wolf started snarling and snapping at Kakudruma, and the lion, tiger, and other jackals were right behind him, roaring and howling in anger.

37   "Leave this jungle at once," roared the lion, "and don't ever come back. If we catch you here, we will tear you to pieces."

38   All of the animals chased Kakudruma through the jungle to the edge of the river, and Kakudruma had no choice but to jump into the water to escape. As he swam across, the blue dye in his fur washed away, and he was once again simply a normal jackal.

39   From that day forward, Kakudruma was banned from the jungle. He once again had to hunt for himself and sneak into the village to get food. Every time he went to the village, he had to be sure to avoid the dogs, because they had heard about his trick and were angry that they had been fooled, too. Each time they caught him in the village, they would torment Kakudruma and chase him away.

40   Kakudruma spent the rest of his life living alone on the edge of the jungle. He became a mere shadow. At night, he would hear the howling of the other jackals and cry himself to sleep, for even more than being king, he missed the company of the other animals he had enjoyed in the old days.

Vocabulary: Using a Thesaurus

A **thesaurus** is a printed or digital list of words, in alphabetical order, along with their synonyms, or words that have the same or nearly the same meaning. Antonyms, or words with opposite meanings, are also listed in some entries. When context clues aren't enough, you can usually figure out the meaning of an unfamiliar word by looking at its antonyms and synonyms. Thesauruses are especially handy when you are writing and searching for the perfect word.

Try It Read this sentence from "The Blue Jackal."

"Come out here, you **scoundrel**," barked the lead dog from outside.

Look at this entry for the word *scoundrel* in a thesaurus.

scoundrel *noun.* a wicked, evil, or mean person <Some *scoundrel* stole her purse.> **Synonyms** crook, evildoer, fiend, rapscallion, rascal, rogue, villain, wretch **Near Antonyms** angel, hero, innocent, saint

> Discuss

Which synonyms are closest to the meaning of *scoundrel* as it is used in the sentence from the selection?

Each of the words below appears in the text. Use a thesaurus to look up the word and write three synonyms. Then write your own definition for the word.

1. **commotion**, p. 19 _____

_____

2. **profess**, p. 17 _____

_____

3. **revered**, p. 17 _____

_____

Respond to Text: Analyze Points of View

"The Blue Jackal" is written from the third-person point of view by a narrator who is outside the story. The jackal is the main character, and the author tells what happens mainly from the jackal's point of view. However, the author also reveals the outlook and points of view of other characters. As the story unfolds, the reader sees the feelings, perspectives, and actions of several minor characters in addition to those of the main character. Through noticing what different characters say and do and how others react to them, the reader perceives their points of view.

Try It Think about the different characters in the story, and analyze how the author develops their points of view.

> Discuss

What do the different animals feel about what the jackal does? What changes do various characters undergo as a result of the jackal's actions? How do their points of view change during the course of the story? How does the jackal's point of view change from the beginning to the middle to the end of the story?

On Your Own There are several characters in this story— Kakudruma, the lion, the pack of dogs, the tiger, the wolf, and the pack of jackals. Write a paragraph analyzing how the author develops and contrasts the points of view and outlooks of the jackal and one other character in the story. Examine how the character's point of view contrasts with the jackal's during the course of the story. Use the guide on the next page to help you write your response. Then write your paragraph on a separate sheet of paper.

Checklist for a Good Response

A good paragraph

✔ begins with a strong topic sentence.

✔ includes details about the main character's feelings and actions.

✔ includes details about one other character's feelings and reactions.

✔ includes details about the way the characters' points of view change in the story.

✔ ends with a conclusion that sums up the main points.

My Analysis of the Characters' Points of View

1. **Topic Sentence:** In your first sentence, tell the reader which character's point of view you are analyzing and contrasting with that of the jackal.

   I am analyzing the points of view of the jackal and _____.

2. **Detail Sentences:** The sentences of your paragraph should include details about the characters' points of view at each major point in the story.

   Detail Sentence 1: At the beginning of the story, the point of view of

   the jackal is _____, and the point of view of

   _____ is _____.

   Detail Sentence 2: When the jackal turns blue and takes over ruling the

   jungle, _____.

   Detail Sentence 3: After the jackal has ruled for a while, the

   _____.

   Detail Sentence 4: When the jackal is exposed as a fraud, the _____

   _____.

3. **Concluding Sentence:** Write a concluding sentence that sums up how the author develops the points of view of the jackal and the other character.

   _____

   _____

   _____

On a separate sheet of paper, write your paragraph.

Read on Your Own

Read the myth independently three times, using the skills you have learned. Then answer the Comprehension Check questions.

First Read	Practice the first-read skills you learned in this lesson.
Second Read	Practice the second-read skills you learned in this lesson.
Third Read	Think critically about the selection.

Strife

Draw and Support Inferences What textual evidence leads you to infer that Agelus is a kind man? Underline them. The first one has been done for you.

Point of View Circle the words in the text that tell you this story is told in the third person.

1   In the times when the Greek gods and goddesses lived on Mount Olympus and mingled with mortals on Earth, King Priam and Queen Hecuba of Troy were awaiting the birth of their first child.

2   One night, Queen Hecuba woke up screaming in terror. "I dreamed that our child was a boy and that he had set fire to the whole city of Troy. Everyone died in the flames," she sobbed.

3   King Priam told his brother, who was a seer,[1] about his wife's dream and asked for advice. His brother said, "The child will bring the destruction of Troy and the death of all its citizens. He must not be allowed to live, so as soon as he is born, have him killed."

4   King Priam and Queen Hecuba wept, but when the baby was born, they called the herdsman Agelus. "Take this baby to Mount Ida and leave him to die," they said. "He won't survive the cold, and **scavengers** will eat his body. He must not live to destroy Troy."

5   With a heavy heart, Agelus departed for Mount Ida with the infant. Halfway up the mountain, he placed the baby on a rock. Five days later, Agelus returned to make sure the infant was dead, but to his surprise, the baby was alive and looking at him with bright blue eyes.

6   "Well, look at you!" exclaimed Agelus in wonder. "I suppose if you've survived this long on your own, you aren't meant to die yet. I can't take you back to your parents, so I'll raise you as my son." Agelus did just that, naming the boy Paris. As he grew up, Paris became known throughout the land for his beauty, wit, and wisdom. It was obvious to everyone that he was of noble birth, and before long, his parents acknowledged him again as their son, despite the dire prophecy.

[1] **seer** someone who can read the future

7   Twenty years later, all of the Greek gods and goddesses were invited to a big wedding on Mount Pelion, where Peleus, a Greek hero, and Thetis, a sea goddess, were getting married. It was going to be a very grand party, and everyone was excited.

8   Unfortunately, one goddess had been left off the guest list. Eris, the goddess of strife, discord, and rivalry, was not invited. She was the least popular of all the gods and goddesses because she grew larger and stronger when people were unhappy.

9   When Eris complained to Hera, queen of the gods, about the snub, Hera said, "No one wants you there because you take delight in causing problems. Your favorite thing is to go onto battlefields and make soldiers miserable, and we don't want you at the wedding. You thrive on anger and bloodshed."

10   "Do you not know who I am?" Eris shrieked in response. "I am a goddess! It is my **birthright** to be at this wedding!"

11   "I don't care about your birthright," snapped Hera. "If you come to this wedding, you will only cause trouble, so you are not invited, and that is final."

12   Eris was infuriated at Hera's refusal to invite her and vowed revenge. "They thought I would cause trouble as a guest? Wait until they see the trouble I cause when I'm *not* invited."

13   Eris traveled to Mount Olympus, where she stole a golden apple from the tree of Hesperides. The tree had been given to Hera as a wedding present, and she treasured its beautiful fruit.

14   Once Eris had the apple, she inscribed "For the Fairest" on it and laughed. "Now let's see what happens," she sneered as she set off to crash the wedding on Mount Pelion.

Summarize Think about how you would summarize why Eris was left off the guest list.

Critical Thinking Was Eris justified in plotting revenge on Hera?

Figurative Language
Box the simile on this page.

Figurative Language
Circle the example of personification on this page.

Critical Thinking Why are the three goddesses not more suspicious of an apple coming from Eris?

15   When she arrived at the wedding, guards turned Eris away because she hadn't been invited, but she pushed past them, regally announcing that she was just there to deliver a present.

16   "Here is my contribution to the wedding party," she yelled to the crowd. "See how you like this!" And with that, she tossed the golden apple into the crowd. It landed at the feet of the three most powerful goddesses, Hera, Athena, and Aphrodite.

17   The crowd fell silent as Hera handed the apple to Zeus and said, "It says 'For the Fairest.' You must decide which of us that is." But Zeus knew better than to judge a beauty competition among these three powerful goddesses. He announced he would find an impartial judge, and then he sent a messenger to Mount Ida to ask Paris if he would make the decision, for Paris had recently judged another contest and was known far and wide for being a fair and honest judge. Paris sent back word that he would judge the contest.

18   All of the wedding guests agreed to go home for the night and gather the next morning on Mount Ida. When they arrived, Paris was there, standing ready to judge. All nature was still, seeming to hold its breath as it awaited Paris's judgment.

19   Zeus handed Paris the golden apple and said, "Eris gave this apple, as golden as the morning sun, to the fairest of the goddesses. But we cannot agree on who that is. You must judge Hera, Athena, and Aphrodite and decide."

20   Hera stepped up first. As she slowly turned in front of Paris, she offered him great things if he selected her as the fairest. "If you choose me," she purred, "I will make you ruler of the most powerful kingdom on Earth."

21   Athena presented herself next for judgment, and not to be outdone by Hera, she also offered Paris a reward for picking her. "When you name me as the fairest, I will give you the three most precious gifts a man can have: victory in all battles, glory, and wisdom."

22   Aphrodite went last. She knew she had to come up with something more enticing than what the other two goddesses had offered, so after thinking a minute, she stood before Paris. She smiled at him, her smile a blinding sunburst, and said, "If you award the apple to me, my darling Paris, I will win you the love of the most beautiful woman in the world, Queen Helen of Sparta."

Figurative Language
Underline the metaphor in paragraph 22.

23   Paris stepped away from the crowd to think for a few minutes. The three goddesses looked on nervously as he made up his mind.

24   "It is my judgment," he said, "that the golden apple rightfully belongs to Aphrodite. She is the fairest of all the goddesses."

25   Furious, Hera and Athena stomped off, returning to Mount Olympus to pout and make plans for mischief.

26   Aphrodite smiled her blazing smile at Paris again, who handed her the apple. "You have made the right choice, my beautiful young man, but there is one catch. Queen Helen of Sparta may be the most beautiful woman on Earth, but she is also married to King Menelaus. You are going to have to win her from her husband."

27   The next morning, Aphrodite transported Paris to the gates of Sparta, where she requested an audience with the king. When they were shown in, Aphrodite introduced Paris to the king and queen as Paris, the son of the king of Troy, his rightful title.

28   The king and queen invited Paris to stay at the palace as a royal guest and threw night after night of parties for him. Paris was so dazzled by Helen's beauty that he didn't say much to her, but after three nights of watching her from across the room, Paris presented himself and declared his love for Helen. King Menelaus was very angry and ordered Paris to leave the palace at dawn.

Summarize Think about how you would summarize the cause of the Trojan War.

Critical Thinking *Strife* means "conflict." Is it a good title for this myth?

29   Before he left, Paris crept into Helen's bedchamber, wrapped her in a blanket, and carried her out of the palace. From there, he took her straight to his parents' palace at Troy.

30   When King Menelaus discovered that his wife had been kidnapped, he roared with fury and scattered messengers like birds throughout the land. "If you ever loved Helen, you must come to her defense. She has been stolen from me, and her honor is at stake!"

31   From all around, Helen's former suitors responded, sending armies of men to surround the walls of Troy. King Menelaus offered to call back the armies if Paris would return Helen, but, proudly, Paris refused.

32   Thus began the ten years of the Trojan War, the longest and most famous in all history—and all because one goddess didn't get invited to a wedding.

✅ Comprehension Check

1. What can you infer about King Priam and Queen Hecuba based on their actions?

    _____

    _____

2. Summarize why Eris was left off the guest list.

    _____

    _____

    _____

3. Look at this thesaurus entry for the word *birthright*.

    birthright *noun.*
    Synonyms *claim, inheritance, due*

    Which of these three synonyms is closest to the meaning of *birthright* as it is used in the selection? Why?

    _____

    _____

4. Summarize what happens while Paris is staying at the palace of King Menelaus.

    _____

    _____

5. Read this sentence from the selection.

   Take this baby to Mount Ida and leave him to die. . . . He won't survive the cold, and scavengers will eat his body.

   What context clues in the sentence help you to understand the meaning of *scavengers*?

   _____

   _____

6. What is Hera's point of view on the judgment of Paris?

   _____

   _____

   _____

7. On the last page of the selection, find an example of a simile. What does it mean?

   _____

   _____

8. What can you infer about King Menelaus from the message he sends across the land after Helen is kidnapped?

   _____

   _____

   _____

Historical Fiction

Historical fiction stories and novels are set in specific and familiar time periods. The characters and events may be ones that actually existed, or they may be created entirely from the author's imagination. Either way, historical fiction uses details of the time period to provide a realistic, engaging setting for the story. Look at this photo of a New York City street around 1900. What kind of story might someone tell about the time period shown?

Skills Focus

The Collector

| Narrative Point of View | Determine Theme |

The Summer Things Fell Apart / Letter from Neshoba County Jail

| Compare and Contrast | Historical Fiction |

Practice the Skill

Looking at the **narrative point of view** of a story answers the question *Who is telling the story*? There are different points of view, but all of them represent the vantage point from which the writer has chosen to tell the story.

In the **first-person point of view**, one of the characters is actually telling the story, using the pronouns *I* and *we*. Readers get to know this character well, but they know only what that character knows and observe and experience only what that character observes and experiences.

In the **third-person point of view**, the narrator focuses on the thoughts and feelings of just one character. Readers observe the action through the eyes and with the feelings of this character, but the character is not telling the story directly. The narrator is outside of the story.

In the **third-person-omniscient point of view**, the person telling the story knows everything that is happening in the story and has access to what every character says, does, feels, and thinks. The word *omniscient* means "all knowing." In the **third-person-limited point of view**, the narrator has access to the thoughts, feelings, and memories of just the main character.

Try It Read this excerpt from a story.

> At dawn, Tanya saddled up her horse and set out for the woods at the edge of the village of Farnsworth, where her best friend, Sarah, lived. She was glad to be getting out of the house. She had been holed up too long. At the same moment, Sarah was riding through the wood in the other direction, still reeling from her conversation with her mother. She'd had it with her family. She needed a real break. *I'll stay with Tanya*, she thought.

> Discuss

Identify the narrative point of view in this story. Who are the characters the narrator describes? Draw a box around their names. Whose actions or thoughts are being revealed? Underline their actions. Double underline their feelings and thoughts. What is the point of view?

As you read, complete the Narrative Point of View Chart on page 283.

Practice the Skill

A **theme** is the central idea of a story. It is the idea or message about life, society, or human nature that the writer wishes to convey about the subject of the story. A theme is expressed in a statement or sentence, such as "Love is more powerful than anything else." A theme is rarely directly stated in a story. Most often, you have to think about all the elements in the story—the details of the plot; the thoughts, words, and actions of the characters; and the story's ending. You use these things to figure out the theme of the story as it develops. Also, stories can sometimes have more than one theme.

Try It Read the following story excerpt.

"Margaret! It is good to see you!" Jacob cried, flustered. "I thought your family had moved out of the county!"

"Oh, we did. I'm just here with Papa; he's at the general store," Margaret said. "I'm sorry that I never wrote you." She was talking to Jacob, but she kept glancing over his shoulder, as if she were more interested in wagons being unloaded than in talking to him.

Has she forgotten me so quickly? Jacob wondered. "That's quite alright! There's no blame!" he said with a forced laugh. Margaret was even prettier than he'd remembered. "Perhaps I can come to call on you soon at the farm."

> **Discuss** **What details point to the story's theme? Ask yourself questions such as *What idea or message about human nature lies beneath the words? What does their dialogue really reveal?* Look for textual evidence that supports your thinking.**

As you read, record your answers to questions about determining theme on the Close Reading Worksheet on page 284.

Purpose for Reading
Read along with your teacher. Each time, read for a different purpose.

First Read Focus on narrative point of view.

Second Read Focus on determining theme.

Third Read Focus on thinking critically about the selection.

From what point of view is the story being told? Provide textual evidence for your answer on the **Narrative Point of View Chart**.

What clues tell you that this story is set in the past?

1   Feyvl and Zippora Kluger did their big shopping on Sundays, when busy Orchard Street really came to life. You could get almost anything on Orchard Street on a Sunday and, if you had a talent for **haggling**, you could get it cheap. Zippora claimed that anything—*anything*—could be gotten for practically any price if you were willing to bargain.

2   Sundays weren't quiet down on Orchard, though—the sidewalks were crowded with recently arrived immigrants from Eastern Europe, and if you walked in the street, you had to sidestep horse-drawn carts crossing Delancey Street and shut your ears to the shouts of the merchants selling their wares. Feyvl, who liked to spend Sundays relaxing with the newspaper in their gas lamp–lit tenement apartment, was always in a hurry to get back home, but Zippora liked to stop wherever she saw a sale. Since most of the best sales happened later in the day, Feyvl was often forced to spend all afternoon trailing his wife. This was not the most unpleasant task in the world, however, as Feyvl was completely smitten by his pretty wife of three months.

3   On this particular Sunday, just as the Klugers were about to head home, Zippora noticed a storefront with a handwritten sign in the window saying BIG SALE. She begged Feyvl to stop so she could have a look.

4   Feyvl sighed heavily and said, "You know what's in there—junk."

5   "Oh, *please*, Feyvl, please!" Zippora said, pouting in that way she knew he found so irresistible. Of course, Feyvl agreed.

6   Together, they walked into the store and were greeted by the friendly owner.

7   "Anything you see, fifty cents," the woman said, "and anything you don't see, twenty-five cents." Feyvl liked her attitude.

8   Zippora circled the piles of old furniture, secondhand clothing, rusty tools, and empty picture frames, which she immediately examined. Feyvl wandered around bored, until a glint from under some rags caught his eye. Pushing the rags aside, he found a strange object—a small metal box that was tarnished and dull. *I know exactly what it is—a spice box.* He took it to the shop owner and offered her a quarter.

9   "I found this under some rags," he said. The woman shrugged as she wrapped it. "It's just a tchotchke—a trinket."

10   Feyvl smiled pleasantly. *Oh, it's much more than that.*

11   When the couple returned home with their purchases, Feyvl unwrapped his find.

12   "It is lovely, Feyvl," Zippora said. "But what is it?"

13   "It's a spice box. Wait until I shine it up. It will be beautiful. The person who made this was a true artist," he said in an admiring voice.

Which line in paragraph 8 suggests that the narrator sees what Feyvl does? What lines on this page show that the narrator has access to Feyvl's thoughts? Write your answers on the **Narrative Point of View Chart**.

Circle the line in the text that tells you that Feyvl appreciates art and well-made things.

Underline the private thoughts revealed in paragraph 14. Think about what they tell you about the narrator's point of view.

What are Zippora's private thoughts about the two new spice boxes? What does this information tell you about the narrator's point of view? Write your ideas in the **Narrative Point of View Chart.**

How is Feyvl changing? Explain your answer using textual evidence.

What does paragraph 19 suggest about the reasons many Eastern Europeans came to the United States?

14   Zippora furrowed her brow. *We already have a spice box*. However, she smiled indulgently at her husband. The little box made him happy. Plus, she was impressed by his ability to see beauty in an everyday object.

15   The next Sunday, after a full day of shopping, Zippora saw another sign—BIG SALE TODAY—and this time Feyvl had no problem going in.

16   They found themselves in another musty shop, and once again, Zippora searched for picture frames. She seized on a bad painting of a sunrise, but it was ornately framed. Feyvl strolled the aisles in search of another spice box, and to his amazement, he found two. He could barely contain his delight.

17   "Two more spice boxes!" Zippora cried in dismay. What would they do with more boxes? Then she had a realization and, smiling, she said, "Feyvl, I do believe you are collector."

18   Feyvl rather liked the sound of it—*collector*—and he said the word a few times out loud. As he imagined having an entire room filled with his treasures, he wondered why these trinkets made him feel such pride and pleasure.

19   Suddenly, he was glad he had come to America, where he had many sources of happiness: his lovely wife, a decent job, his comfortable home, and now his *collection* of spice boxes. He was not yet a man of wealth and **substance**, but these little boxes made him feel like a person of worth.

20   Soon, Feyvl had amassed a dozen spice boxes, so he built a cabinet to display them. Then every week he and Zippora lovingly polished each one with a special **chamois** to prevent the objects from growing tarnished. Zippora was amazed by how quickly the collection had grown. Feyvl, she could see, was developing a good eye and was now selecting them carefully for their artistry and beauty—just as she chose her picture frames.

21   Zippora now felt honored to be married to a collector of spice boxes so fine that they were housed in a special case. She took every opportunity to show visitors, including her picture frame customers, Feyvl's collectibles. She lovingly called them the "Kluger Collection" and gave Feyvl the nickname the "King of Collectibles," which pleased him very much.

22   Once Feyvl became choosier about the spice boxes he'd add to his collection, he had to search harder and more carefully for them. No longer could he wander through junk shops of Orchard Street looking for deals. Now he visited antiques shops in fancier parts of the city. The owners of these shops were glad to have a new customer who appreciated their wares. To them, Feyvl was more than the king of collectibles; he was a true collector.

<u>Underline</u> instances on this page where the narrator tells what Zippora is thinking and how she feels.

How would you describe what is happening to Feyvl?

What function does the spice box collection serve in the story? What do you think it represents?

What is revealed about the narrator toward the end of the story? Write your answer on the **Narrative Point of View Chart** and answer the question below the chart.

What is a universal truth about material things that is reflected in this story? State a theme you found in the story.

Analyze

In the end, did Kluger's collection have any value? Cite textual evidence to support your ideas.

23   Time passed, and the Klugers moved to Brooklyn into a beautiful house which, after many years on the Lower East Side, was like a dream come true.

24   The Kluger Collection was transferred to the new home and continued to grow. It became well known in the neighborhood and was the subject of a few local newspaper articles. Sometimes, neighbors would bring objects for Feyvl to appraise. Feyvl soon gave up his job so he could travel in search of spice boxes. Zippora, for her part, had a thriving business restoring antique picture frames that paid all the bills. In the midst of all this, the Klugers had five children, all happy and healthy.

25   Eventually, the Klugers transformed the first floor of the house into a museum they lovingly called "The Kluger Collection." The younger generation knew the story of this collection—how their papa had found one box in a junk shop and over many years developed a fine collection. They were only metal boxes, but the children had their favorites, and when they married, they took "their" spice boxes to their new homes.

26   It has been sixty years since Feyvl collected his last spice box. Since then, all the boxes have been distributed among his children and their children and grandchildren. Today, every one of Feyvl and Zippora's descendants has a small silver box, and each one is a reminder of a special man who discovered the beauty in everyday things and found value as their collector.

Vocabulary: Context Clues

Sometimes you need to look up the meaning of an unfamiliar word in a dictionary. Often, though, you can figure out a word's meaning from the way it is used in a sentence or from surrounding words. These are called **context clues**, and they fall into several categories, such as example, explanation, description, antonym, and synonym.

Try It Look at each example. The meaning of the word in boldface can be figured out from the underlined context clue.

example	I enjoy **sedentary** activities, such as <u>reading and napping</u>.
definition	I ate some **tainted** fish the other day, which made me wonder if all the fish in the store were <u>rotten</u>.
description	George is the type of <u>person whom everyone likes and enjoys being with</u>. He is the most **charismatic** person I know.
antonym	Shawn was **reluctant** to swim laps in the pool; on the other hand, he was <u>eager</u> to goof off with his friends.
synonym	Kasey felt **compassion** and <u>pity</u> for the hurt bird, so she decided to take it home and nurse it back to health.

Discuss Talk about how the different kinds of context clues help you understand the boldface words.

Find the following words in "The Collector." Underline the context clues that help you understand them. Then write a new sentence using each word.

1. haggling, p. 34 _____

_____

2. substance, p. 36 _____

_____

3. chamois, p. 37 _____

_____

Practice the Skill

Compare and Contrast

Making critical comparisons between two texts can help you understand what you read. This means identifying the ways that two stories are alike (**compare**) and different (**contrast**). There are many ways stories can be compared. You can consider plots, settings, characters, or themes. You can look at genres, formats, and points of view. When comparing texts, look at the way information is presented in each text and evaluate the quality of that information.

It can be especially rewarding to compare fiction and primary-account texts on the same topic or from the same period of history. Comparing the story "The Summer Things Fell Apart" with the primary account "Letter from Neshoba County Jail" will help you get a deeper insight into complex concepts such as racism and segregation.

Try It Read the following article.

Many American citizens resisted the Vietnam War because they felt it was unnecessary or unjust. One form of resistance centered around the Selective Service. This was a system designed to bolster the number of troops by "drafting" common citizens to fight. It worked like a lottery, where all eligible men were given a number corresponding to their birthday. When the military needed more troops, it would announce a number, and anyone holding it was required by law for report for duty.

Because so many were opposed to or feared the war, they devised methods to avoid service. To be eligible, men had to be mentally and physically sound. This led many to fake mental and physical deficiencies or, more extremely, to pay doctors to falsify their medical records. Others simply fled the country until the war ended. Such a move would be expensive. This meant that evading military service, for the most part, was only an option for the wealthy. Poorer draftees had to choose between fighting in combat or being sent to prison.

> Discuss **What would you expect to find in a historical fiction account of a person being drafted into military service? How might that account differ from the article above? Think about the personal feelings involved in being drafted.**

As you read, complete the Venn Diagram on page 285.

Practice the Skill

Second Read **Historical Fiction**

Historical fiction stories and novels take place in the past. They are not strictly factual accounts of historic events. Rather, they are reconstructions that capture the spirit of a bygone era with realistic detail. A story may deal with actual historic characters, or it may contain a mixture of fictional and historic characters. It may focus on a single event, or it may portray a broader view in which plot developments occur against the backdrop of history.

Try It Read this brief description of a popular movie based on a historic event.

Titanic (1997), an American film, is a fictional account of a true event—the sinking of the passenger liner RMS *Titanic* in the Atlantic Ocean on April 15, 1912. Leonardo DiCaprio and Kate Winslet star as members of different social classes who fall in love during the ship's ill-fated voyage. While not historically accurate, the film does include scenes with various historic characters. A reconstruction of the *Titanic* was built in California, and scale models and computer-generated imagery were used to re-create the sinking. The deep-sea film crew shot at the site of the real shipwreck eleven times in 1995, spending more time with the ship than its original passengers ever had a chance to.

Discuss **Discuss ideas about the ways in which the movie *Titanic* is factually accurate and ways in which it is fictional. How did the movie crew make the ship and its sinking as realistic as possible? What aspects of the film would have to have been made up? Now, brainstorm ideas about real historic events you would like to create movies about and how you might add an element of fiction to them, such as adding purely fictional characters or plot twists.**

As you read, record your answers to questions about the genre of historical fiction on the Close Reading Worksheet on page 286. ✏️➤

The Summer Things Fell Apart

How do Shelby's mother and Uncle Terry differ on their feelings about Shelby going to Alabama? Why? As you read the story, write your answer on the **Venn Diagram**.

From what you've read so far, which aspects of the setting are crucial in establishing the historic context? Explain.

1   In the years to come, people would refer to the summer of 1964 as "Freedom Summer," but Shelby Hammond would always think of it as the summer things fell apart. That year, her father died, her mother returned to work, and her uncle Terry, who had been living with them in New York, was preparing to leave for graduate school in the fall. Shelby was to be sent to her grandparents in Montgomery, Alabama, for the summer, in order to give Shelby's mother time to mourn her husband's death and figure out what to do with the rest of her life.

2   Shelby's mom and uncle were divided about whether or not sending Shelby down South was a good idea and would argue about it often in the weeks before Shelby was to leave. Uncle Terry was offended by the idea of his niece being under the thumb of "those people," but her mother thought it was fine—for a time. *Come on, Terry, do you really think they're about to take her to a Klan meeting?* she'd overheard her mother saying.

3   The week before she was to leave, her mother and uncle took her to an Indian restaurant in Manhattan they liked, as a send-off. Her mother was in high spirits, but her uncle was morose, as usual.

4   "I hate to sound like a broken record, Shel," her mother said, spearing an appetizer, "but do not engage them. You don't have to agree with them, but don't argue. It wouldn't do any good, and it would just get him mad." It was clear that by *him* she meant Grandpa.

5   "What—just walk away?" said Shelby. It felt like she was getting stage directions from a movie director.

6   "Bad move, Ellen," said Terry. "Don't tell her that. You want to turn your daughter into a zombie? Someone who can't think for herself?"

7   "Stop fighting!" Shelby cried, hands over her ears.

8   They did and slunk back into their chairs like chastised children.

9   "Look, guys, you don't have to give me step-by-step instructions," Shelby said. "I'm not an imbecile."

10   *Why make such a big fuss about spending time with a couple of old people?* Shelby wondered. If they were racists, she felt sorry for them. It's not like they were *doing* anything—they'd never *do* anything to hurt other people.

11   Grandma she remembered only as a polite, diminutive person who had a precise way of doing things, and while not cold, she had never been excessively warm either. She remembered Grandpa as gruff.

In what way is Terry unlike Shelby's mother? Box an argument that Shelby's mother makes, and then circle a contrasting argument that Terry makes.

What assumption is Shelby making? Why?

How does the author use the character of Shelby to help readers understand this time in history?

Read this sentence from the selection: *She knew her grandfather's answer would be "Because that's the way it is," even though he hired black men to work in his feed and seed business.* What point is the author making here?

12   "I hope you understand, Shel—I need some time to—to—," her mother broke off, choking back a sob in the making.

13   "I don't mind, Mom," Shelby said a little too quickly. "It's only for a few weeks, and it'll give me a chance to see another part of the country." Terry snorted loudly enough to make people in the restaurant turn around.

14   Shelby was not naïve. She was aware of how negroes were forced to live in the South, but her knowledge of the situation was mainly the stuff of TV news reports and heated conversations in meeting halls and living rooms. She had a feeling she was in for a rude awakening.

15   Sure enough, after a few days in Montgomery, Shelby knew why her uncle had left home and why he never talked to his father, as well as why Terry's infrequent conversations with his mother were hushed and secretive. Grandpa was "gruff," all right, but without the heart of gold that makes gruffness bearable.

16   Living in Montgomery was like living in Alice's Looking Glass, where nothing looked familiar or made sense. Her mother and uncle had prepared her for the dual water fountains and bathrooms, the Colored Only or White Only signs everywhere you looked, but it was still shocking to see firsthand

17   Shelby knew better than to ask why this was so. She knew why, of course—it was the law—but she yearned to know *why*. She knew her grandfather's answer would be "Because that's the way it is," even though he hired black men to work in his feed and seed business.

18   She would have to follow her mother's advice and keep her mouth shut around Grandpa. She would keep her opinions to herself, and she would be seen and not heard—*because that's the way it was.*

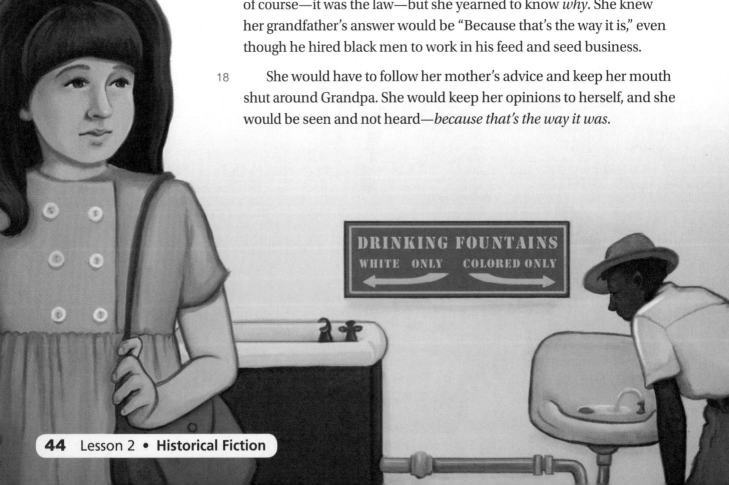

DRINKING FOUNTAINS
WHITE ONLY   COLORED ONLY

19   One evening, Shelby and her grandfather were watching *The Jack Benny Show* on TV, and the guest was Nat King Cole, the great African American musician. Predictably, this was enough to set off her grandfather. He snarled at the TV. Slamming down his glass of water, he got up and changed the channel, went back to his chair, and cursed, "This younger generation and its fancy ideas of everybody getting along." As Shelby got up, ostensibly to help her grandma in the kitchen, she heard him grumble, "That's not the way it works!"

20   "You didn't like the show?" her grandmother said, bending over a pan of biscuits.

21   "Grandpa's angry at something on TV, some black musician."

      "Don't you worry about him, honey—your grandpa is completely harmless."

22   "What's he so angry about?"

23   "Oh—a lot of things," said her grandmother. "Disappointments, mostly. He's never been as successful as he wanted, but he doesn't like things to change, either. He thinks other people are to blame for the way things have turned out—and to tell you truth, so do I. Things were so much simpler when people kept to themselves, before all this fuss about civil rights. What about *our* civil rights?" She leaned over confidentially and whispered, "I know some of them are fine, dear, but we're all too different to really get along together."

24   Shelby grabbed a fist-sized biscuit from the tray and stuffed it into her mouth as quickly as possible. She felt invisible, blotted out. She had tried to follow her mother's advice, to "not engage," but it was getting harder.

25   And if she *did* engage, what would she say? What words would she use? *Grandpa, how come you say they're not as good as we are, yet you depend on them to operate your business?* She knew when something was wrong, but not how to explain it to someone who didn't. She wasn't old enough or smart enough to formulate the words that would convince her grandfather of his folly.

What is a difference between Grandpa's and Grandma's reactions to the world changing? Circle a reason that Grandpa gives, and box a reason that Grandma gives.

Underline a detail on this page that places the story in historical context.

Box a sentence that shows how Shelby is different from her mother and Uncle Terry.

Why does Shelby resolve to ask Grandpa what she does?

26   She would call her mother and Terry and she'd ask them to send her a ticket back to New York. She'd insist on it, throw a fit, threaten to be a runaway, tell them how she couldn't bear to listen to her grandparents, but neither could she talk back, and it was driving her crazy. She'd tell them she was suffocating, and they'd understand.

27   But *would* they? What did *they* do when they were living under her grandparents' roof? Her mother had played the "good girl," the peacemaker, never speaking her mind, unsure of herself to this day. Her uncle had quit the scene altogether, moved North, and erased his past just like that. Since then, he had carried a chip on his shoulder a mile wide.

28   Well, she would do neither, because she was not her mother, nor was she her uncle. She'd go back in that room, where her grandfather sat chuckling in front of the TV again. She'd take a seat next to him on the couch. Then, when the show was over, she'd ask him some questions—not about civil rights or segregation but about his childhood, his brothers and sisters, what games he liked to play, about his father and mother and the house they lived in. That would be a start.

29   If Shelby could gently bring Grandpa out and make him think about the world and the people in it in new ways, then perhaps she would prove to be smart enough after all.

Letter from Neshoba County Jail

This letter is a fictional work that models the characteristics and text features common in authentic texts of this type.

August 23, 1964

Dear Mother,

1   First, I want to I apologize for saying I would be at the shore with Trish and her family for the month of August. I told myself I had to lie about it, because I didn't want you and Daddy to worry. The truth is, it was more complex than that: I didn't want you and Daddy to stop me from what I planned to do. I told myself that I'd be home in Maine by the time you got back from Europe so that you would never have to know— obviously, I was wrong.

2   Here is the story: I'm being held in the Neshoba County Jail along with two friends, who are black. All of us are charged with trying to integrate a white-only lunch counter at a Woolworth's department store. I would have been ignored if I wasn't with them, but that wasn't the point. I wanted to be arrested along with them, so we joined hands and refused to let the police break us apart.

3   We have a New York lawyer, Tom Wittig, who is helping us for free, or *pro bono*, because he believes in our case. He's confident he can get us out on bail by the end of the week, in which case I'll be home this weekend, and we can have a long talk. For now, I'm just happy knowing that this letter will get to you, as Mr. Wittig has promised.

Compare and contrast how Shelby from the previous story and the writer here take action to deal with racism differently. Record your ideas on the **Venn Diagram.**

Underline two details about the setting on this page that establish historical context.

What distinction does the writer make between her old and her current beliefs? Circle a phrase that shows an old belief, and box a phrase that shows a new one.

What does the fact that this is a primary account tell you about the writer's observations of this period in history? How does it differ from the fictional account? ✏️

4   I'm okay, considering I am writing this from a jail cell—although it's easier for me than it is for my friends, who are being punished not because of what they did but because of who they are. Although I knew very well that arrest was a possibility, the reality of being here, of hearing that steel door shut behind me, is something I did not, and could not, know about. I never want it to happen again, I know that, but if the country continues to persecute its black citizens, I will have to follow my conscience.

5   I know this all will be a shock to you, but I'm simply not the same person I was when you saw me last—I guess you could say that I've become a political activist. I haven't spoken to you about this part of my life, as I know how much you and Daddy hate to talk about anything "unpleasant." And I know how you (and especially Daddy) feel about integration and racial matters in general.

6   It wasn't so long ago that I wanted the kind of life you had, full of travel and parties and beautiful things, but I've come to believe that, as a good citizen, I have to try to help people who are powerless and oppressed. Maybe you feel betrayed—and not just because I lied to you. You might think I'm rejecting you and everything you've done for me, but please believe me when I tell you that this is not true. If there's one thing you've taught me, it's that it's always better to stick by your principles, and that's what I'm doing. You raised a good daughter, and I really hope that you can be proud of what I am doing.

All my love,

Laura

Connect

How are the backgrounds of Shelby and Laura similar? Why is this important?

People march in support of civil rights in 1964.

Vocabulary: Eliminate Wordiness and Redundancy

Wordiness means using more words than necessary when speaking or writing. Many factors contribute to wordiness, including using complicated words or phrases when a simple one will do. **Redundancy** means repeating the same concept when there is no need to do so. To write successfully, you should always be mindful of wordiness and redundancy. Look out for it when proofreading your work. When you eliminate wordiness and redundancy, your message comes across clearly and concisely.

Try It This paragraph, based on the story you just read, contains wordiness and redundancies caused by the overuse of synonyms.

> Sure enough, after a few days in Montgomery, Shelby knew why her uncle had left home as an adolescent **teenager** and why he never **talked to** or conversed with his father, as well as why Terry's infrequent conversations with his mother were **secretive** and clandestine. Grandpa was "gruff" was one way to describe it, of course, and lacking the heart of gold that makes gruffness bearable.

Discuss **What wordiness and redundancies can you find in the paragraph?**

Find the redundant word or phrase for each boldface word and cross it out. Write the unnecessary synonym on the line below. Then use the synonym in a new sentence.

1. teenager _____

_____

2. talked _____

_____

3. secretive _____

_____

Respond to Text: Compare and Contrast Texts

"The Summer Things Fell Apart" and "Letter from Neshoba County Jail" both deal with the South during the mid–1960s, a time when laws enforcing racial segregation in public places were being challenged. "The Summer Things Fell Apart" is historical fiction. "Letter from Neshoba County Jail" is a primary account of a made-up event in the form of a letter. Although the accounts share a historic context, they are written for different purposes and from different vantage points.

Try It Think about what you learned about comparing and contrasting a fictional portrayal and a primary account of the same period.

 Discuss

What are some similarities between "The Summer Things Fell Apart" and "Letter from Neshoba County Jail"? What are some differences? What were the different writers' purposes for writing? Make sure your answer is supported by sound reasoning and evidence from the text.

On Your Own Write your ideas about the similarities and differences between the fictional "The Summer Things Fell Apart" and the primary account of the same period, "Letter from Neshoba County Jail." Include details from the text and things you may know. Use the next page to help you plan your response. Then write your paragraph on a separate sheet of paper.

Checklist for a Good Response

A good paragraph

✔ identifies ways that the fictional portrayal and the primary account are different and ways they are similar.

✔ explains the reasoning behind your ideas.

✔ includes evidence from the text and other things you know.

✔ shows your understanding of the two texts in their historic context.

✔ includes a topic sentence, supporting ideas, and a concluding statement.

Compare and Contrast Texts

1. **Topic Sentence** Include this information in your first sentence:

   Based on my reading, the stories are similar because _____

   _____ and different

   because _____

   _____ .

2. **Explain Your Answer** The sentences of your paragraph should provide details that support your answer. Use this chart to organize your ideas.

Selection	"The Summer Things Fell Apart"	"Letter from Neshoba County Jail"
Genre		
Author		
Author's purpose		
Narrator		
Objectivity		

3. **Concluding Sentence** Your final sentence should restate your conclusions with a new twist.

   _____

   _____

On a separate sheet of paper, write your paragraph.

Read on Your Own

Read the selections independently three times, using the skills you have learned. Then answer the Comprehension Check questions.

First Read — Practice the first-read skills you learned in this lesson.

Second Read — Practice the second-read skills you learned in this lesson.

Third Read — Think critically about the selections.

Hidden

Narrative Point of View Think about the point of view from which this story is told.

Historical Fiction When and where is this story set? (Circle) the details that tell you. The first one has been circled for you.

1   "I ran into Eva Mueller yesterday," announced Mrs. Grunwald, sweeping away crumbs from the breakfast table. She waited for her husband to look up from his copy of (Der Speigel.)

2   "Oh?" He rubbed his eyes and glanced at the clock on the wall. He was late for work, but he was procrastinating, so today he didn't mind his wife's gabbing.

3   "I want to tell you what she told me, but you mustn't tell anybody," pleaded Mrs. Grunwald. "Promise me."

4   "What's this all about, Lotte?" grumbled Mr. Grunwald as he downed the rest of his coffee.

5   "The Muellers are taking in a little Jewish boy. They will pretend he's Eva's nephew."

6   Mr. Grunwald rocked back in his chair, shocked—he admired the Muellers for this enormous act of bravery and compassion, but mostly he was terrified for them. They had a daughter Helgi's age. Why put her in such terrible jeopardy for the sake of a stranger's child?

7   "Evil things are happening here in Germany, Lotte," he said. "The Gestapo are storming through every house now. I don't tell you everything; despicable things are going on in this city."

8   The clock over the sink ticked off the seconds, and Mrs. Grunwald thought how very strange it was that most of the time you couldn't even hear it, while today the noise was practically deafening.

9   To break the silence, he continued, "It's not right to take risks like that if you have a child, Lotte. People must put their own children first."

10   Mrs. Grunwald turned her back on her husband and asked, "How long will you be at that shop today?"

11   "I have no idea—there are thousands of buttons to sort and catalogue," he said, then quickly added, "by myself now, of course."

12   "Oh yes, I nearly forgot," Mrs. Grunwald said, "the poor old woman. How did she take it when you demanded she leave?"

13   "She was distraught, of course," Mr. Grunwald insisted; he didn't like being deceitful with his wife. The fact is, he'd never really demanded the old lady leave.

14   Mr. Grunwald's job, known as "rubbish removal," was to oversee the takeover of Jewish-owned businesses. When he'd first gotten the order from local party headquarters to take over the old lady's button shop in the village, he was not happy, though it could have been worse. Some people put up a fight, but the lady who owned the shop was old and docile, despite the fact that she must have foreseen what was coming, for many shops along the main avenue were boarded up, their windows smashed or covered with obscenities, while others had opened under new management.

15   After weeks of upending innocent people's lives, closing their businesses, and leaving them with no means of income, he was feeling the moral and emotional weight of his task. That was lucky for old Mrs. Steingesser, whose chatty, oblivious ways made Mr. Grunwald's job all the more difficult.

16   When he'd first arrived at the button shop with an Order to Vacate, the seventy-four-year-old owner, Freda Steingesser, appeared neither surprised nor upset—if anything, she seemed glad to see him and even offered him a cup of tea.

17   She had fifteen minutes to collect her things, Mr. Grunwald told her, but she chattered on as if she hadn't a care in the world. It occurred to him then that Mrs. Steingesser thought she still owned the shop and believed that he was there to help her sort her buttons; that in fact Freda Steingesser was not in her right mind.

Historical Fiction
Underline historical aspects in the story that heighten the suspense and drama.

Critical Thinking
Think about why Mr. Grunwald might have lied to his wife about Mrs. Steingesser.

Narrative Point of View As the narrator reveals Mr. Grunwald's thoughts on this page, how does the character's outlook on the situation change?

Determine Theme Think about a major theme in the story regarding how we treat others.

Critical Thinking Think about what the story suggests about why people hate others.

18   With each passing day, it got harder and harder to tell Mrs. Steingesser his original intentions, but now it was a week later, and the head office would want their report. If they figured out the old lady was still occupying her store, he knew what they'd do—they would come to the store, drag her out, humiliate her, and kick her to the curb.

19   So today she'd have to clear out. But where would she go? The store was her home; she had no one, so she would die.

20   Fleetingly, Mr. Grunwald let himself imagine Mrs. Steingesser in his upstairs bedroom; she could be an aged relative from the provinces come to stay. He in fact knew someone who could fix the papers.

21   But no, he had to consider his daughter, Helgi—if they were caught hiding a Jew, the authorities would take the old woman and Helgi, too. Mr. Grunwald turned the quandary over and over in his mind, considering the sides of the dilemma and the repercussions each choice would have not only on poor old Freda, but on his family.

22   Suddenly he was pounding on the table and shouting, "*No!* They cannot do this to people. This is inhuman!"

23   "*What's* inhuman? What are you talking about?" asked Helgi as she breezed into the room, swiped an apple from the bowl, and bit it.

24   "They shut down that little button shop," explained her mother. "We were wondering how the old lady was."

25   "Who cares?" Helgi said. "I mean, she's a Jew, right? Don't you know anything? Jews are dangerous. They steal our jobs, and—"

26   "*Enough!*" Mr. Grunwald fiercely interrupted.

27   Helgi looked like she'd been slapped in the face. She stood there, frozen in place, looking like the nine-year-old girl she actually was, and then she burst out crying and ran to her room.

28   "Ernst, she doesn't know what she's saying!"

29   "No, and she never will—unless we do something about it."

30   "And that would be . . ."

31   "We're going to have to take the old lady in, hide her here, and fix her papers. She can't keep her shop, but we can do this for her and, more important, we *must* do it, for the sake of our child. Helgi has to learn that these things she hears, they're not true. She's being indoctrinated with filthy lies, and I won't stand for it!"

Letter to a Granddaughter

My darling granddaughter,

1   I'm not feeling quite up to our usual weekly phone chat, so I'm dictating a letter to one of the nice nurses they have here, who said she'll drop it in the mail on her way home. I have to get something off my chest.

2   I have kept something from you, mainly out of respect for your mother's wishes, because the whole subject makes her anxious and depressed. You'd never know it, though, as she keeps "all that" well hidden, but I suppose keeping things well hidden is a family trait.

3   For one thing, I am not who you think I am. I am not Kryztyna Kowalczyk, a Polish Catholic farm girl whose family emigrated to America when she was a baby—I am Miriam Zelinsky, the child of Jewish parents, the only one in her family to survive the war.

4   Here's the truth: I grew up a small town in Poland called Oleszyce, where the Jews, who were in the minority, kept an uneasy peace with the rest of the population. Anti-Semitism existed, for sure, but it was not until the Nazis came in 1939 that the real horrors began. They arrived all at once—on motorcycles, on horseback, in motorcades—and they arrived with laws that forbade us Jews from leaving the ghetto.[1] The Gentiles, or non-Jewish citizens, didn't stick up for us, for they knew what would happen if they did.

5   Because of my red hair and fair skin, I could pass as a Pole, so I'd sneak out of the ghetto into the non-Jewish areas and smuggle in food, toiletries, clothing, and shoes. I had to be careful about not giving myself away, so I had to think about things like my eyes, for eyes can be a dead giveaway. I was told that Jews trying to "pass" often revealed themselves by the sadness in their eyes. Piotr had those eyes. He was my fiancée, and we were going to get married after the war.

6   One day, he and I were on a train, returning to the Jewish ghetto with supplies, when suddenly the train began to slow down—the bottom went out of my stomach when I saw the checkpoint up ahead. Our papers were in order, but Piotr's Polish was bad—he'd only emigrated from Russia a year before—and I knew that if they questioned him, they'd discover we were Jews, not legally allowed past the confines of the ghetto, and we'd be . . . I didn't want to think about it.

[1]**ghetto** a section of a city in which Jews were required to live

Narrative Point of View How do you know that the account is told from the first-person point of view? Circle evidence in the first two paragraphs.

Critical Thinking Think about what you find out from this account that you didn't know from reading "Hidden."

Compare and Contrast
Think about how you would compare and contrast the couple in "Hidden" with the letter writer's depiction of the people she asked for help.

Historical Fiction Think about how the selections are similar in terms of how the period is depicted.

Critical Thinking Think about how it could be both easier and more difficult to hide your true identity as time goes on.

7   So I yelled at Piotr to jump. He didn't want to; he could play a deaf-mute, he said, arguing that our chances would be better than they'd be jumping off a moving train. But in the end I convinced him, and I jumped first. Then, Piotr jumped from the train and hit his head on an iron railing. It looked like he was killed right away, and I could only pray he didn't suffer.

8   Panicked and heartbroken, I ran and ran, back to the farmer who gave us the supplies, told him what had happened, and asked him for shelter. He refused, afraid the Germans would kill his family. I went to a neighboring farm, but they, too, refused. Nobody would help me. In a way I don't blame them, and I don't hate them for it, because I don't know how I would have acted if I'd been in their position.

9   I made my way to Krakow, and by chance they were **recruiting** Polish boys and girls for farm work in Germany. That's how I ended up working and living with a farmer the whole time during the war. And under assumed papers, I went with them to church, I went to confession—they were Catholics, so I was a Catholic, too. And when I emigrated to America after the war, I arrived as Kryztyna Mniewski. I met your grandfather at a church social, and I'm sorry to say that it took me a long time to tell *him*, rest his soul. We waited too long to tell your mother—perhaps if we had done it sooner. . . . She was upset by what I'd told her, and if ever the subject came up, she would go silent and become saddened. She made me promise not to tell you, saying she'd do it herself someday, but I fear she never will.

10   Anyway, I was lying here thinking about all this, and it made me think that if I'm going to be remembered, it should be the actual me that you all are remembering.

11   Please tell me what you think of all this, and the next time you visit, we can have a long talk about it.

All my love,
Grandma

✔ Comprehension Check

1. How would "Hidden" be different if it were a first-person narrative told by Mrs. Grunwald?

   _____

   _____

   _____

2. What theme is expressed in "Hidden?"

   _____

   _____

   _____

3. Compare how people hide in the two selections.

   _____

   _____

   _____

4. How does the historical setting in "Hidden" create dramatic tension?

   _____

   _____

   _____

5. What do you learn in "Letter to a Granddaughter" that helps you to understand "Hidden"?

_____

_____

_____

6. What do these two selections reveal about how dangerous times can require a different approach to moral questions, such as when to tell the truth?

_____

_____

_____

7. Read these sentences from "Letter to a Granddaughter."

   I made my way to Krakow and by chance they were recruiting Polish boys and girls for farm work in Germany. That's how I ended up working and living with a farmer the whole time during the war.

   Circle the word or words that help you understand the meaning of the word *recruiting*.

8. Read this sentence based on the selections.

   The situation was dangerously dire, and people literally started beginning to be seriously terrified and scared out of their wits.

   Circle the words you think the sentence should do without. Make sure the sentence still conveys all its essential information.

Lesson 3

Drama

Drama is fiction that is written to be performed by actors on a stage. Dramas are made up of acts and scenes, and the story is told mainly through the characters' dialogue. Just like other forms of fiction, dramas—also called plays—can be tragic, comic, romantic, or any combination of those things, and they can be set in the past, present, or future. Is the actor in the photo performing in a drama set in the past, present, or future? How can you tell?

Skills Focus

The Lost River, Act 1

Cause and Effect   Dramatic Structure

The Lost River, Act 2

Cite Textual Evidence   Character, Setting, and Plot

Practice the Skill

First Read Cause and Effect

A **cause** is what makes something happen; the **effect** is what happens. For example, imagine that a character in a drama insults another character. The effect might be an act of violence, and the cause would be the insult. Cause and effect can also be more subtle. One character in love with another might be motivated by this love to do any number of things, like behave foolishly or speak with great kindness toward the love interest. Each small action can be seen as an effect of this single cause. Also, an effect may be the cause of another effect, and so on.

The clues linking cause and effect lie in the text. If you look carefully, you can find them. Some will be plain as day; others may require a little investigating.

Try It Read this dramatic scene.

KARIN: (*on her horse, Trixie*) Whoa, Trixie, slow down. It was just a prairie dog running across the trail.

ANDRE: (*riding at a distance behind Karin*) Karin! I can't keep up! Trixie is running too fast.

Discuss **What causes Trixie to run so fast? Underline this cause. What effect does this have? Double underline one effect.**

Read on to find another example of cause and effect.

ANDRE: (*losing sight of Karin; speaking to himself*) I can't believe Karin took off like that. Is she mad at me? What did I do? (*angrily*) Fine. If she's going to be that way, I'm heading back home.

Discuss **What causes Andre to be upset? Underline this cause. What effect does it have? Double underline one effect.**

As you read, complete the Cause-and-Effect Chart on page 287.

Practice the Skill

Second Read Dramatic Structure

Dramatic structure is how the writer shapes the things that happen in the story of the drama, or play. Plays are usually divided into acts, like novels are often divided into chapters. Within each act are one or more scenes that move the plot along. Like other fiction, dramas involve a conflict that builds up until it reaches a climax, or high point, before being resolved. Each scene works to develop the conflict and the characters and to reveal the play's theme. In plays, the dramatic structure is clarified by elements such as these:

- **Act** and **scene** breaks indicate a change in place or time or of the characters on stage.

- **Dialogue tags** tell you who is speaking.

- **Stage directions** give physical directions for how characters speak or move on stage and can also tell where and when the scene is set.

- A **soliloquy** is a speech given by a character alone on stage. The character directly addresses the audience and reveals his or her inner thoughts and feelings.

Try It Read this scene from a play.

> ALEXA: (*Obviously frustrated, she gazes out the castle window. The moon is visible.*) I still don't know what to do. Clearly Father wishes for me to marry the count. (*looks sadly at painting of her father on the wall*) Father loves me and would never wish an unhappy alliance, even if it did benefit our nation. (*looks back out the window*) Tell me, Moon. (*pauses*) What sort of man might this count be beyond his silks, furs, and golden rings?

Discuss Draw a box around the dialogue tag. Who is speaking? Circle the stage directions. How does the character speak and move? Where is the scene set? How can you tell this is a soliloquy?

As you read, record your answers to questions about dramatic structure on the Close Reading Worksheet on page 288.

Purpose for Reading
Read along with your teacher. Each time, read for a different purpose.

First Read   Focus on cause and effect.

Second Read   Focus on dramatic structure.

Third Read   Focus on thinking critically about the drama.

The Lost River,
Act 1

CAST OF CHARACTERS

ABIGAIL, thirteen-year-old girl

LAURA, mother of Abigail

THOMAS, electrical engineer, father of Abigail

MRS. CLEMSON, town librarian

ROBBIE, twelve-year-old boy and store clerk

Scene 1

What causes Abigail to be so upset? <u>Double underline</u> the effect she thinks this will have. Write both things on the **Cause-and-Effect Chart**.

When and where is this scene set? How do you know?

SETTING: *The entry hall of a large house in Boston, 1927. Thomas and Laura Gooden and Abigail stand as porters carry out trunks and cases marked "FRAGILE." They're dressed in tweed traveling clothes. A touring car's motor can be heard chugging outside. Above them is a crystal chandelier.*

1 ABIGAIL: (*stomping her foot so the chandelier tinkles*) I won't go!

2 LAURA: A few months in the country will do you nothing but good.

3 ABIGAIL: Good? This is exile, that's what it is. It's **banishment**. I'll lose every friend I ever had.

4 THOMAS: (*clearly amused*) It's not exile, Crumpet.[1] It's an adventure.

5 ABIGAIL: Don't call me Crumpet. I'm nearly fourteen.

---

[1]**crumpet** a small, unsweetened cake, used here as a pet name

6   LAURA: (*leaning on her husband's arm*) Oh, Abigail. When the marvelous lamps your father has designed turn on, **illuminating** Virginia's Natural Bridge, it's going to be the proudest night of our lives. Imagine, the first lighting of that great stone archway. It's history. And you know who's throwing the switch, don't you?

7   ABIGAIL: President Coolidge.[2] Hmph. I'm not going and that's it. (*She stomps her foot again, and Laura and Thomas look up nervously at the chandelier.*)

8   THOMAS: (*putting on huge gloves and a pair of goggles*) Got to get on the road. Days of hard traveling between here and the Shenandoah.[3]

9   ABIGAIL: You look like a bug.

10   THOMAS: (*hugging her, smoothing her hair*) I can't say how, Crumpet, but I have a feeling you won't regret a minute of this.

Scene 2

SETTING: *The Goodens in the touring car. Backdrop is a lovely mountain view. Thomas and Laura sit in front, Abigail in the back.*

11   THOMAS: (*shouting over the engine*) Electricity, Abby—it's a wonder of the modern world.

12   LAURA: (*shouting*) This town's going to be famous, Abigail, once your father's done installing the light show. Folks will **flock** there. They'll come swarming in from all over the country.

13   ABIGAIL: (*shouting*) Why should I care about a town I've never even heard of before? I bet they have no soda fountains, no concerts, no dances—no anything. What am I supposed to do with myself?

[2]**Coolidge** Calvin Coolidge (1872–1933), thirtieth president of the United States
[3]**Shenandoah** a river valley in western Virginia and West Virginia

What are the effects of the loud car engine in scene 2? Write your answers on the **Cause-and-Effect Chart**.

Circle the stage direction that helps you know why everyone is shouting in scene 2.

What is the effect on the audience of Thomas telling his daughter he has "a feeling" she won't regret the trip at the end of scene 1?

Scene 3

Underline what causes Thomas and Laura to come up with an occupation for their daughter. Write your answer on the **Cause-and-Effect Chart**.

How do Thomas and Laura feel at the start of this scene? Circle the stage directions that tell you.

SETTING: *Days later, in a Virginia hotel room. Thomas and Laura are alone. He is seated, stripping off his gloves and goggles. She is unpacking a mess of bags and trunks.*

14 THOMAS: (*frustrated*) Well. That was a long ride.

15 LAURA: (*exhausted*) Oh yes. Did we have to make the last leg all in one day?

16 THOMAS: Did you really want to spend another night in some one-room roadhouse with . . . (*nods toward the door to the other room, indicating Abigail*)

17 LAURA: (*peers out the window*) Thomas, we absolutely must find something to engage Abigail. She's so used to life in Boston, all that activity. She's going to drive us mad.

18 THOMAS: How about we make Abby a proposition? If she writes a book about the natural bridge—and properly researches it—we'll bind it and publish it back in Boston.

19 LAURA: She could illustrate it, too. She'd love that.

20 THOMAS: What she's going to love is the investigation. Imagine, the **interrogation** of every poor soul in town! Gathering evidence. It's what she does.

21 LAURA: Abigail does have a mad passion for mystery stories.

22 THOMAS: Excellent. Let her indulge that passion. My mind will be set on lighting that bridge. (*smiles thoughtfully*) Laura, I'm going to create the brightest glow the world has ever seen.

23 LAURA: (*hugging him*) I know that you are, Thomas. I'll go and see to Abigail.

Scene 4

SETTING: *The local library the following day. The librarian, Mrs. Clemson, sits behind a desk. Abigail bursts in wearing an explorer's outfit—heavy canvas pants, a sun hat, and her father's huge gloves. It's clear this is not her first visit today.*

24 ABIGAIL: (*wipes her muddy boots on the mat*) Hello, Mrs. Clemson. So was it George Washington who carved that big GW into the Natural Bridge? It says 1750, so I figured—

25 MRS. CLEMSON: Your boots are a horror, Miss Gooden. But yes, that mark was left by the father of our country, and another founder, Thomas Jefferson, purchased this whole area for a mere twenty shillings . . .

26 ABIGAIL: (*pulling out her lunch and tearing into it*) That's all interesting, I guess. Just not, you know, very.

27 MRS. CLEMSON: (*changing the subject*) You are a very special child, Miss Gooden. I find it frankly **distasteful** that a girl of your tender years should be allowed to wander unattended, in such strange attire and in such a filthy state, rather than attending to more pleasant pursuits.

28 ABIGAIL: I'm going to put it all in my book, Mrs. Clemson. Boring or not. I just wish there was something more. See, if I had a clue about what I'm missing, my investigation would be easier.

29 MRS. CLEMSON: I think it's time you left the library in peace. What you need is a guide. And I know just the one. Go to the soda fountain on Cherry Lane. Robbie Lyme knows these hills better than any boy his age has a right to.

30 ABIGAIL: (*almost speechless with delight*) There's a *soda fountain*? Here?

What cause-and-effect relationship results in Mrs. Clemson finding a way to get Abigail out of the library? Put your answers into the **Cause-and-Effect Chart**.

What role do costumes play in this scene?

Scene 5

SETTING: *The soda fountain a few minutes later. Robbie Lyme, a twelve-year-old boy who looks young for his age, works the counter.*

What cause-and-effect relationship results from Robbie's mention of Sir Arthur Conan Doyle? Write your answers on the **Cause-and-Effect Chart.**

31   ABIGAIL: Sarsaparilla,[4] please. Are you Robbie Lyme?

32   ROBBIE: (*slides the drink down the counter*) That's me. And you're Abigail Gooden. Staying at the St. Francis Hotel, I believe.

33   ABIGAIL: You're a regular Sherlock Holmes, Robbie. A little young, aren't you?

34   ROBBIE: (*brightens*) I've read everything Sir Arthur Conan Doyle ever wrote. And despite appearances, I'm twelve.

Circle the stage direction that helps you know a soliloquy is being used at the end of this scene. What makes it a soliloquy?

35   ABIGAIL: OK. (*looks both ways, slides a nickel across the counter*) Have a sarsaparilla on me, and I'll explain the case. (*Robbie draws a soda.*) I'm investigating the Natural Bridge. How it got here, what it is. Everything about it.

36   ROBBIE: Then you need to see the caverns, where the bridge came from. But it's maybe not for a girl. They're deeper than the tallest building. They only just got discovered.

37   ABIGAIL: (*eyes filled with wonder*) That's what I want—to see the caverns.

38   ROBBIE: All right. I'll show you. But you can't get scared or cry. Deal?

39   ABIGAIL: (*shakes his hand*) It's a deal, Mr. Watson. (*Abigail walks to the front of the stage. The scene goes dark. A spotlight shines on her, alone.*) He may look like a little boy, but if he knows about this place like Mrs. Clemson says, he's the guide I need. Maybe Dad was right: This summer may not be a total loss after all.

[4]**sarsaparilla** a sweet soft drink, similar to root beer, popular in the late-nineteenth and early twentieth centuries

Interpret

Why does Abigail become so excited when she hears that there is a soda fountain in town?

Vocabulary: Synonyms and Antonyms

In your reading, you will come across words that have similar meanings to other words. Such words are called **synonyms**. *Grumpy*, *cranky*, and *crotchety* are synonyms. **Antonyms** are words that have opposite or nearly opposite meanings. *Black* and *white* are antonyms. If you find an unfamiliar word, it sometimes helps to look at the context, the words and sentences that surround it, for a synonym or antonym to help you figure out the unfamiliar word's meaning.

Try It Read this excerpt from *The Lost River*.

> LAURA: (*shouting*) This town's going to be famous, Abigail, once your father's done installing the light show. Folks will **flock** there. They'll come swarming in from all over the country.

Discuss **Which word or phrase in the excerpt is a synonym for *flock*? Draw a box around the words that help you figure this out. Discuss how the words mean the same thing, as used here.**

Find the following words in *The Lost River*. Look at the context for a synonym or antonym. Write each synonym or antonym on the lines provided, indicate which it is, and provide a definition.

1. **banishment**, p. 62 _____

_____

2. **illuminating**, p. 63 _____

_____

3. **interrogation**, p. 64 _____

_____

4. **distasteful**, p. 65 _____

_____

Practice the Skill

First Read **Cite Textual Evidence**

Textual evidence is anything you can find in written material that supports your analysis, or explanation of what something means. When you cite textual evidence, you show exactly what text supports your analysis.

For example, if an analysis of act 1 of *The Lost River* leads you to conclude that Abigail shares her father's outsized ambition, you would need to show specific text from the play that shows this similarity. You could point to Thomas Gooden's claim that he will "create the brightest glow the world has ever seen" and Abigail's wish for "something more" as support for this analysis.

As you read and form ideas about a text, consider which actual words from the text support your analysis.

Try It Read this scene from a play.

JUAN: (*staring at his phone*) I can't believe Isabel doesn't even text me back. All she has to say is yes or no, but she has to say something, doesn't she? By now, she has to get that I want to take her to the dance.

ESTELLA: Not necessarily. Maybe she's not going to be around, or maybe someone else asked her. (*trying to catch Juan's attention, but he's focused on his phone*) There are other girls in the world besides Isabel.

JUAN: (*not listening, playing with his phone*) Right, sure. Maybe she's in class so she can't use her phone. That's probably it.

ESTELLA: Oh, no doubt. (*blows out her cheeks*) A girl *not* talking to you is a sure sign she's interested. But a girl sitting right next to you? (*She slides closer to him.*) Listening to your problems? She couldn't possibly want to go to a dance with you, right?

JUAN: (*staring at his phone*) What?

Discuss How is Estella feeling? What does she want? Circle the text that supports your ideas.

As you read, complete the **Cite Textual Evidence Chart** on page 289.

Practice the Skill

In a drama, **plot** involves the conflict characters face and the events that occur in which they work to solve the conflict. The action of the plot is framed by the setting and told through the words and actions of the characters. **Setting** refers to the time, place, and circumstances in which a story occurs. The **characters** are the people or animals that take part in the action.

Often, setting will shape both the characters and plot. For instance, in a drama with a historical setting, the characters are limited in their words and actions by the common practices, customs, and the technology of that time and place. Other times, the events of the drama are shaped by the setting. For example, a fierce snowstorm may trap rivals in a remote cabin and force them to work together or perish.

Try It Read this scene from a play.

> SETTING: *A tropical island with the sound of breaking waves in the background. Tilden and Glen sit playing chess on an improvised board, using shells and sea creatures as playing pieces.*
>
> TILDEN: Your move. Is that fiddler crab a knight or your king?
>
> GLEN: I can't remember. I didn't think it was possible to be this unbelievably, stunningly bored. My brain's turning into mush.
>
> TILDEN: (*eyeing movement on the board*) Well, whichever it is, your knight or your king, it's walking away.
>
> GLEN: I don't get it, Tilden. (*grabs the crab and moves it*) We've been wrecked on this beach for three weeks, and you never complain about anything. The endless diet of coconuts, the broiling days, the freezing nights. (*yawns*)
>
> TILDEN: I don't know, Glen. (*turns a playing piece in his fingers*) Maybe it's that, for me, life has always been a bit of a desert island? I've got the routine down. (*sets the piece down*) I believe that's checkmate.

> **Discuss** Draw a box around details that describe the setting. How does the setting affect what the characters do and say?

As you read, record your answers to questions about character, setting, and plot on the **Close Reading Worksheet** on page 290. ✏️➡️

Purpose for Reading
Read along with your teacher. Each time, read for a different purpose.

First Read — Focus on citing textual evidence to support your ideas.

Second Read — Focus on the drama's character, setting, and plot.

Third Read — Focus on thinking critically about the drama.

The Lost River,
Act 2

Scene 1

How does Abigail feel about the progress of her investigation? Circle evidence that supports your ideas. Record your answers in the **Cite Textual Evidence Chart**.

What does the waterfall in this setting and the observation it prompts help reveal about Abigail's character?

SETTING: *A clearing deep in the forest a month later. Abigail is perched on a small stump, sketching. We hear the sound of a waterfall offstage.*

1   ABIGAIL: This waterfall is called the Lace Fan. So delicate, like those dresses mother wants me to wear. (*glances down at her stained canvas trousers*) What would she think of the saltpeter[1] mines nearby? That foul smell? Robbie says they supplied gunpowder for the Revolution, the War of 1812, *and* the Civil War. (*notes these things down*)

(*Robbie enters the clearing.*)

2   ABIGAIL: (*doesn't look up*) You're late.

3   ROBBIE: Shop had a new shipment of gas canisters. No bubbles, no soda.

4   ABIGAIL: For the millionth time, Robbie. It's been a whole summer. When are you going to take me to the caverns?

5   ROBBIE: (*looking at her thoughtfully*) When I know you're up to it. Maybe tomorrow.

6   ABIGAIL: Always tomorrow. (*blows out her bangs*) So, what's on for today, then?

7   ROBBIE: The oldest tree in the world. The *arbor vitae*.

[1]**saltpeter**   naturally occurring potassium nitrate, a substance used to make explosives (especially gunpowder)

8   ABIGAIL: Wait. Let me guess. It's Latin. *The Tree of Life.*

9   ROBBIE: (*nods, impressed*) You're good.

10   ABIGAIL: (*getting to her feet*) Come, Watson. The game's afoot.[2]

(*An image of the 1,600-year-old Tree of Life is projected on a backdrop. Robbie and Abigail enter.*)

11   ABIGAIL: (*pausing, a bit out of breath*) So that's it, eh? The oldest tree in the world . . .

12   ROBBIE: Well, 1,600 years. That much is for sure.

(*A chugging sound, almost like a distant freight train, fills the air.*)

13   ABIGAIL: (*looking around*) What is that?

14   ROBBIE: (*shaken*) The Lost River. An old native legend. No one's really seen it, at least not in modern times. But sometimes, in the deep woods, you can hear it.

15   ABIGAIL: Why on earth did you not tell me about this, Robbie?

16   ROBBIE: Because it's like I said, no one ever sees it. It's probably not even real.

17   ABIGAIL: But we can hear it so clearly. Let's chase it down, Robbie. (*turning to him*) We'll make history! (*walks to other side of stage*)

(*The chugging sound fades.*)

18   ROBBIE: It's too late, it's already going away.

[2]**the game's afoot** Sherlock Holmes quoted these words from Shakespeare to his assistant, Dr. Watson, to say their suspect (game) is on the run and the chase is on.

Circle evidence that Abigail considers Robbie to be her assistant.

What is the conflict at this point?

19 ABIGAIL: (*waving for him to join her*) Come on, Robbie! I can tell where the sound came from. But we have to go now, while I can still remember—just through those sycamore trees . . .

20 ROBBIE: (*hesitant*) No. Not that way.

21 ABIGAIL: (*smiling, crosses to Robbie*) You know where it is! You have an idea where to look, don't you?

22 ROBBIE: (*turns away from her*) In the caverns.

23 ABIGAIL: So, let's go down there! (*stomps her foot*) Today!

24 ROBBIE: It's not that simple—we'd need candles. And rope. And extra clothes. It's cold down there. We have to plan it.

25 ABIGAIL: So we'll plan it, then. We'll go tomorrow.

26 ROBBIE: I can't get off work. All these tourists are coming in for your dad's light show.

How does Abigail know that Robbie is afraid?

27 ABIGAIL: (*her eyes and mouth open wide*) You've never been in the caverns, have you, Robbie? (*Robbie looks nervous.*) That's why you haven't taken me yet. It's not because I'm a girl. It's because you're afraid. Aren't you?

28 ROBBIE: (*shrugging*) Sort of. I guess. (*pauses*) I don't like closed spaces.

29 ABIGAIL: Please, Robbie. (*places her hands on his shoulders*) Summer's almost over. I have to see the caverns.

30   ROBBIE: (*nods thoughtfully*) We'll need lots of lights. And you can't leave me alone. Not even for a second.

31   ABIGAIL: I'll be right by your side. We're a team, Robbie. Always. (*She ruffles his hair.*) Holmes and Watson.

Scene 2

SETTING: *The caverns. A wall of limestone shines in the glow of Robbie's lamp. The light bathes Abigail as she climbs through a passage ahead of him.*

32   ABIGAIL: It's like the mountain's breathing on me. Brrrr. Pretty dark down here.

33   ROBBIE: Well, that's just great. (*He stops walking; the light above stops moving.*)

34   ABIGAIL: Robbie? Are you coming? Robbie you have to come through right now, or *I'm* going to get scared.

35   ROBBIE: (*joining her*) Well, you look plenty scary. (*Abigail's face is lit from below.*)

36   ABIGAIL: That's because you've got the wick too low. Turn it up, Robbie.

(*Both stand stunned as the increased light dances on slick pink walls, shining stalactites.*)

37   ABIGAIL: Robbie. It's beautiful. Like an underground cathedral or Boston all lit up on New Year's Eve. But better.

38   ROBBIE: (*hushed*) It's **dynamic**, a living cave. I read that it grows a little deeper every year. Water seeps through cracks and erodes the limestone. It's how the bridge formed.

39   ABIGAIL: Listen. Can you hear it? (*There's a far-off crash of water.*)

40   ROBBIE: The Lost River.

41   ABIGAIL: Let's go deeper. (*Robbie sits.*) Oh, Robbie, I'm sorry. Look, we don't have to actually see it—we can hear it. Hearing's as good as seeing, right? (*She sits next to him.*)

How does Abigail's attitude change in scene 2? Circle evidence that supports your ideas. Record your answers in the **Cite Textual Evidence Chart**.

Draw a box around details that describe the cave. How does the cave setting affect the characters' actions?

Circle evidence that Abigail is no longer as concerned with her Boston friends as she was at the beginning of the play.

In what way is the descent into the caverns actually a high point for Abigail?

42 ROBBIE: Some folks say there are tunnels down there that will take you back to any point in your life you want. Like magic. You just step out at the hole you choose. Start all over again from there. Like some moment, a time you wish you'd taken a different turn.

43 ABIGAIL: (*looking at Robbie*) You know what? I'd always come out here. It's been like magic. The things you've shown me: the *arbor vitae*, the Lace Fan, even the saltpeter mines. (*grinning widely*) You won't find any of that in Boston!

44 ROBBIE: Just listen. All that dripping. The cavern's getting bigger. Even while we're sitting here. That has to be true, right? (*Abigail nods, leaning in to him.*) Each drip we hear, that's time. It's like we're inside a big clock, and that clock is the world.

45 ABIGAIL: Those are big thoughts, Robbie.

46 ROBBIE: For such a young boy. That's what you're thinking, isn't it?

47 ABIGAIL: For anyone, Robbie. My friends at home? They'd be far more interested to hear that sarsaparilla tastes exactly like root beer. They'd ask, "What were the dances and parties like? Did you meet the president?" And here I am, sitting in the heartbeat of the world— thanks to you.

(*Robbie raises the lamp, and the walls glisten again in a magnificent display.*)

48 ROBBIE: Hey! Isn't tonight your father's big show?

49 ABIGAIL: (*startled*) Oh, gosh, it is! (*sighs, watches the lights dance*) Honestly though, Robbie . . . the greatest light show in the world? It's right here.

Scene 3

SETTING: *Under the Natural Bridge at twilight. Laura, Abigail, and Robbie wait for the light show. A **generator** rumbles offstage.*

50 ROBBIE: Gosh, Mrs. Gooden, these are prime seats. Thanks so much for inviting me. I've never seen so many people in one place.

51 LAURA: (*pointing, handing them a pair of binoculars*) Look, you two! You can see Calvin Coolidge. He's talking to your father about something.

52 ABIGAIL: (*smiling as she peers through the binoculars*) Dad's making sure the president of the United States knows how to turn on the lights!

53 LAURA: Trust me, it will all go like clockwork. Knowing your father, he's got backups to his backups. I've seen almost as little of your father this summer as I have of you, Abigail. Remind me what it is you two have been up to?

54 ABIGAIL: Oh, you know. Just poking around.

55 LAURA: Well, whatever it is, I think it's **created** some kind of magical effect on you. You seem changed somehow, Abby. If I didn't know better I might even say transformed. But that would take some very strong magic, indeed.

> How do Laura's words support what you have already learned about the summer's effect on Abigail?

56 ABIGAIL: (*flashing Robbie a secret smile in the dark*) Oh, there's magic in these hills. (*as if to herself*) More than I ever imagined.

(*The lights suddenly flash on, bathing the whole scene in bright light. All three characters break into huge grins.*)

57 THOMAS: (*voice booming over a loudspeaker*) Tonight you witness history . . .

Scene 4

SETTING: *Back in Boston a month later. Abigail, Thomas, and Laura are looking at a leather-bound copy of Abigail's book, which lies on a table in the parlor of their Beacon Hill home. Summer has turned to fall. Rain lashes the windows.*

How has Abigail changed over the course of the play? What evidence supports that analysis? Record your answers in the **Cite Textual Evidence Chart**.

58 THOMAS: So, how does it feel, Abby? Finally finishing your epic work. (*reading the title page out loud*) The Lost River.

59 ABIGAIL: I don't know. It's like having to leave everything all over again. When I was turning the sketches into paintings, I felt myself going back in time.

60 LAURA: (*teasing*) Who'd have ever **predicted** that Abigail Gooden would become **sentimental** about her exile?

Draw boxes around the details of setting. How does the setting reflect Abigail's character in the final scene?

61 ABIGAIL: Mother, please. I know I was a terrible snob. It hurts to think about it, actually. It's hard to believe I'll probably never go back there again.

62 LAURA: (*puts a hand on Abigail's shoulder*) When you live something deeply, Crumpet, it stays with you forever.

63 ABIGAIL: (*turns the pages, a little wistful*) Do you suppose Robbie will ever see this?

64 THOMAS: You know one thing's for sure. If a copy of this book found its way into the local library, that boy would run across it. Such a reader, that one.

65 ABIGAIL: Of course! If we sent it to Mrs. Clemson she'd have to shelve it. (*goes to the window, looking out but not seeing Boston*) So one rainy Saturday, Robbie will come into the library, looking for the latest Sherlock Holmes. And there it will be, our book. Waiting for him.

66 LAURA: I guess it isn't a lost river after all.

67 ABIGAIL: (*weighs the book in her hands*) No, not lost at all. Not anymore.

Judge

Will the changes to Abigail's character be permanent? Why or why not?

Vocabulary: Greek and Latin Roots

Greek and **Latin roots** are the basic word parts that have been borrowed from these languages. These roots convey the basic meaning of a word. For example, the word *patronize* means "to give support or aid," like a parent would. It contains a root that comes from the Latin word *pater*, which means "father."

Try It Read this sentence from *The Lost River*.

> LAURA: (*teasing*) Who'd have ever predicted that Abigail Gooden would become **sentimental** about her exile?

The word *sentimental* contains the Latin root *sent*, meaning "to feel." Based on the meaning of this root, what does the word *sentimental* mean?

Discuss **Brainstorm all the words you can think of with the root *sent* or *sens*, and use each one in a different sentence.**

The following words with Greek or Latin roots appear in act 2 of *The Lost River*. Read the meaning of the root, and write a definition for the word. Reread the word in context to check that your definition is correct.

1. **dynamic**, p. 73 The Greek root *dyna* means "power or force." _____

   _____

2. **generator**, p. 75 The Latin root *gen* means "birth or produce." _____

   _____

3. **created**, p. 75 The Latin root *crea* means "to make." _____

   _____

4. **predicted**, p. 76 The Latin root *dict* means "to speak." _____

   _____

Respond to Text: How Setting Affects Character

The Lost River is set in Boston and Virginia. These different settings help shape the events of the plot by creating a conflict. The settings also help shape the characters by showing how someone can change as a result of a change in surroundings.

Try It Think about the dramatic elements in this play and how they work together to shape the reader's experience.

 Discuss **What does the setting at the drama's start tell you about the Gooden family? How do you know this? What does Abigail's initial reaction to their summer vacation say about her?**

On Your Own Write a paragraph that compares and contrasts Abigail's life in Boston to her life in Virginia and how she changes as a result of the change in settings. Briefly describe each setting. Cite evidence from the play to support your conclusions. Use the next page to help you plan your response. Then write your paragraph on a separate sheet of paper.

Checklist for a Good Response

A good paragraph

✔ clearly states the comparisons being made.

✔ describes the settings.

✔ explains how Abigail changes and why.

✔ includes details from the text to support your conclusions.

✔ shows your understanding of the information.

✔ includes a topic sentence, supporting ideas, and a concluding statement.

Comparing and Contrasting Characters in Different Settings

1. **Topic Sentence** Include this information in your first sentence:

   When Abigail lives in Boston, she _____.

   but when she moves to Virginia, she _____.

2. **Detail Sentences** The sentences of your paragraph should cite evidence that explain your conclusions. Use this chart to organize your ideas.

What Abigail is like in Boston	What Abigail is like in Virginia
The setting at the start suggests that the Goodens are well off.	
Abigail's attitude about going to Virginia shows she might be snobbish and spoiled.	
Abigail seems unwilling to accept change.	

3. **Concluding Sentence** Your final sentence should restate your conclusions with a new twist.

   _____

   _____

   _____

On a separate sheet of paper, write your paragraph.

Read on Your Own

Read the drama independently three times, using the skills you have learned. Then answer the Comprehension Check questions.

First Read Practice the first-read skills you learned in this lesson.

Second Read Practice the second-read skills you learned in this lesson.

Third Read Think critically about the drama.

Circle in the Woods

CAST OF CHARACTERS

BRIANNA, teen girl; assertive and forceful

DEREK, teen boy; Brianna's male counterpart

TAFFY, teen girl; a complainer

ALAN, teen boy; not part of original group

HUAN, one of Operation Leadership's coordinators

Scene 1

Cite Textual Evidence Circle textual evidence that shows how Brianna and Derek are dealing with their situation. Some details have been circled for you.

SETTING: *The summer of 1973. A forest clearing. Brianna, Derek, and Taffy enter through the brush, dressed for a day hike, in 1970s-era shorts, T-shirts, and boots.*

1   BRIANNA: (*leading the others into the clearing*) I can't believe they let you into Operation Leadership—

2   DEREK: Settle down, Brianna. Your comments aren't helping the situation.

3   TAFFY: Where are we? Where are the other groups? Are they lost, too?

Character, Setting, and Plot Draw a box around the text that describes the setting. Think about how it might affect the plot.

4   DEREK: Look, Brianna, can't you see this is exactly what **Operation Leadership** is all about? Giving us the chance to be real leaders. It's important that we can cope with trouble.

5   BRIANNA: Ha! You? Talking about coping? Like how you coped when you broke our compass? Or when it turned out I was *right* that we were following the orange trail markers and not the red ones?

6   ALAN: (*stumbling into the clearing*) Hey, guys. What group are you?

7   BRIANNA and DEREK (*together, through gritted teeth, eyes locked*): The Wolverines.

8   ALAN: I started with the Grizzlies. But I stopped to tie my shoe and when I looked up, poof. I was alone. (*extends his hand*) I'm Alan.

9   BRIANNA: There's a group called the Grizzlies? Are you sure?

10 TAFFY: (*addressing Alan*) Dude, you are, like, really **pale**. I've never seen anyone so white.

11 DEREK: (*extends his hand*) Derek. (*unfolds a map*) Let me show you where we are.

12 BRIANNA: (*snippy*) Our fearless leader, consulting his upside-down map. (*Derek sheepishly reverses the map.*) We're just going in circles.

13 ALAN: At least I'm not lost anymore.

14 TAFFY: You think finding us means you're not lost? It just confirms that you *are* lost. (*holds out her hand, palm up*) Hey, is it raining? Now we're going to be wet *and* lost!

15 DEREK: Leadership asserts itself, Brianna. It doesn't wait for everyone else to catch up. That's why we all just met today—so leadership can come to the fore naturally.

(*As Brianna and Derek consult the map, Alan climbs a tree at the edge of the stage. The sound of rain grows louder, and Taffy starts crying.*)

16 BRIANNA: Leadership is about understanding people, not just asserting yourself.

17 DEREK: So you're the understanding one? Is that how you see it?

18 BRIANNA: More so than you. Look what you've done to Taffy.

19 ALAN: (*from up in the tree, pointing*) Hey. I see some shelter over there.

Cause and Effect
Underline what causes Taffy to start crying. Think about the effect her crying has on other characters.

Dramatic Structure
Think about how the stage directions help you understand the plot and the play's action.

Scene 2

Character, Setting, and Plot Think about how the setting shapes the plot in this scene.

SETTING: *An abandoned cabin. Derek has spread the map on a table, Brianna is half looking at it, arms crossed. Taffy sits in a broken chair, head in her hands.*

20 DEREK: (*examining the map*) Hey. This place isn't on the map.

21 BRIANNA: That's because it's the wrong map, and it always has been.

22 DEREK: No way.

23 TAFFY: What does it matter if it's on the map? We're still stuck in the woods. What if we never get out?

24 BRIANNA: Who knew a forest could be this big? Or this cold? (*rubs her arms*) Brrr.

25 ALAN: (*entering the cabin with a load of firewood*) I checked out the chimney, and it looks clear. (*He begins building a fire while Brianna and Derek go back to the map, each tugging it in a different direction; Taffy drags her chair over to watch Alan work. As the fire begins to crackle, Derek looks up from the map.*)

26 DEREK: Hey. That's actually a pretty good idea. (*He goes to the fire Alan has started, and he begins carelessly heaping more and more wood on it.*)

27 ALAN: Hey, um. That's kind of a lot . . .

28 DEREK: (*chuckling*) Brianna's cold; we can't have that. A leader serves his people.

(*The fire swiftly becomes a raging inferno. Taffy wanders offstage.*)

29 TAFFY: (*offstage*) Flames are coming out of the chimney! Get out of there, now!

Scene 3

SETTING: *In the woods again, a red glow can be seen in the distance. The rain has stopped.*

Cite Textual Evidence
Think about how Alan is changing. Circle evidence that supports your ideas.

30   TAFFY: See it? That red glow?

31   ALAN: The woods are on fire.

32   BRIANNA: Well, that's just great, Derek. Had to build the biggest fire, didn't you?

33   TAFFY: It doesn't matter—listen.

(*The wind comes up, and the sound of the flames is a roar. All turn to Alan.*)

34   BRIANNA: Alan. Get us out of here.

(*Alan kneels, scoops up a bunch of leaves, and tosses them in the air.*)

35   ALAN: (*speaking with authority*) The wind is going that way. (*points stage right, then points left*) So, if we go that way, we'll stay behind the fire. Follow me. (*They all do.*)

(*The lights go black. When the lights come back up, they are still in the woods. A red, flickering glow bathes the stage. Characters pant as they catch their breaths, their faces blackened with soot. It's clear they're all scared, except for Alan.*)

36   DEREK: Are you sure this is the right way?

37   ALAN: (*sniffs the air*) There's a river this way—the road follows the river. Come on. It's the only way.

Scene 4

Dramatic Structure
Think about how the author resolves the plot.

Critical Thinking
Think about possible explanations for who Alan was, both logical and extraordinary.

SETTING: *Brianna, Derek, and Taffy sit by the side of a road, completely stunned, holding blankets around their shoulders. Flashing red and blue lights suggest emergency vehicles. Huan, a camp counselor, kneels before them. Sound indicates it is still raining.*

38   HUAN: I'm just so glad you guys are okay. The EMTs who checked you out say you're fine, just a little shaken up. The fire's under control—the rain helped with that. All the other hikers got out safely, too. (*taps a clipboard*) All present and accounted for.

39   DEREK: Thanks . . . It was quite an experience.

(*Brianna opens her mouth to speak, then just shakes her head.*)

40   HUAN: If you don't mind, I'm curious: Which one of you led the way out of there?

41   DEREK: It was Alan. He was just here, right? He has to be here.

42   BRIANNA: It was like he knew exactly where to go. Alan saved us.

43   TAFFY: He said he was with the Grizzlies group. Really pale kid?

44   HUAN: (*flipping through the pages on the clipboard over and over; finally looks up*) There's no Alan. There's no Grizzlies group, either.

45   BRIANNA: But that's . . . that's impossible.

46   HUAN: I was right here when you came out of the woods. There was no one else, just the three of you.

(*They all stand frozen in the rain, smoke whipping around them.*)

✅ Comprehension Check

1. Why didn't the characters get to know one another before the hike? What evidence supports this?

_____

_____

_____

2. Who starts the out-of-control fire in the cabin? What element of the plot structure shows this action?

_____

_____

3. What effect does Alan's climbing the tree have?

_____

_____

4. In which scene can you find the climax, or high point, of the drama? What happens in that scene?

_____

_____

5. What motivates Derek to throw more wood on the fire?

_____

_____

6. What aspect of the setting explains why the characters do not use a GPS to find their location or use a cell phone to call for help?

_____

_____

7. Read these lines from the play.

DEREK: Look, Brianna, can't you see this is exactly what Operation Leadership is all about? Giving us the chance to be real leaders.

The Latin root *oper* means "work." What other words share this root? What do you think the word *operation* means based on the meaning of the root and the context of the sentence?

_____

_____

8. Read these lines from the play.

TAFFY: (*addressing Alan*) Dude, you are, like, really pale. I've never seen anyone so white.

Circle the word that is a synonym for *pale*. Think of an antonym for *pale*, and write a sentence using the antonym.

_____

_____

_____

Lesson 4
Poetry

Poetry has been an essential part of human expression since the beginning of language. As the oldest literary genre, poetry was recited and sung long before it was ever written down. Even today, one of the most effective ways to appreciate a poem is to hear it spoken or sung.

Poetry uses rhythmic language to express truths about things that exist in our world and about what it means to be human. Each reader responds differently to a poem, depending on his or her own experiences. What thoughts might you bring to a poem about skateboarding? What words would you use to describe the photo below?

Skills Focus

The Lake Isle of Innisfree / I wandered lonely as a cloud / The Cat and the Moon

Visualize   **Rhyme, Alliteration, Assonance**

The Ballad of King Arthur / Annabel Lee / Shall I compare thee to a summer's day? / The Oven Bird

Paraphrase   **Poetic Structure: Narrative Poem and Sonnet**

Practice the Skill

First Read **Visualize**

Suppose you had a friend who had never seen snow. How would you describe the experience of snow? Would a picture or video of snow be enough? What words could help your friend **visualize** snow?

Visualization means forming a mental image inside your head, in what is called "the mind's eye." A poet's words help you form a mental image of what is being described. Visualization is essential to understanding a poem and bringing it to life. Two important tools help you visualize a poet's words: your experience in the world and your imagination. This means you won't always visualize the same thing as the next reader. As long as the poet has left room for interpretation in his or her images, this is normal and acceptable. It helps explain why the same poem can affect readers differently.

Try It Read these lines from the poem "Snow in the Suburbs" by Thomas Hardy.

> Every branch big with it,
>
> Bent every twig with it;
>
> Every fork like a white web-foot;
>
> Every street and pavement mute:
>
> Some flakes have lost their way, and grope back upward, when
>
> Meeting those meandering down they turn and descend again.

Discuss > What words help you visualize the snow? Circle the key words. Note that the word *mute* means "silent." Why might the pavement be described as "mute"? What in your experience helps you visualize the scene the poet describes?

> **As you read, complete the Visualization Chart on page 291.**

Practice the Skill

Second Read Rhyme, Alliteration, Assonance

Poetry is written to be heard, and poets choose words with sounds that suit their subject matter. For example, the words of a lullaby usually sound soft and musical, while the words in a poem about a raging sea might crash around your ears. Three common poetic devices, or methods, that poets use to achieve these effects are rhyme, alliteration, and assonance.

Rhyme, the repetition of sounds at the ends of words, is the most familiar poetic device. Rhymes please the ear and the mind. They create a sense of completion and make a poem easier to remember. They usually come at the end of a line and follow a pattern called a rhyme scheme. Common rhyme schemes include alternating rhyming lines and pairs of rhyming lines called couplets.

Alliteration, the repetition of the initial consonant sounds in words, is another way that poets play with word sounds. In our national anthem, "Oh **s**ay can you **s**ee," "**r**ockets' **r**ed," and "**s**tar **s**pangled" are examples of alliteration.

Assonance is the repetition of similar vowel sounds within words. Repeated vowel sounds are appealing to the ear, as in Alfred, Lord Tennyson's description of an eagle that "cl**a**sps the cr**a**g with crooked h**a**nds."

When you read a poem, listen for its unique sounds. Read the poem aloud. What different kinds of sounds do you hear? What mood or feeling do these sounds convey? How do the sounds suit the subject of the poem?

Try It Read these opening lines from the poem "Silver" by Walter de la Mare.

> Slowly, silently, now the moon
>
> Walks the night in her silver shoon;
>
> This way and that, she peers, and sees
>
> Silver fruit upon silver trees;

Discuss **What rhyming words do you hear in these lines? Underline them. What alliteration do you hear? Box the words. How do these sounds contribute to the description of the moonlit night?**

As you read, record your answers to questions about poetic devices on the Close Reading Worksheet on page 292.

Purpose for Reading

Read the poems with your teacher. Each time, read for a different purpose.

First Read Focus on visualization.

Second Read Focus on rhyme, alliteration, and assonance.

Third Read Focus on evaluating the poems critically.

What do you visualize as you read the poem? (Circle) words that help you visualize. Describe or draw your answer on the **Visualization Chart.**

In the first stanza, underline the first pair of rhyming words. Double underline the second pair of rhyming words. Do the rhymes alternate, or are they in couplets?

Where is the speaker when he or she hears "lake water lapping"?

The Lake Isle of Innisfree

W. B. Yeats

I will arise and go now, and go to Innisfree,
And a small cabin build there, of clay and wattles[1] made;
Nine bean-rows will I have there, a hive for the honey-bee,
And live alone in the bee-loud glade.

5   And I shall have some peace there, for peace comes dropping slow,
Dropping from the veils of the morning to where the cricket sings;
There midnight's all a glimmer, and noon a purple glow,
And evening full of the linnet's[2] wings.

I will arise and go now, for always night and day
10 I hear lake water lapping with low sounds by the shore;
While I stand on the roadway, or on the pavements grey,
I hear it in the deep heart's core.

[1]**wattles** woven branches
[2]**linnet** small brown bird

I wandered lonely as a cloud

William Wordsworth

I wandered lonely as a cloud
That floats on high o'er vales[1] and hills,
When all at once I saw a crowd,
A host, of golden daffodils;
5   Beside the lake, beneath the trees,
Fluttering and dancing in the breeze.

Continuous as the stars that shine
And twinkle on the milky way,
They stretched in never-ending line
10   Along the margin of a bay:
Ten thousand saw I at a glance,
Tossing their heads in sprightly[2] dance.

The waves beside them danced; but they
Out-did the sparkling waves in glee:
15   A poet could not but be gay,
In such a **jocund**[3] company:
I gazed—and gazed—but little thought
What wealth the show to me had brought:

For oft, when on my couch I lie
20   In **vacant** or in pensive[4] mood,
They flash upon that inward eye
Which is the **bliss** of solitude;
And then my heart with pleasure fills,
And dances with the daffodils.

¹**vales** valleys
²**sprightly** lively
³**jocund** joyful
⁴**pensive** thoughtful

What does the word *crowd* help you visualize in the first stanza? Circle words in the poem that help you visualize many daffodils. Add your notes to the **Visualization Chart**.

Underline the rhyming pairs of verses. Where do the couplets appear in the poem?

How is the speaker's memory of the daffodils in this poem similar to the speaker's memory of Innisfree in the previous poem?

The Cat and the Moon

W. B. Yeats

What is the cat doing in the moonlight? Circle phrases that show you. Add your notes to the **Visualization Chart**.

Box words that are examples of alliteration.

The speaker says the cat is "the nearest kin of the moon." What does he or she mean? What do the cat and moon have in common?

The cat went here and there
And the moon spun round like a top,
And the nearest kin of the moon
The creeping cat looked up.
5   Black Minnaloushe stared at the moon,
For wander and wail as he would
The pure cold light in the sky
Troubled his animal blood.
Minnaloushe runs in the grass,
10 Lifting his **delicate** feet.
Do you dance, Minnaloushe, do you dance?
When two close kindred meet
What better than call a dance?
Maybe the moon may learn,
15 Tired of that courtly fashion,
A new dance turn.
Minnaloushe creeps through the grass
From moonlit place to place,
The **sacred** moon overhead
20 Has taken a new phase.
Does Minnaloushe know that his pupils
Will pass from change to change,
And that from round to crescent,
From crescent to round they range?
25 Minnaloushe creeps through the grass
Alone, important and wise,
And lifts to the changing moon
His changing eyes.

Judge

Which of the three poems do you think has the most powerful visual images? What words helped you visualize it?

Vocabulary: Denotation and Connotation

Some words express more than their dictionary definition, or **denotation**. Words can be associated with positive or negative emotions. For example, the word *slender* is positive, while the word *skinny* is negative. *Easygoing* is positive, but *lazy* is negative. These emotional associations are called the **connotations** of words. Neutral words have no special feeling associated with them.

Poets can choose words with positive or negative connotations to add emotional power to a poem.

Try It Read this phrase from "I wandered lonely as a cloud."

> In such a **jocund** company

> Discuss **Brainstorm ideas about the connotation of *jocund*.**

Reread each line in context. Determine the connotation—negative, positive, or neutral—of each word in italics. Then explain the impact of the word's connotation on the poem.

1. "In *vacant* or in pensive mood" p. 91 _____

   _____

2. "Which is the *bliss* of solitude" p. 91 _____

   _____

3. "Lifting his *delicate* feet" p. 92 _____

   _____

4. "the *sacred* moon overhead" p. 92 _____

   _____

Practice the Skill

When you **paraphrase** a poem, you use your own words to restate the poem in prose form. Paraphrasing is a good way to check your understanding of a poem. It can give you a better sense of a poem's meaning or call your attention to something you might not understand. A paraphrase should always be expressed in the same point of view as the poem.

To paraphrase a poem, reread it phrase by phrase, verse by verse. Look up in a dictionary any words you don't know, and think about the connotations of the words the poet used. Focus your attention on any lines that are difficult. Ask yourself, "Does the paraphrase make sense in relation to the rest of the poem? Does it express the poet's meaning?"

Poems are about much more than meaning, of course. They include poetic devices, rhythm, and figurative language. Don't try to bring all of those poetic elements into a paraphrase. For instance, a paraphrase would not address rhyme scheme.

Try It Try paraphrasing these lines written more than four hundred years ago by the poet Robert Herrick.

Gather ye rose-buds while ye may,
    Old Time is still a-flying:
And this same flower that smiles today
    Tomorrow will be dying.

Discuss   Reread the lines and restate them in your own words. What does the speaker mean by "Gather ye rose-buds"? How would you say "Old Time is still a-flying" in your own words?

As you read, complete the Paraphrase Chart on page 293.

Practice the Skill

Second Read **Poetic Structure: Narrative Poem and Sonnet**

Many poems follow a traditional structure, or form, that dictates how the poem is organized. For example, a **narrative poem** tells a story and has a plot, setting, and characters. Narrative poems can be short or very long. There are few rules. They usually rhyme, as older narratives were meant to be sung.

In contrast, a **sonnet** has many rules. Sonnets are commonly fourteen lines long. Some have two parts: an eight-line section that describes a situation or problem, followed by a six-line section that builds on it or adds a new thought. In some sonnets, the last two lines, called a couplet, present a conclusion or third idea. Sonnets usually keep a strict rhythm, or meter, throughout the poem. Most sonnets rhyme and follow a particular rhyming pattern, called a rhyme scheme.

Try It Read the sonnet "To Sleep" by William Wordsworth.

> A flock of sheep that leisurely pass by
> One after one; the sound of rain, and bees
> Murmuring; the fall of rivers, winds and seas,
> Smooth fields, white sheets of water, and pure sky;—
> 5   I've thought of all by turns, and still I lie
> Sleepless; and soon the small birds' melodies
> Must hear, first uttered from my orchard trees,
> And the first cuckoo's melancholy cry.
> Even thus last night, and two nights more I lay,
> 10   And could not win thee, Sleep! by any stealth:
> So do not let me wear tonight away:
> Without Thee what is all the morning's wealth?
> Come, blessed barrier between day and day,
> Dear mother of fresh thoughts and joyous health!

Discuss What is being described in the first eight lines of the sonnet? To whom are the last two stanzas addressed?

As you read, record your answers to questions about poetic structure on the Close Reading Worksheet on page 294.

Purpose for Reading

Read the poems with your teacher. Each time, read for a different purpose.

First Read Focus on paraphrasing.

Second Read Focus on poetic structure.

Third Read Focus on evaluating the poems critically.

The Ballad of King Arthur

In ancient Britain, songs called ballads were sung about legendary heroes. Ballads are a form of narrative poetry. This ballad is about King Arthur's childhood, when a mysterious sword appears near a church gate, firmly lodged in a massive stone. Golden letters on the stone declare that whoever can pull the sword from the stone "shall be Lord and King of all England." A tournament is scheduled for New Year's Day, when all the knights will try to pull the sword from the stone. Arthur's foster brother, Sir Kay, has forgotten his sword and asks Arthur to ride his horse back home to get it.

Paraphrase stanza 1, restating in your own words what Sir Kay says to Arthur. Record your paraphrase on the **Paraphrase Chart**.

What does the dialogue in these verses contribute to narrative form?

"O foster brother! backward speed,
   Ride fast for love of me,
And when thou reachest Ector's[1] house,
   My sword bring back to me."

5   "That will I," said the gallant youth,
      Riding away alone;
But when he reached the castle gate
   He found the wardour[2] gone,

And all the inmates, great and small,
10   Off to the tournament;
Baffled and wroth[3] he turned his horse
      And to the churchyard went.

[1]**Ector** Sir Kay's father
[2]**wardour** guard
[3]**wroth** angry

"Ten thousand pities 'twere," he said,
  "My dearest brother Kay

15 Should at the joust[4] withouten a sword
  Appear in disarray."

So when he found no knights were there
  But to the jousting gone,
Lightly yet fierce the sword he seized,
20 And pulled it from the stone,

And to Sir Kay delivered it,
  Who wist,[5] as soon as seen,
That 'twas the sword from out the stone;
  Then said, "Full well I ween[6]

25 I have the sword, and I must be
  The King of all England."
But when he showed it to his sire[7]
  Sir Ector gave command

That to the church he should repair
30 And swear upon the book
How gat he then the sword; but he,
  Fearing his sire's rebuke,[8]

Told how his foster brother came
  When all the knights were gone,
35 And light and fiercely plucked the sword
  From out the magic stone.

[4]**joust** competition
[5]**wist** understood
[6]**ween** think; suppose
[7]**sire** father
[8]**rebuke** scolding

What does Sir Kay want to do with the sword when he first sees it? Paraphrase what he says in lines 24–26 on the **Paraphrase Chart**.

In what ways would the structure of this ballad make it easy to sing to music?

Circle a detail that shows the events in this ballad didn't actually happen.

"Now try again," Sir Ector said;
　　Whereat they all assayed,[9]
But none save Arthur there availed[10]
40　　To sunder[11] out the blade.

Then happèd it[12] that on Twelfth day
　　The Barons all assay
To pluck the sword, but none **prevail**
　　Save Arthur on that day.

45　Then waxed[13] they wroth, and Candlemas[14]
　　Was fixed for the assay,
Yet still no knight but Arthur
　　Could pluck the sword away.

Then at high feast of Eastertide,
50　　Also at Pentecost,[15]
None but young Arthur loosed the sword—
　　The knights their temper lost.

But when the Lord Archbishop came,
　　All cried with one accord,
55　"We will have Arthur for our King,
　　God wills him for our lord."

And down on bended knee they fell
　　To pay him homage due;
And thus he won Excalibur[16]
60　　And all fair England too.

Soon Scotland, and the North, and Wales,[17]
　　To him obeisance[18] made,
Won by prowess[19] of his knights
　　And of his trusty blade.

[9]**assayed** tried
[10]**availed** managed
[11]**sunder** remove
[12]**happéd it** it happened
[13]**waxed** grew
[14]**Candlemas** religious festival
[15]**Eastertide, Pentecost** religious festivals

[16]**Excalibur** the name of Arthur's sword
[17]**Scotland ... Wales** border regions of Britain
[18]**obeisance** allegiance
[19]**prowess** skill

Annabel Lee

Edgar Allan Poe

It was many and many a year ago,
    In a kingdom by the sea,
That a maiden there lived whom you may know
    By the name of Annabel Lee;
5 And this maiden she lived with no other thought
    Than to love and be loved by me.

I was a child and she was a child,
    In this kingdom by the sea;
But we loved with a love that was more than love—
10   I and my Annabel Lee—
With a love that the winged seraphs[1] of Heaven
    Coveted her and me.

And this was the reason that, long ago,
    In this kingdom by the sea,
15 A wind blew out of a cloud, chilling
    My beautiful Annabel Lee;
So that her highborn kinsmen[2] came
    And bore her away from me,
To shut her up in a sepulchre
20   In this kingdom by the sea.

The angels, not half so happy in Heaven,
    Went envying her and me—
Yes!—that was the reason (as all men know,
    In this kingdom by the sea)
25 That the wind came out of the cloud by night,
    Chilling and killing my Annabel Lee.

[1]**seraphs** a kind of angel
[2]**kinsmen** relatives

> What do lines 21–22 mean? Write a paraphrase of the lines on the **Paraphrase Chart**.

> Underline the lines that tell of a tragic plot twist in the narrative poem.

Duplicating any part of this book is prohibited by law. © 2014 Triumph Learning, LLC

What idea is presented in lines 30–33? Write a paraphrase of those lines on the **Paraphrase Chart**.

Circle the event that shows how the speaker resolves the narrative.

What is the effect of the final stanza?

But our love it was stronger by far than the love
　　Of those who were older than we—
　　Of many far wiser than we—
30 And neither the angels in heaven above,
　　Nor the demons down under the sea,
Can ever dissever my soul from the soul
　　Of the beautiful Annabel Lee—:

For the moon never beams, without bringing me dreams
35　　Of the beautiful Annabel Lee;
And the stars never rise, but I feel the bright eyes
　　Of the beautiful Annabel Lee;
And so, all the night-tide, I lie down by the side
Of my darling—my darling—my life and my bride,
40　　In her **sepulchre** there by the sea—
　　In her tomb by the sounding sea.

Shall I compare thee to a summer's day?

William Shakespeare

Shall I compare thee to a summer's day?
Thou art more lovely and more **temperate**.
Rough winds do shake the darling buds of May,
And summer's lease hath all too short a date.

5   Sometime too hot the eye of heaven shines,
And often is his gold complexion dimm'd;
And every fair from fair sometime declines,
By chance, or nature's changing course, untrimm'd;
But thy eternal summer shall not fade,

10 Nor lose possession of that fair thou ow'st,[1]
Nor shall death brag thou wander'st in his shade,
When in eternal lines to Time thou grow'st.
    So long as men can breathe, or eyes can see,
    So long lives this, and this gives life to thee.

[1] **ow'st** owns

Paraphrase the final couplet and add it to your **Paraphrase Chart**.

Draw boxes around the two main sections of the sonnet. What structural details make this poem a sonnet?

Why does the speaker compare his love to a summer's day? Identify two reasons.

The Oven Bird

Robert Frost

What image is expressed in lines 6–9? Write a paraphrase of the lines on the **Paraphrase Chart**.

Compare

How are the last two poems similar in their ideas about what lasts in the world? How are they different? Explain your viewpoint in writing using textual evidence.

There is a singer everyone has heard,
Loud, a mid-summer and a mid-wood bird,
Who makes the solid tree trunks sound again.
He says that leaves are old and that for flowers
5 Mid-summer is to spring as one to ten.
He says the early petal-fall is past
When pear and cherry bloom went down in showers
On sunny days a moment overcast;
And comes that other fall we name the fall.
10 He says the highway dust is over all.
The bird would cease and be as other birds
But that he knows in singing not to sing.
The question that he frames in all but words
Is what to make of a diminished[1] thing.

[1]**diminished** reduced; lessened

Vocabulary: Using Context Clues

When you encounter an unfamiliar word in a poem, **context clues** can sometimes help you determine its meaning. A word's context is the words around it, in the same or nearby lines. The meaning of those other words and of the poem as a whole can help you figure out the unfamiliar word's meaning.

To figure out the meaning of an unfamiliar word in a poem, reread the surrounding lines. Think about the meaning of the other words and of the entire poem. Compare the unfamiliar word to words that are similar.

Try It Read these opening lines from Shakespeare's sonnet.

Shall I compare thee to a summer's day?

Thou art more lovely and more **temperate**.

Discuss **If you are not sure about the meaning of *temperate*, what words might help you? Underline them. What words do you know that are similar to *temperate*? What is Shakespeare expressing in these lines? Try to guess at the meaning of the word.**

The following words are from the poems you have just read. Reread each word and the surrounding text of the poem. List any words or phrases that helped you figure out the word's meaning, and write a definition. Use a dictionary to check your definition.

1. **prevail,** p. 98 from "The Ballad of King Arthur" _____

_____

2. **coveted,** p. 99 from "Annabel Lee" _____

_____

3. **sepulchre,** p. 100 from "Annabel Lee" _____

_____

Respond to Text: Compare and Contrast Poetic Structures

Compare and contrast the poetic structure of the narrative poems and sonnets you have just read. Think about how the structure of a narrative poem and a sonnet are different and similar. Consider the impact of these differences on each poem—how the poems read, sound, flow, and communicate their messages.

Try It Think about how the poetic structures of "Annabel Lee" and "The Oven Bird" affect your understanding of each poem's purpose and ideas.

> **Discuss** **What events and imagery does the poet want to relate to the reader in "Annabel Lee"? How does the form of "The Oven Bird" help convey its images and its central idea? How would the poems be different if they were written in the other form? Which parts might they keep, which might they lose, and which might need to be expanded?**

On Your Own Write your own analysis of the poetic structure of the narrative poem "The Ballad of King Arthur." Analyze how the verses organize the events and how the poet's description helps you visualize the action. Compare that to how Shakespeare's sonnet "Shall I compare thee to a summer's day?" presents ideas and imagery. Use the next page to plan your response. Then write your paragraph on a separate sheet of paper.

Checklist for a Good Response

A good paragraph

✔ states the subject of your analysis.

✔ explains the reasons why and in what ways you think each poem's structure is appropriate for its purpose.

✔ includes details from the poem.

✔ shows your understanding of the poem.

✔ includes a topic sentence, supporting ideas, and a concluding statement.

Poetic Structure: Narrative Poem and Sonnet

1. **Topic Sentence** Include this information in your topic sentence:

   The poetic structure of _____ is narrative, while

   _____ is a sonnet.

2. **Detail Sentences** Explain how the structure of each poem affects your understanding and experience of it. Cite details that support your ideas. Use this chart to organize your ideas.

	"The Ballad of King Arthur"	"Shall I compare thee to a summer's day?"
How do the structure and content of the poem work together?		
How does the poem's structure help me understand its tone and purpose?		
How does the poem's structure help me enjoy the poem?		

3. **Concluding Sentence** Your final sentence should restate in a fresh way how the poetic structure of each poem added to your understanding.

   _____

   _____

On a separate sheet of paper, write your paragraph.

Read on Your Own

Read the poems independently three times, using the skills you have learned. Then answer the Comprehension Check questions.

First Read | Practice the first-read skills you learned in this lesson.

Second Read | Practice the second-read skills you learned in this lesson.

Third Read | Think critically about the poems.

The Magnificent Bull

a traditional poem from Africa

Visualize Think about the colors of the bull and the similes the poet uses to help you see the bull in your "mind's eye."

Rhyme, Alliteration, Assonance Box words that show alliteration and circle words that show assonance. Note that the examples don't have to be in the same line. The first two words have been circled for you.

My bull is white like the silver fish in the river
White like the shimmering crane bird on the river bank
White like fresh milk!
His roar is like the thunder to the Turkish cannon on the steep shore

5 My bull is dark like the raincloud in the storm.
He is like summer and winter.
Half of him is dark like the storm cloud,
Half of him is light like sunshine.
His back shines like the morning star.
10 His brow is red like the beak of the Hornbill.
His forehead is like a flag, calling the people from a distance,
He resembles the rainbow.

I will water him at the river.
With my spear I shall drive my enemies.
15 Let them water their herds at the well;
The river belongs to me and my bull.
Drink, my bull, from the river; I am here
To guard you with my spear.

When I Was a Lad

W. S. Gilbert (from the comic opera H.M.S. Pinafore)

Paraphrase Think about how you would paraphrase the second stanza of the poem.

Poetic Structure Think about the narrative structure of this poem. How is it like a story?

Critical Thinking Think about what the speaker accomplishes to become the Ruler of the Queen's Navy. What talents does he show that get him promoted?

In this poem, Gilbert is poking fun at the First Lord of the Admiralty, or "the Ruler of the Queen's Navy," who was a politician and not a sailor or naval commander.

When I was a lad I served a term
As office-boy in an attorney's firm.
I cleaned the windows and I swept the floor,
And I polished up the handle of the big front door.
5   I polished up that handle so successfullee
       That now I am the Ruler of the Queen's Navee.

As office-boy I made such a mark
That they gave me the post of a junior clerk;
I served the writs with a smile so **bland**,
10   And I copied all the letters in a big round hand.
       I copied all the letters in a hand so free
       That now I am the Ruler of the Queen's Navee.

Visualize Think about how you visualize the first stanza on this page. What details from the poem would you include in a drawing?

Rhyme, Alliteration, and Assonance Look at the rhymes in the first stanza on this page. Underline the first pair of rhyming words, box the second pair, and circle the third pair.

In serving writs I made such a name,
That an articled clerk I soon became;

15　I wore clean collars and a brand-new suit
For the pass-examination at the Institute.
　　That pass-examination did so well for me,
　　That now I am the Ruler of the Queen's Navee.

Of legal knowledge I acquired such a grip,
20　That they took me into the partnership,
And that junior partnership, I ween[1]
Was the only ship that I ever had seen.
　　But that kind of ship so suited me
　　That now I am the Ruler of the Queen's Navee.

[1]**ween** think; suppose

25　I grew so rich that I was sent
　　To the House a Member of Parliament.
　　I always voted at my party's call,
　　And I never thought of thinking for myself at all.
　　　　I thought so little they rewarded me
30　　　By making me the Ruler of the Queen's Navee.

　　Now landsmen all, whoever you may be,
　　If you want to rise to the top of the tree—
　　If your soul isn't fettered to an office-stool,
　　Be careful to be guided by this golden rule—
35　　　Stick close to your desks and never go to sea,
　　　　And you all may be rulers of the Queen's Navee.

Rhyme, Alliteration, and Assonance This poem was written to be sung. Think about how the rhymes, alliteration, and assonance make the poem melodic.

Critical Thinking Think about how much experience the speaker of the poem has had on a real ship and how this adds humor to the poem.

To me, fair friend, you never can be old

William Shakespeare

Paraphrase Think about how you would rephrase "mine eye may be deceiv'd."

Poetic Structure There is a shift in the presentation of ideas in this poem. Draw a line to show where this shift occurs.

Critical Thinking Think about what the speaker is telling his friend in the end.

To me, fair friend, you never can be old,
For as you were when first your eye I ey'd,
Such seems your beauty still. Three winters cold
Have from the forests shook three summers' pride,
5 Three beauteous springs to yellow autumn turn'd,
In process of the seasons have I seen,
Three April perfumes in three hot Junes burn'd,
Since first I saw you fresh, which yet are green.
Ah! yet doth beauty, like a dial-hand,
10 Steal from his figure, and no pace perceiv'd;
So your sweet hue, which methinks still doth stand,
Hath motion, and mine eye may be deceiv'd:
     For fear of which, hear this, thou age unbred:
     Ere you were born was beauty's summer dead.

✅ Comprehension Check

1. In line 3 of "The Magnificent Bull," the bull is compared to fresh milk. How does this comparison help you visualize the bull?

_____

_____

2. Paraphrase these lines from "To me, fair friend, you never can be old."

   To me, fair friend, you never can be old,
   For as you were when first your eye I ey'd,
   Such seems your beauty still.

_____

_____

3. In the first stanza of "The Magnificent Bull," which image stands out as different from the rest? Why is it different?

_____

_____

4. Read this line from "When I Was a Lad."

   I served the writs with a smile so bland,

   How would the meaning of this line change if the word *bland* were replaced with *mild* or *calm*, both of which have similar denotations?

_____

_____

5. How is the narrative structure of "When I Was a Lad" suitable for the subject of the poem?

    _____

    _____

    _____

6. In "To me, fair friend, you never can be old," how does the poet make use of images of nature to develop his subject?

    _____

    _____

7. Look at the last lines of "To me, fair friend, you never can be old."

    For fear of which, hear this, thou age unbred:
    Ere you were born was beauty's summer dead.

    What is an example of assonance here? What about alliteration? How are the rhymes different from the rest of the rhymes in the poem?

    _____

    _____

8. Read this line from "The Magnificent Bull."

    His brow is red like the beak of the Hornbill.

    What word is a context clue that gives you an idea of what a "Hornbill" is? What is a Hornbill?

    _____

    _____

Lesson 5
Scientific Texts

Scientific texts provide factual information about topics that are related to science. Scientific texts can appear in magazines, newspapers, books, or on Web sites. You might read an article about earthquakes in an encyclopedia, for example, to research a school project or just because you are interested in the subject. Scientific texts can vary from simple, informative articles to highly technical papers, so it is important to locate the kind of text you can understand. Since being specific is crucial to scientific investigation, you will likely encounter technical vocabulary along the way. Be sure to have a dictionary on hand to help with difficult words and concepts. If you read an article about the work being done by the researcher shown here, what kinds of information would you want to learn?

Skills Focus

The Puzzling Platypus

Central Idea and Supporting Details

Analyze Interactions

Discovering Deep-Sea Vents

Summarize

Distinguish among Facts, Reasoned Judgments, and Speculation

Practice the Skill

Every scientific text has a central idea. The **central idea** is the most important concept the author wants to convey. To identify the central idea, read the selection and think about what it is mostly about. Sometimes, the author will state the central idea directly in the title of a selection or in a topic sentence. Other times, you will need to look for important details that support a central idea that is not directly stated. **Supporting details** are facts and information that build on the central idea. Each new detail adds information to deepen your understanding of the central idea.

To determine the central idea and supporting details as you read, ask yourself: *Is the central idea obvious, or am I still figuring out what it is? Why did the author include this detail? Does it help me understand the main idea of the whole selection?*

Try It Read the paragraphs below.

California is home to the world's tallest trees: giant redwoods and sequoias. Many people think these trees are the same because of their similar bark color and amazing size. But the species have significant differences.

Giant redwoods grow only along the coast of northern California. They require a moist, humid climate. The daily fog that rolls in from the ocean provides the perfect environment. Giant redwoods are the tallest trees in the world, often exceeding three hundred feet in height.

Sequoias, on the other hand, are found on the western slope of the Sierra Nevada. They require a drier climate. Though they are not as tall as redwoods, they are considered the largest trees in the world. Their bases can grow to be thirty-five feet in diameter.

> **Discuss** As you read, look for the author's central idea. Is it stated directly, or do you have to use supporting details to find it? Underline the central idea. Circle details the author provides to support the central idea.

As you read, complete the Central Idea and Details Chart on page 295.

Practice the Skill

Second Read Analyze Interactions

People's beliefs and ideas can influence how they interact with the world around them, and vice versa. This is especially true in science. For example, someone can begin a scientific experiment assuming a particular outcome. If the results are not what the scientist expects, he or she then has to change his or her expectations. Then he or she will conduct more experiments. In this way, the scientist is interacting with ideas and events. Analyzing the interactions between ideas, events, and people can help you understand scientific texts and help with reading comprehension in general.

Try It Read the paragraphs below.

For centuries, people believed that the disease malaria was caused by bad air in swampy, marshy regions. In fact, the word *malaria* means "bad air" in Italian. People believed that swampy areas released dangerous gases at night. As a result, they avoided building homes near swamps, marshes, and other bodies of standing water, and they made sure to stay inside at night.

In time, it was determined that malaria is actually caused by a microorganism spread by mosquitoes. Even though people based their original prevention measures on incorrect information, their actions were effective. Mosquitoes breed in the standing water found in swamps and marshes, and they are most active after sunset. The idea that swampy night air caused the disease, though wrong, prevented some illnesses and led scientists to look in the right place for the true cause.

> Discuss > **How did people's ideas about the cause of malaria affect their actions? What evidence influenced their understanding of malaria? How do you think finding the true cause of malaria changed people's behavior?**

As you read, record your answers to questions about analyzing interactions on the Close Reading Worksheet on page 296. ✏️

Purpose for Reading
Read along with your teacher. Each time, read for a different purpose.

First Read	Focus on identifying the central idea and supporting details.
Second Read	Focus on analyzing interactions.
Third Read	Focus on evaluating the selection critically.

The Puzzling Platypus

What is the central idea conveyed in paragraphs 1 and 2? <u>Underline it.</u> Then (circle) some details that support this idea. Record your answers on the **Central Idea and Details Chart**.

1   In 1798, the governor of the Australian state of New South Wales, Captain John Hunter, sent an interesting animal specimen to a renowned society of educated men in England. When the members of the society opened that package, they found the pelt of a creature unlike any they had ever seen. It had the bill and webbed feet of a duck, the tail of a beaver, and the body and fur of an otter. Convinced it was the work of a clever **taxidermist** who had sewn pieces of different animals together, they sent it off to the zoologist George Shaw at the British Museum for further study.

How did scientists' established beliefs about animals affect their reaction to the platypus pelt?

2   When Shaw saw the pelt, he, too, was convinced it was a hoax. He was so sure that a duck's bill had been sewn onto the body of an otterlike creature that he took out scissors and searched for stitches. He even tried to pry the bill off the pelt. Today, the famous specimen is on display at the British Museum of Natural History in London, and Shaw's scissor marks can be seen on the bill, which is still securely attached to its hide.

What to Call It?

3   Whenever a new species of animal is discovered, zoologists have to create a scientific name for it. Because of this animal's uniqueness, there was initial confusion over what to call it. In addition, the original name Shaw gave it—*platypus,* meaning "flat-footed"—had already been assigned to a type of beetle and, therefore, had to be changed. The name *Ornithorhynchus anatinus*, which means "bird snout, ducklike," was eventually accepted as its scientific name. However, the name platypus has stuck as the common name. Therefore, this creature is known to most of us as the duck-billed platypus.

Physical Characteristics and Habitat

4   Without a doubt, the platypus is one of the oddest animals on the planet. An average platypus is fifteen inches long and weighs three pounds. It has a thick coat of three layers of fur. The first layer keeps the animal warm by trapping air next to the skin, and the second provides insulation. Finally, the third, or outer layer, has long, flat hairs that help the platypus detect nearby objects as it moves among them.

5   The platypus is a **monotreme**, or egg-laying mammal. The only other member of that group is the echidna, or spiny anteater, which is also found in Australia. The word *monotreme* means "one hole." This means that the animal has one opening for mating, laying eggs, and excreting waste. The platypus is venomous, which is extremely rare among mammals.

6   The platypus is a strong but not fast swimmer. To swim, a platypus uses its webbed front paws to paddle and its rear paws and tail to steer. When it goes underwater, folds of skin cover its eyes and ears, keeping the water out. The platypus's nostrils have a watertight seal. This allows the animal to stay submerged for a minute or two at a time.

7   The platypus is found along the eastern coast of Australia and all over the island of Tasmania, which is part of Australia. It lives next to freshwater rivers, streams, and lakes. Its habitat extends from freezing mountain streams to warm, tropical waters. The platypus is a solitary creature, but individual territories may overlap.

8   While the platypus spends most of its time swimming and hunting in the water, it lives on land. Its webbed feet have sharp claws that help it dig burrows in riverbanks and lakeshores to sleep in during the day. When the animal is on land, the webbing retracts to allow the platypus to use its claws for running.

9   The platypus mostly hunts at night, making it a nocturnal creature. This is one reason it took scientists so long to learn about the animal. Spotting a platypus in its natural environment is rare.

Circle three details that support the idea that "the platypus is one of the oddest animals on the planet." Record your answers on the **Central Idea and Details Chart.**

Why is spotting a platypus in the wild so rare?

Australia

The darker color represents platypus habitats in Australia and Tasmania

Tasmania

What is the central idea of the section titled "Food"? What details support it? Record your answers on the **Central Idea and Details Chart.**

How has human settlement affected the platypus?

Food

10   The platypus is a bottom-feeder, meaning that it gets its food from the bottom of a body of water. The creature has **electroreceptors** in its bill that sense the electrical currents emitted when prey move their muscles. Using its bill, the platypus scoops up larvae, shellfish, and worms from the river or lake bottom. Each trip to the bottom for food lasts up to two minutes. A platypus can make up to seventy-five dives in an hour and spend up to twelve hours a day hunting. It eats about 30 percent of its body weight each day.

11   Surprisingly, this tireless hunter does not have teeth! Instead, it has hard, bony plates in its mouth. After each dive, the platypus floats on the surface and grinds its food against the plates using pebbles and silt scooped from the lake bottom. It takes between ten and twenty seconds to eat its catch, and then the animal dives for the bottom again.

Predators

12   Predators of the platypus include snakes, large lizards called goannas, rats, and foxes. Platypuses are also threatened by pollution in their waterways and the development of land that is their natural habitat. These animals were hunted for their fur through the early twentieth century and are now on the list of protected species, but they are not currently at risk of extinction.

13   Platypuses may look cute and cuddly, but they do have ways of defending themselves. The male platypus has a bony stinger, called a spur, behind the heel of each rear paw. When the platypus strikes, the spur emits venom strong enough to kill a dog or cause excruciating pain in a human that can continue for months. In addition to defending itself from predators, the male platypus uses its claws and spur to fight other males for territory and mates.

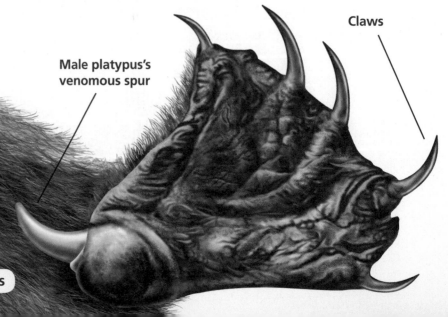

Claws

Male platypus's venomous spur

Offspring

14   Even in reproduction, platypuses are unique. They are among only two mammals on Earth that lay eggs. They mate once a year, usually between June and October. Once a male and female have mated, the male platypus has nothing more to do with the female or with caring for the offspring.

15   Egg development occurs in three stages. In the first, the **embryo** relies on the yolk sac for nutrition. During the second stage, the embryo develops digits on its front and rear feet. In the third stage of development, the embryo grows an egg tooth that it uses to break out of its shell. This egg tooth drops out after hatching.

16   The eggs develop in the female platypus for twenty-eight days before she lays them in a nest. In contrast, chicken eggs develop for one day before being laid. The female platypus lays two to four eggs each year. When she is ready to lay her eggs, the female creates a nesting burrow and seals herself and the eggs inside. To keep them warm, she holds the eggs between her tail and body. Once the eggs are laid, the female incubates[1] them for about ten days until, finally, the platypuses hatch.

17   There is no official name for a baby platypus, but some biologists have suggested the term "platypup." When it is born, a baby platypus is the size of a lima bean. It is hairless, blind, and completely defenseless.

18   Platypuses differ from other mammals in yet another way. Mammals are the class of animals that are warm-blooded vertebrates, meaning that they have a spine. Their skin has fur, and the females have milk-producing mammary glands that provide nourishment for their young. However, unlike other mammals, the female platypus does not have nipples. Instead, to nurse its young, it secretes milk from special glands. The milk then puddles on the mother's fur, and the baby platypus licks it up. Its mother nurses it for three to four months before it learns to swim.

[1]**incubate** to sit or rest on (eggs) so as to hatch by body warmth

Circle two details in the section titled "Offspring" that support the central idea that platypuses are unique animals. Record your answers on the **Central Idea and Details Chart.**

What reproductive characteristics might have made it difficult for nineteenth-century scientists to accept the platypus as a mammal?

How does the Aboriginal legend contribute to the central idea that the platypus is a distinctive animal? Record your answer on the **Central Idea and Details Chart.**

Box two sentences that show a nonscientific way in which people relate to events in the natural world.

Why might Australians have adopted the platypus as an icon?

Analyze

How did the discovery of the platypus change the way scientists view the animal world?

Platypus and Australian Culture

19   Long before the Europeans first arrived in Australia and marveled at this curious creature, native Australians, or Aborigines, knew about the platypus. In the Aboriginal culture, the time when Earth was being created is called the Dreamtime. Members of Aboriginal tribes passed stories and legends about the Dreamtime from one generation to the next.

20   According to legend, the platypus was created when a female duck mated with a water rat. The resulting offspring had its mother's bill and webbed feet and its father's legs and fur. When the platypus was old enough, all the animals of the land, water, and air sought to have it join their groups. But the platypus declined, opting to be in a category all its own.

21   Today the platypus is an iconic symbol of Australia. It is a mascot at national sports events and is on their twenty-cent coin. The Australian state of New South Wales has adopted it as its animal emblem.

Aboriginal vase depicting a platypus

Vocabulary: Use a Dictionary to Determine a Word's Pronunciation and Part of Speech

Beyond providing definitions of words, dictionaries give other important information. By looking up a word in a **dictionary**, you can find its part of speech—whether it is a noun, verb, adjective, adverb, or other kind of word. Dictionaries also show syllabication, or how a word breaks into syllables, and how a word is pronounced. **Pronunciation guides** display and explain special symbols that are used to show how a word is pronounced, or how it should be spoken, and are especially useful for longer technical words. Here is an example.

sol•u•ble ('sol yə bəl) *adjective.* able to be dissolved in a liquid

The apostrophe in the pronunciation above tells you which syllable to stress the most when saying the word. Many online dictionaries have audio recordings of pronunciations available as well.

Try It Read the sentence below. Use a dictionary to look up the boldface word's part of speech and pronunciation.

The platypus is a **monotreme**, or egg-laying mammal.

> Discuss   **What part of speech is *monotreme*? How is it pronounced? Did you already know how to pronounce it?**

Look up each word in a dictionary. Write down its part of speech and definition, and practice pronouncing the word.

1. **taxidermist**, p. 116 _____

_____

2. **electroreceptors**, p. 118 _____

_____

3. **embryo**, p. 119 _____

_____

Practice the Skill

When you summarize a selection, you restate its content briefly in your own words. To summarize a text, you must read the whole selection first. Then think about the central idea and any key supporting information. A summary should be short and include only the major pieces of information presented in the selection. It should not include minor details.

When you write a summary, stick to the facts. Your summary should not include your opinion or feelings on the information presented. It also should not include any knowledge you might have on the subject that is not presented in the selection.

Try It Read the paragraphs below.

Giant pandas are native to China. They used to inhabit the lowlands, but development and deforestation have driven them into the mountains. Currently there are only about 1,600 pandas left in the wild. But China, with the assistance of other countries, including the United States, is working to restore panda populations.

In breeding centers built specifically to house pandas, Chinese zoologists now have about three hundred pandas in captivity. The United States is helping by hosting pairs of pandas at zoos around the country. When the cubs born to these pairs are old enough, they are sent back to China to be part of its breeding program and to eventually be introduced to the wild.

Discuss **What is the central idea of the selection? Circle it. What are the most important supporting details? How would you summarize the selection?**

As you read, record your answers to questions about summarizing on the Close Reading Worksheet on page 297.

Practice the Skill

Not all scientific texts are created equal. The best are those filled with hard **facts** that can be proved true and **reasoned judgments** based on careful research findings. These texts will include interviews with experts, data from research, and evidence gathered from well-documented experiments.

Some scientific articles include **speculation**, which is an opinion or educated guess on an issue without the established facts to back it up. Speculation is not a problem in itself, but scientific texts that present a lot of speculation without proof or evidence are weaker than those based on facts and reasoned judgments.

As you read, be careful to distinguish between the author's use of facts, reasoned judgments, and speculation to decide whether the article is reliable.

Try It Read the paragraphs below.

Planetary scientists have long theorized that there was once water on Mars. Photos taken by orbiting satellites showed what looked like canyons and riverbeds on the planet's surface. It was thought that these geological formations must have been carved out by flowing water.

Now, thanks to the Mars rover *Curiosity*, researchers have proof that the red planet once had flowing water. *Curiosity* has sent back images of rounded gravel and pebbles. "The shapes tell you [the rocks] were transported, and the sizes tell you they couldn't be transported by wind. They were transported by water flow," said Rebecca Williams, a geologist at the Planetary Science Institute in Tucson, Arizona.

The next step for geologists will be to determine how much water was there, when, and for how long. It is almost certain that they will discover ancient oceans and rivers that once teemed with life, proving once and for all we're not alone in the universe.

> Discuss › **As you read the selection, think about the information presented. Are there facts? How about reasoned judgments based on research? Underline any speculation that is not backed up by research.**

As you read, complete the Facts, Reasoned Judgments, and Speculation Chart on page 298.

Purpose for Reading

Read along with your teacher. Each time, read for a different purpose.

| First Read | Focus on summarizing. |

| Second Read | Focus on distinguishing among facts, reasoned judgments, and speculation. |

| Third Read | Focus on evaluating the selection critically. |

Discovering Deep-Sea Vents

Summarize the main idea of the text on this page. ✎

Circle a fact and underline an example of speculation in paragraph 4, and write them in the columns on the **Facts, Reasoned Judgments, and Speculation Chart**.

1   In 1977, researchers aboard a deep-sea submersible called *Alvin* made a discovery that changed how scientists view the development of life on Earth. *Alvin* was first launched in 1964 by the Woods Hole Oceanographic Institute in Massachusetts. It was the first submersible built to carry passengers into the extreme depths of the oceans. Its titanium hull is able to withstand the crushing pressure and icy cold that exist in the deep. *Alvin* has been upgraded many times over its life span. Currently, *Alvin* is able to explore for six to ten hours, although it can support life for seventy-two hours in an emergency. Arrayed on the vehicle's exterior are banks of lights that allow scientists to see at depths where sunlight doesn't penetrate.

2   Scientists had long believed that life could not exist without sunlight. The process of photosynthesis allows plants to utilize the sun's energy to produce food. When other organisms feed on the plants, they consume nutrients that were made with the sun's energy. All of life on land relies on photosynthesis for its existence.

3   While scientists believed that organisms might exist at extreme depths, they **theorized** that they fed on rotting plant and animal material that sank from near the surface or that they came closer to the surface for food. This meant that these bottom-dwellers were still part of the accepted food chain.

4   So in 1977, when the researchers aboard *Alvin* explored the depths near the Galápagos Islands in the Pacific Ocean, they were expecting to find a barren ocean floor, devoid of life. Instead, they were shocked to find giant tubeworms thriving on the edge of deep-water hydrothermal vents.

How Hydrothermal Vents Are Formed

5   Earth's outer crust is composed of plates that move slowly over the mantle. Sometimes magma, or molten rock, from inside Earth wells up at plate boundaries, causing the plates to spread apart. This can produce volcanoes on land or underwater. On the ocean floor, spreading at plate boundaries can allow cold ocean water to seep into Earth's crust and make contact with the hot magma below.

6   When the sinking water makes contact with the magma, it becomes heated to temperatures high enough to melt metal. At this point, minerals from the surrounding rock dissolve in the water. The hot water is less dense and more buoyant than the magma. Therefore, it rises to the surface like a hot-air balloon. After it passes through the crust to the ocean floor, the superheated water blasts out like a jet through cracks called hydrothermal vents.

7   As the hot water exiting the vents mixes with cold ocean water, the minerals separate out of the mixture and fall to the ocean floor. These deposits create chimneys out of which superhot water continues to vent. Some vent chimneys have been measured at more than fifteen stories high, with openings forty feet wide.

> Summarize the process by which hydrothermal vents are formed.

> What physical property of water causes most of the action in the process described here? How?

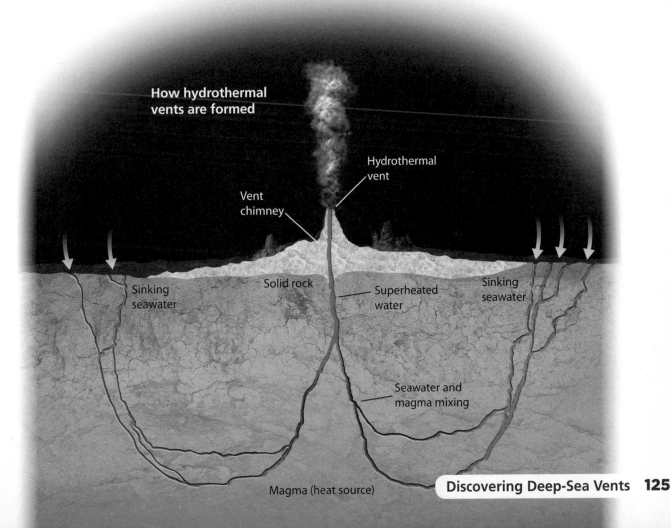

How hydrothermal vents are formed

Hydrothermal vent

Vent chimney

Sinking seawater

Solid rock

Superheated water

Sinking seawater

Seawater and magma mixing

Magma (heat source)

Different Kinds of Vents

8   Based on their study of land-based geology, geologists had predicted the presence of hydrothermal vents on the ocean floor long before they had the ability to observe them. On land, examples of geothermal vents are hot springs and geysers. Old Faithful in Yellowstone National Park is one famous geyser. Water from the surface of Earth seeps downward until it encounters magma. The water then heats up, expands, and is forced up and out. Old Faithful erupts on a predictable schedule.

9   There are two categories of underwater chimneys. "Black smokers" billow what looks like black clouds of smoke. These clouds are actually dissolved metals from deep in Earth's crust mixing with sulfur in the seawater. This creates tiny black particles. The water temperature at the mouths of black smokers is between 350 and 400 degrees Celsius (662–752 degrees Fahrenheit).

10   The water mixture emitted from "white smokers" moves less rapidly and isn't as hot. Water temperatures at the mouths of white smokers range from 250 to 300 degrees Celsius (482–572 degrees Fahrenheit). The mixture billowing out of these chimneys appears white because it doesn't contain dissolved metals.

11   At the mouth of a hydrothermal vent, the hot water mixes with the cold ocean water, triggering a chemical reaction. As the water from the vent mixes with oxygenated ocean water, hydrogen sulfide is released. This turns the water around the vent into a toxic stew, **inhospitable** to almost all life-forms. Yet, as the researchers aboard *Alvin* in 1977 discovered, some life flourishes in this lightless environment.

Life around Hydrothermal Vents

12   At the very edges of these vents live bacteria that are able to use the minerals in the water to create energy, instead of depending on the sun's energy. These organisms turn the heat and minerals into energy through a process called **chemosynthesis**. On land, organisms such as plants depend on the sunlight's energy, and larger organisms depend on plants. In the same way, larger deep-sea organisms feed on the bacteria that create their own energy. In both cases, this creates a self-sustaining ecosystem.

A hydrothermal vent

13   In time, scientists discovered more than three hundred species of life surrounding deep-sea vents, including new types of bacteria, algae, shrimp, tubeworms, and crabs. These organisms are able to thrive in the extreme heat and pressure of the ocean depths in addition to withstanding a highly acidic, lightless environment.

Summarize the symbiotic relationship between the bacteria and tubeworms living near hydrothermal vents.

14   The thermophilic bacteria are the foundation of an amazing food chain. For instance, tubeworms have no means of creating energy, so they require an outside energy source to survive. Some bacteria survive by living inside host organisms that provide shelter and nutrients. How do these organisms work together to survive? The bacteria use tubeworms as their host organism. Tubeworms have red, featherlike plumes that they use to absorb hydrogen sulfide that comes from the vents. The bacteria living in their tissues then use the hydrogen sulfide to create energy for the tubeworms. Each organism relies on the other to survive. This kind of relationship is called a symbiotic relationship.

Box an example of a reasoned judgment in paragraph 15.

15   Another surprising characteristic of these deep-sea organisms is how large they grow to become. Scientists theorized that the extreme conditions of the deep ocean would prevent any organisms there from growing very large. Instead, the creatures around hydrothermal vents display gigantism. This means they grow larger at extreme depths than similar species do in shallower water.

What may have been some of the earliest life-forms on Earth? What is your evidence?

16   An example is the tubeworm. At shallow depths, tubeworms grow to be several inches long. But scientists have discovered tubeworms around deep-sea vents that have measured more than seven feet in length.

17   Many scientists believe that the first life-forms on Earth developed in superheated, sulfuric conditions similar to those around deep-sea hydrothermal vents. By studying the organisms that thrive at the vents, researchers hope to gain insights into how life began and evolved on this planet.

Tubeworm

18   DNA analysis of ocean vent bacteria shows that they are related to primitive life-forms that existed during **Precambrian** times, more than 500 million years ago. Researchers believe that the bacteria evolved as the chimneys formed.

What type of evidence is the last sentence of paragraph 19? Write this sentence in the correct column on the **Facts, Reasoned Judgments, and Speculation Chart.**

Connect

How does the discovery of deep-sea vents and life around them connect the sciences of geology, biology, and space exploration? Support your answer with evidence from the text.

Beyond the Sea

19   Studying organisms from hydrothermal vents may also provide clues to the existence of life elsewhere in the solar system. Living organisms require water, energy, and carbon[1] to survive. Previously, it was assumed that this energy had to come from sunlight. This considerably narrowed down the locations where life could exist. But now that we know organisms can produce energy by chemosynthesis, researchers have been considering other places that might provide these three crucial ingredients, even without adequate energy from sunlight. So far, they have come up with two possibilities farther out in the solar system. The planet Mars and Jupiter's moon Europa may have had the conditions necessary to support life.

20   While there are plans to eventually explore Europa, NASA already landed a rover called *Curiosity* on Mars in August 2012. One of *Curiosity*'s missions is to look for evidence of water and life on the planet's surface. Research on the ecosystems surrounding hydrothermal vents will help scientists as they study Mars. These unlikely colonies of life in our deepest oceans have become an essential tool for the study of biology on Earth—and beyond.

[1] **carbon** a chemical element found in all organisms

A red spotted siphonophore, a type of jellyfish

Vocabulary: Domain-Specific Vocabulary: Science Terms

When reading scientific texts, you are likely to come across words and terms that you have not seen before. These specialized words are used in a particular field of study to describe things like chemical processes (*evaporation*) or geological phenomena (*erosion*). As you read a scientific text, look for context clues to help you determine the meaning of science terms. Keep a dictionary at hand so you can look up any unfamiliar terms whose meaning you cannot determine from the context.

Try It Read the sentences from "Discovering Deep-Sea Vents."

> This turns the water around the vent into a toxic stew, **inhospitable** to almost all life-forms. Yet, as the researchers aboard *Alvin* in 1977 discovered, some life flourishes in this lightless environment.

Discuss **Use context clues to figure out the the meaning of *inhospitable*. What words and phrases help you? Use a dictionary to check your answer.**

The scientific terms below are in "Discovering Deep-Sea Vents." Find each term in the selection and try to figure out its meaning from its context. Then look up each term and provide a definition.

1. **theorized**, p. 124 _____

_____

2. **chemosynthesis**, p. 126 _____

_____

3. **Precambrian**, p. 127 _____

_____

Respond to Text: Determine Author's Purpose

When an author writes a piece of nonfiction, he or she does so for a reason. In order to properly understand the information in a nonfiction text, you need to understand the author's purpose. Sometimes that purpose is clear from the start, but other times you will have to determine it as you read. Think about whether the author is presenting facts about a topic, trying to persuade you to believe something, or making an argument to refute the work of others. Once you have identified an author's purpose, you can evaluate whether the author succeeded in his or her goals. Most science writers are writing to inform, to convey information about a topic. A good scientific article is the result of an author achieving his or her purpose clearly.

Try It Think about the author's purpose for writing "The Puzzling Platypus."

> Discuss   **What is the author's purpose in writing the selection? How is the information in the selection presented? Is the piece successful? Is the author's purpose achieved?**

On Your Own Consider the author's purpose for writing "Discovering Deep-Sea Vents." Is it to persuade you to accept a theory, to explain a scientific principle, or to make an argument? Evaluate the author's purpose by analyzing the facts and judgments presented. Use the chart on the next page to organize details that support your ideas. Then write a paragraph about the author's purpose on a separate sheet of paper.

Checklist for a Good Response

A good paragraph

✔ states the author's purpose.

✔ presents specific details to support your conclusion.

✔ cites research presented in the selection.

✔ clearly states the central idea and supporting details.

✔ evaluates the author's effectiveness.

✔ clearly states the conclusion.

My Analysis of Author's Purpose

1. **Topic Sentence** Include this information in your first sentence:
   The author's purpose in "Discovering Deep-Sea Vents" is to

   _____

   _____

2. **Explain Your Answer** The sentences of your paragraph should provide details that explain your answer. Use this chart to organize your ideas.

Facts or Judgments Presented	Author's Treatment of Facts	What This Suggests about Author's Purpose

3. **Concluding Sentence** Your final sentence should restate your conclusions with a new twist.

   _____

   _____

   _____

On a separate sheet of paper, write your paragraph.

Read on Your Own

Read the selection independently three times, using the skills you have learned. Then answer the Comprehension Check questions.

First Read — Practice the first-read skills you learned in this lesson.

Second Read — Practice the second-read skills you learned in this lesson.

Third Read — Think critically about the selection.

The Large Hadron Collider

Central Idea and Supporting Details
Underline the sentence that states the central idea on this page.

Distinguish Facts, Reasoned Judgments, and Speculation
Circle two facts about the Large Hadron Collider. One fact is already circled for you.

1   Scientists believe that the universe was formed by an explosion called the Big Bang. Since then, the universe has been cooling and losing energy. Scientists are seeking to discover what the universe was like in the milliseconds right after the Big Bang. This will help them understand how the universe formed and why it is the way it is today.

2   The Conseil Européen pour la Recherche Nucléaire, or CERN, employs scientists from around the world to achieve this goal. Most of the studies are taking place at a facility located outside of Geneva, Switzerland. It is called the Large Hadron Collider, or LHC.

3   Located between 50 and 175 meters below the ground beneath the border of Switzerland and France, the LHC is the world's largest science experiment. It is a circular tunnel 16.8 miles in circumference in which scientists collide particles. Every object in the universe is composed of tiny particles. Commonly known particles include the proton, neutron, and electron, but there are many others. When scientists collide particular types of these particles, reactions occur which can give the scientists insights into many crucial scientific mysteries.

4   To conduct their experiments, scientists send two beams of particles zipping in opposite directions around a giant tunnel in the LHC. First, they build up energy in the particles by accelerating them faster and faster. They do this because the more energy a particle has, the more it resembles what existed immediately after the universe was created. When the particles have nearly reached the speed of light, scientists allow the beams to cross and the particles to smash together. The theory is that these explosions should closely resemble explosions that occurred right after the Big Bang.

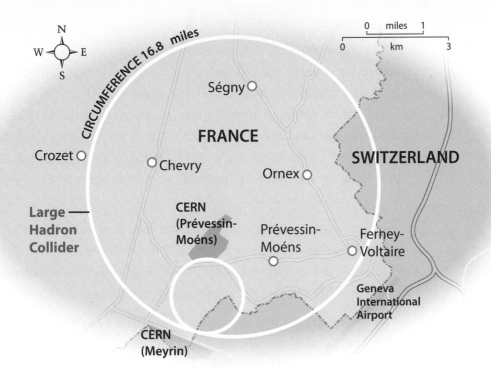

N
W ← → E
S

CIRCUMFERENCE 16.8 miles

0   miles   1
0   km   3

Ségny ○

FRANCE

Crozet ○   ○ Chevry

Ornex ○

SWITZERLAND

**CERN
(Prévessin-
Moéns)**

Prévessin-
Moéns

Ferney-
○ Voltaire

Large —
Hadron
Collider

Geneva
International
Airport

**CERN
(Meyrin)**

The location of the Large Hadron Collider. The smaller white circle shows
the super proton synchrotron, which boosts the speeds of particles going
into the LHC.

5   Construction on the LHC began in 2000. CERN built it in the tunnel
that had been dug for the Large Electron-Positron collider, which had
been decommissioned. Using a preexisting tunnel meant that CERN
could avoid the cost of clearing the miles of land that would be needed.
In addition, the earth surrounding the LHC acts as an excellent
radiation shield.

6   The first beams of particles were accelerated on September 10, 2008.
Shortly thereafter, a fault in the equipment forced the LHC to be shut
down for repair. It powered back up in November 2009. Since then,
researchers have been sending beams of hadron particles speeding
around the LHC at almost the speed of light.

What Are Hadrons?

7   Hadrons are atomic particles that are relatively large. The word
hadron comes from the Greek word *adros*, meaning "bulky." Protons
are a kind of hadron particle that exists in the nucleus of every atom.
Because protons have an electrical charge, they can be affected by
magnets. Researchers at CERN use massive magnets to accelerate and
steer the protons around the LHC.

Summarize
Think about how you
would summarize
paragraph 7.

Critical Thinking
Think about why scientists
use protons in the LHC.

The Collider

8   The collider itself contains two two-millimeter-wide beam pipes that travel completely around the loop. These are surrounded by superconducting electromagnets. These magnets are made of coils of electrical cables wrapped around iron. The electromagnets in the LHC contain about ten thousand tons of iron. That's more than was used to build the Eiffel Tower. When currents of electricity are run through the coils, they create the powerful magnetic fields that allow researchers to control the particle beams.

9   For superconducting magnets to work, they have to be kept cold— very cold. The electromagnets at the LHC are cooled by liquid helium. They are kept at a temperature of –271 degrees Celsius (–456 degrees Fahrenheit). That's colder than the darkest reaches of outer space.

10   In addition to the LHC, the facility has smaller particle accelerators and four huge underground chambers that house equipment to monitor particles after their collisions.

11   The detecting equipment produces so much data that CERN requires a vast grid of networked computers around the world to process it.

How It Works

12   The LHC is actually the final step in a ladder of particle accelerators. Several smaller accelerators are located around the LHC. These get particles up to speed in stages before shooting them into the two beam tubes of the LHC. Researchers also conduct experiments on the particles while they are gathering speed and energy in the smaller accelerators.

13   The hadrons are put into the two LHC beam tubes traveling in opposite directions. It takes them twenty minutes to reach their maximum speed of .999999991 times the speed of light. Traveling that fast, the hadrons make an unbelievable 11,245 circuits of the 26.55-kilometer (16.8-mile) circular collider each second.

14   The beams of hadrons can last for up to ten hours before the particles decay. During that time, they will travel a total distance of ten billion kilometers. That means the particles travel the distance from Earth to Neptune and back again—in less than half a day.

15   The massive electromagnets "steer" the hadrons around the loop. Meanwhile, radio **frequencies** are used to boost the energy level of the particles on each lap. These boosters help the particles gather speed the same way pushing someone on a swing makes him or her go faster. The beam tubes intersect at four locations in the collider. These intersection points are where the particles collide. It's also where the detectors are located to observe the collisions.

16   When the beams of particles reach maximum speed and energy, scientists allow them to collide. These collisions produce thousands of new particles. The four detectors are so sensitive that they can record 600 million collision events per second. After the collisions, researchers study the results to look for particles that behave in new, distinctive ways.

Distinguish among Facts, Reasoned Judgments, and Speculation
Circle a judgment based on reasoned research.

An artist's rendering of the interior of the Large Hadron Collider and the geographic area that it covers in France and Switzerland.

17   In addition to studying the creation of the universe, researchers at CERN are using the LHC to answer other big questions.

18   Matter is anything that has mass and takes up space, including solids, liquids, and gasses. Yet all the visible matter in the universe is only 4 percent of the total that exists. The remaining 96 percent is made of something scientists call dark matter and dark energy. Scientists are hoping their experiments at the LHC will help them identify what dark matter and dark energy are made of.

19   Scientists theorize that the Big Bang created matter and antimatter. Antimatter are particles that are the opposites of matter particles. If the two kinds of particles meet, they will destroy one another. For instance, if a proton and an antiproton come into contact, both will disappear forever. In theory, for every piece of matter in the universe, there should be an equal amount of antimatter. Scientists have not been able to find any antimatter anywhere. Particle studies at the LHC are working to produce and observe antimatter.

20   Another big question that researchers are working to answer is why objects that have no internal structure have mass. For example, particles are made up mostly of empty space, and yet they have mass, or weight. Scientists haven't been able to answer where this mass comes from.

21   In July 2012, CERN announced that its researchers had reached a major milestone. The LHC had produced a new particle called the Higgs boson. This particle is believed to be what gives other particles their mass.

What's Next

22   While researchers have made huge gains in their understanding of the universe thanks to their work at the LHC, there is still much work to be done. Now that they have evidence of the Higgs boson particle, researchers need to discover where it comes from and how it works. As scientists are able to generate hadron particles with more and more energy and produce new particles from collisions, they will be able to look back in time to the beginning of the universe. Perhaps one day they will understand what triggered the Big Bang and created the universe we know.

✅ Comprehension Check

1. What is the central idea of the selection?

   _____

   _____

   _____

2. Why is it important to generate as much energy as possible in these experiments?

   _____

   _____

   _____

3. Use a dictionary to determine the pronunciation and part of speech of the word *nucleus*. What does the word mean?

   _____

   _____

   _____

4. What was one factor that influenced CERN to build the LHC where it did?

   _____

   _____

   _____

5. Below are three definitions of the word *frequency*. Which one best fits the use of *frequencies* on page 135? Explain your choice.

> **frequency** ('frē-kwən(t)-sē) *noun.* **1:** the rate of occurrence; **2:** specific intervals at which waves occur; **3:** number of items in a given category

_____

_____

6. Summarize what happens in the LHC when it is running.

_____

_____

_____

7. On page 136, what is one reasoned judgment based on research?

_____

_____

_____

8. Knowing that the LHC produces new particles through collisions, what can you infer about the questions scientists hope to answer with the LHC?

_____

_____

_____

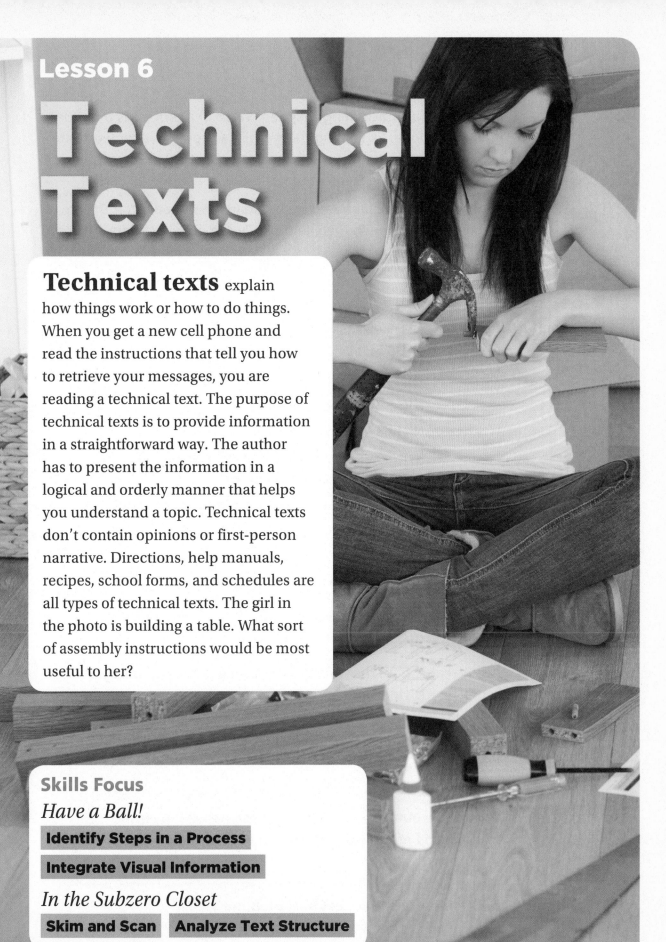

Lesson 6
Technical Texts

Technical texts explain how things work or how to do things. When you get a new cell phone and read the instructions that tell you how to retrieve your messages, you are reading a technical text. The purpose of technical texts is to provide information in a straightforward way. The author has to present the information in a logical and orderly manner that helps you understand a topic. Technical texts don't contain opinions or first-person narrative. Directions, help manuals, recipes, school forms, and schedules are all types of technical texts. The girl in the photo is building a table. What sort of assembly instructions would be most useful to her?

Skills Focus

Have a Ball!

Identify Steps in a Process

Integrate Visual Information

In the Subzero Closet

Skim and Scan   **Analyze Text Structure**

Practice the Skill

Sequence is the order in which things happen. **Steps in a process** is the order in which things must be done. Explaining the steps in a process is an important part of a technical text. Imagine that you are preparing a recipe for cupcakes. What would happen if the recipe steps were written in the wrong order?

Steps in a process are often numbered or placed in a bulleted list. If they're not, sequence words like *first*, *next*, *then*, and *finally* can help you identify them.

Try It Read this recipe.

Vanilla Cupcakes

- Preheat oven to 350°.
- In a medium-size bowl, blend ½ cup softened butter and 1 cup sugar.
- Add 2 eggs, one at a time, then beat together.
- Stir in 2 teaspoons vanilla extract.
- Next, in a separate bowl, stir together 1½ cups all-purpose flour, ½ teaspoon baking powder, and ¼ teaspoon salt.
- Add dry mix to butter and egg mixture, then stir in ⅔ cup cold milk.
- Pour batter into cupcake pan and bake for 18–24 minutes.

Discuss **Draw a box around the design element and sequence words.**

Read the following paragraph and box the sequence words.

First plug the cable from the wall into the CABLE IN port on the cable box. Then, connect the video and audio cables from the OUT port on the cable box to the IN port on your television. Next, plug the power cords for the cable box and your television into an electrical outlet. Finally, turn on the television and cable box. Wait for the cable box to boot up.

Discuss **What is the outcome of following these steps? How is the organization of this text different from that of the recipe?**

As you read, complete the Process Chart on page 299.

Practice the Skill

Technical texts often contain graphics and other visual elements that present information in a visual form. A **diagram** can show you details about the way something works or how a task must be done. Diagrams are especially useful for showing complicated assembly processes. Most diagrams include some text, usually in the form of labels or ordered steps. A **time line** can clearly display the order in which a certain technology developed. An **illustration** shows how something looks or how a thing is done. As you read, take the time to look at and study any graphic elements on the page and see how the visuals work with the text to convey information.

Try It Read the paragraph and study the diagram.

A pulley is a simple machine used to lift an object, or load. A fixed pulley uses a small wheel attached to a supporting structure and a rope. By pulling down on the rope, you pull up on the load. If you pull the rope down 10 feet, the load goes up 10 feet. The fixed pulley changes only the direction of the force. It does not change the size of the force. So, to lift a 50-pound load, you still need to apply 50 pounds of force.

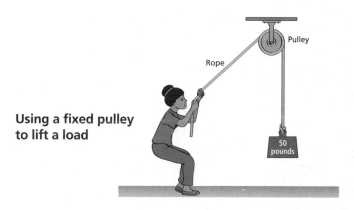

Using a fixed pulley to lift a load

Pulley

Rope

50 pounds

Discuss What can you learn from reading the paragraph and looking at the diagram? Circle the parts of the paragraph that relate directly to the diagram and tell how the diagram helped you understand the text.

As you read, record your answers to questions about integrating visual information on the Close Reading Worksheet on page 300.

Have a Ball!

Circle the part of the time line that tells you what the events on it describe.

Why might FIFA introduce an official World Cup ball every four years?

1   Every four years, millions of **fans** around the world shout and cheer as the biggest sporting tournament on the globe, soccer's World Cup, takes place. The World Cup athletes also shout, but it's not always words of encouragement. Sometimes they're yelling about the ball.

2   The International Federation of Association Football, or FIFA, is the organization that runs international soccer and organizes the World Cup competition. Before every World Cup series gets underway, FIFA announces a new official ball for it. And with every World Cup, there seems to be controversy surrounding the newly designed ball.

3   In 2010, goaltenders grumbled about the Jabulani, the official ball for the World Cup that took place in South Africa. They said it was dreadful and compared it to a beach ball. The makers of the Jabulani defended their soccer ball, saying that it was perfectly round and extremely aerodynamic. It wasn't the first time that players complained about the official World Cup soccer ball, and it probably won't be the **last**.

History of the Soccer Ball

1863

1850 — 1880 — 1910 — 1940

1930

Charles Goodyear's vulcanized rubber soccer ball is first used in official game in Boston.

Soccer balls are made from stronger rubber.

In the first FIFA World Cup, one soccer ball from each team is used during alternate halves of each match.

142   Lesson 6 • Technical Texts

The Buckminster Ball

4   The classic black-and-white soccer ball is known to some as the Buckminster soccer ball. It is named for a design developed by an architect named Richard Buckminster Fuller, who came up with the design when he was exploring ways to most efficiently use materials to build dome-shaped buildings.

5   Earlier soccer balls were always sewn by hand and had a lace-up seam, similar to footballs. Most were made from leather, which couldn't be shaped into a single segment that created a sphere. The heavy laces and water-absorbing leather made the balls heavy and dangerous to players. The Buckminster ball is made of geometric shapes that are sewn together. There are twenty hexagons and twelve pentagons in the classic Buckminster ball. When the different shapes are sewn together and the ball is inflated, they create a round surface. The black-and-white panels help players judge the spin and swerve of a moving ball.

Soccer Ball Basics

6   Over forty million soccer balls of all kinds are made every year. The least expensive have parts that are glued together, while the most expensive balls are still hand stitched. In the middle price range are soccer balls stitched together by machines.

Draw a |box| around the sentences that tell how soccer balls were put together before the Buckminster ball was designed.

Circle the soccer balls in the time line that can be described as having a "lace-up seam, similar to footballs."

Why are soccer balls sewn by hand the most expensive?

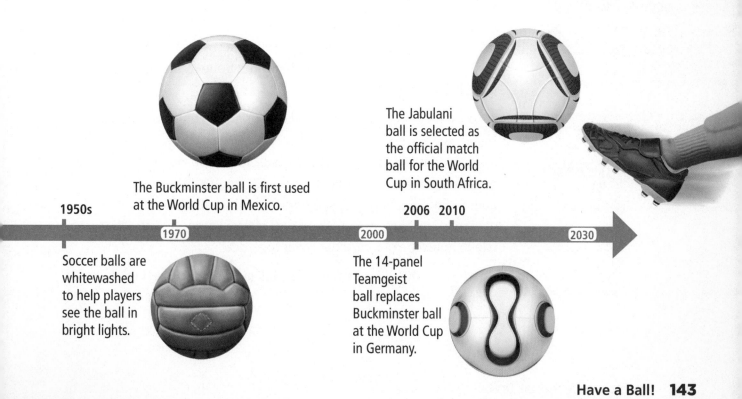

The Buckminster ball is first used at the World Cup in Mexico.

The Jabulani ball is selected as the official match ball for the World Cup in South Africa.

1950s   1970   2000   2006 2010   2030

Soccer balls are whitewashed to help players see the ball in bright lights.

The 14-panel Teamgeist ball replaces Buckminster ball at the World Cup in Germany.

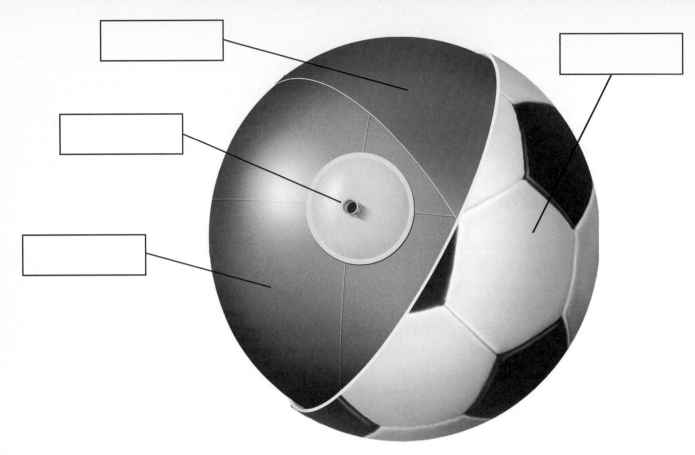

Parts of a soccer ball

Label the parts of the diagram above according to the information on this page. Circle text in paragraph 9 about the part of the soccer ball that is not shown in the diagram.

Why could playing with a heavy, wet leather soccer ball lead to injury?

7   Most soccer balls today have four main parts. In the center of the ball is the bladder, which holds the air. Named after the animal body part used to make balls in ancient times, the modern bladder is made from either natural or synthetic rubber. The bladder has a valve through which air can **pass** in order to inflate or deflate it.

8   Between the bladder and the cover are multiple layers of lining material. Made from polyester or cotton or a combination of the two, the lining helps the ball keep its shape and bounce. Some balls have foam linings as well.

9   Next comes the ball's cover, which wraps the outside of the ball. In the past, covers were often made from leather. However, because animal hides absorb water, leather balls tended to get very heavy when wet, which sometimes led to injuries. Consequently, most soccer balls today are made from synthetic, or artificial, leather. The cover also contains another important part of the soccer ball—the stitching, which holds the pieces of the cover together.

10   How are the different parts formed and put together? Let's take a look.

Building the Bladder

11   First, a soccer ball manufacturer has to decide whether to use natural rubber, synthetic rubber, or another material to make the ball's bladder. There are many factors involved in this decision, including cost and availability of the materials. Natural rubber is softer, but it does not hold air as well as synthetic rubber, which means natural rubber balls must be reinflated more often (at least once a week).

12   Then the manufacturer uses a **mold** to form the bladder. Workers heat the rubber and pour it into a machine where it is funneled into the mold. The mold is shaped like a balloon. Water surrounds the mold and helps cool the bladder evenly. The material wrinkles as it cools, but when the bladder is ready to come off the mold, workers remove it and fill it partially with air to smooth the bladder out.

What are the first and second steps that manufacturers take when making a soccer ball bladder? Record your answers in the **Process Chart**.

How does the diagram help you understand water's role in the process?

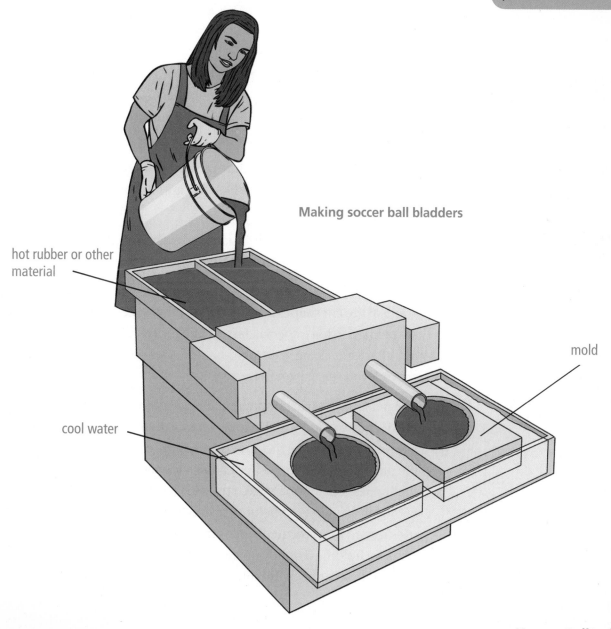

Making soccer ball bladders

hot rubber or other material

cool water

mold

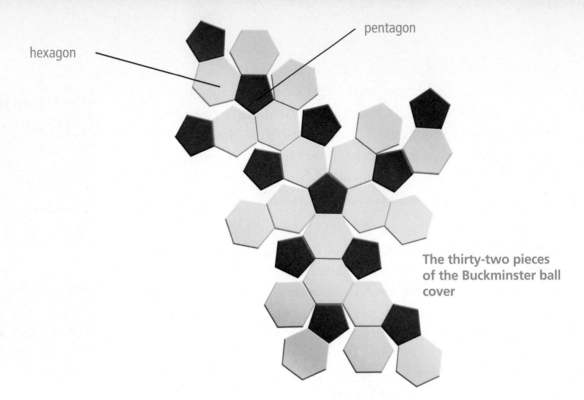

hexagon

pentagon

The thirty-two pieces of the Buckminster ball cover

Assembling the Lining and the Cover

13   The process by which a soccer ball's cover is assembled depends on the cover design and whether the manufacturer uses glue, machine stitching, or hand stitching. Here's how a hand-stitched Buckminster ball, the world's most popular soccer ball, is made.

1. Layers of lining are glued with strong adhesive to sheets of cover material such as synthetic leather. A high-end ball will have four layers of lining.

2. The sheets are put through a machine that cuts out the hexagonal and pentagonal shapes and also **punches** the stitch holes around the edges of the shapes.

3. Some of the cut shapes are taken to another area, where they are painted using a special, fast-drying process. This is how the manufacturer's company logo, as well as any other coloring or artwork you see, get on the soccer ball.

4. The person who will be stitching the ball is given a kit containing the thirty-two pieces of the cover and the ball's bladder. The stitcher follows a pattern, like the one shown in the diagram above, to put all the pieces together in the right order. One by one, he or she stitches the shapes together by hand, attaching a white hexagon to each side of one black pentagon before moving to the next shape. The stitcher uses thread that is coated with wax. The wax melts when the stitch is made, holding it tightly in place. The stitcher works with the cover inside out, so none of the stitches will show on the surface.

What steps are taken after the bladder is molded? Record your answers as steps 3 to 5 in the **Process Chart**.

How does the pattern in the diagram help you see how the Buckminster ball is put together?

5. The last stitches are the trickiest. When the cover is almost completely sewn, the stitcher turns it right side out and places the bladder inside. Then the stitcher uses a special needle to close the final seam. After that, an inspector checks the ball to make sure that no stitches have been missed.

6. The ball is then pumped up with air to ensure that the bladder was not punctured during the stitching process. It is weighed and measured to meet FIFA regulations. If the ball inflates as it should, then it is deflated again and packed to be shipped to retailers.

14   Manufacturers have quality control measures in place throughout the process to make sure that the soccer balls meet FIFA standards. International rules define the standards for shape, size, and weight of professional balls. All soccer balls used in international competitions must be spherical. They must be between 27 and 28 inches in circumference and weigh between 14 and 16 ounces.

What happens before the last stitches are sewn? What happens after they are sewn? Record your answer as steps 6, 7, and 8 in the **Process Chart**.

Why does FIFA need to have international rules for a regulation soccer ball's size, shape, and weight?

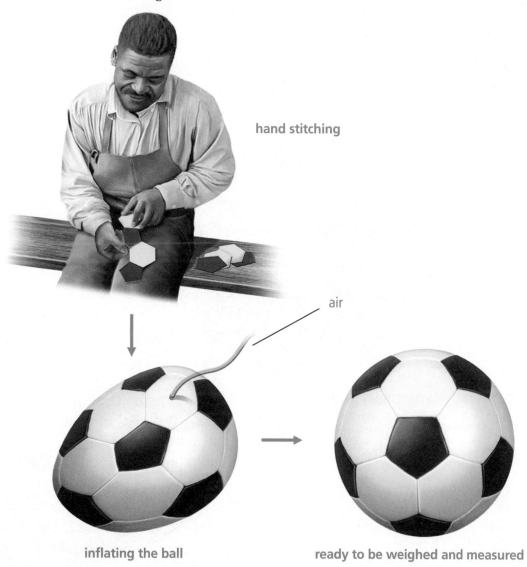

hand stitching

air

inflating the ball

ready to be weighed and measured

Draw a box around what happens after the positioning sensor and computer chip determine if a ball was in or out-of-bounds.

15   Technology is influencing soccer in new and interesting ways. One futuristic change is the CTRUS soccer ball, which is airless. Instead of the traditional bladder, this soccer ball has an interior frame. It bounces like a regular soccer ball, but it never needs to be inflated. The ball doesn't lose air during a game and isn't affected by altitude, which influences the air pressure in traditional balls.

16   Furthermore, the ball contains a position sensor that can tell where on the field the ball is. Imagine there is a close play. At first, the referees aren't sure if the ball was in or out-of-bounds. The CTRUS ball can tell them. The sensor determines whether the ball crossed the lines of play, then a computer **chip** analyzes that information and sends a message to the ball's frame. Next, the truly amazing thing happens: the ball changes color to signal to the players, referees, and fans that it was in or out-of-**bounds**. The same technology causes a similar color change when the ball goes over the goal line.

17   The CTRUS ball can also record the force with which it was kicked and the speed at which it travels. This new soccer ball even has a camera with a ball-view shot of the field. Say cheese!

Analyze

Why could the CTRUS ball be called "the chameleon of soccer balls"?

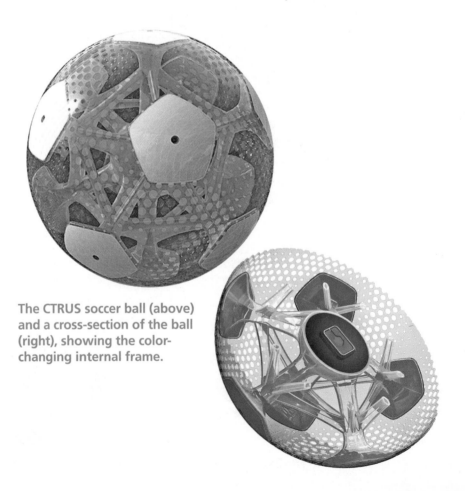

The CTRUS soccer ball (above) and a cross-section of the ball (right), showing the color-changing internal frame.

Vocabulary: Determine the Meanings of Multiple-Meaning Words

Many words and phrases have multiple meanings, and often the only way to figure out a word's correct meaning is to look at the other words around it—the context in which it is used. Imagine you and a friend are at your school's computer lab. If your friend says, "My mouse isn't working," you probably don't think of the small rodent. You know from the context that your friend means there's a problem with the computer's mouse. On the other hand, if your friend yells, "A mouse!" you know that he or she has most likely spotted the small rodent.

Try It Read this sentence from "Have a Ball!"

> Every four years, millions of **fans** around the world shout and cheer as the biggest sporting tournament on the globe, soccer's World Cup, takes place.

Discuss Which meaning of *fan* is correct: A) a machine that moves air, or B) an admirer or enthusiast? What context clues help you know?

Find these words in the selection, and circle the correct meaning.

	Meaning 1	**Meaning 2**
last, p. 142	A. to remain fresh, endure	B. final, after all others
pass, p. 144	A. to go by or move past	B. to happen
mold, p. 145	A. a type of fungus	B. a hollow form used to shape a liquid substance when it cools

Write the definition of each word below, based on its context in the selection.

punches, p. 146 _____

chip, p. 148 _____

bounds, p. 148 _____

Practice the Skill

When you **skim** a text, you read a selection quickly to get an overview of the main ideas in the text. Read the title. Then read the entire first paragraph and the first sentence of each remaining paragraph. Look at headings, subheads, and graphics. Look for boldfaced or italicized words. Read the final paragraph. This will help you decide where you should read more carefully for details. Imagine you are writing a report about the moons of Jupiter. You are in the library and can't find a book about that specific topic, but you find several that are about planets, the solar system, and moons. How will you know which ones will be best to use for sources? If you skim a chapter or two, as well as the contents page and the index, you'll be able to tell quickly which books have the best information about Jupiter's moons.

Once you have the books home, you can **scan** them by moving your eyes quickly down the pages, looking for the specific information, such as the word *Jupiter* or *moon* or the names of Jupiter's moons. Scanning for key words helps you find the exact information you need.

Try It Skim and scan these paragraphs.

> Did your bicycle chain break? Don't worry. There's no need to drag your bike to the bike shop. You can fix it yourself with just a hammer, or a chain tool if you have one, and an adult to help you.
>
> Before you get started, you should understand how chains work. Each link of a bike chain is held together by a steel pin or peg. With a chain tool or hammer, you can push the pins in and out. This will allow you to remove and attach links.
>
> It's a dirty job, so make sure you put on some old clothes before you get started. When you're ready, you should first flip your bike upside down so you can get to the chain easily.

> Discuss **What overview of the selection can you get by skimming it? What sort of information will the selection provide when you read it more thoroughly? Scan the paragraphs, looking for the tool(s) you will need. Double underline them.**

As you read, complete the Skim and Scan Chart on page 301.

Practice the Skill

Second Read Analyze Text Structure

Text structure is how a selection's ideas are arranged to help readers more easily understand what they are reading. Nonfiction texts are structured so that the different parts relate to one another and to the whole selection in the way that most clearly presents the ideas. To identify text structure, ask yourself: *How does a particular sentence give me insight into the ideas the author is trying to convey? How does the paragraph relate to the ones before and after it?*

Here are two major text structures used with nonfiction texts.

Structure	Definition	Clue Words and Phrases	
Description	lists characteristics, features, or examples to describe a topic, person, place, thing, or idea	such as for example in fact	for instance to illustrate in addition
Compare and Contrast	explains how two or more things, ideas, or people are alike or different	is similar to alike also yet	is different from instead but however

Keep in mind that a single selection may be structured using more than one style.

Try It Read these paragraphs.

Feeding your bearded dragon is simple. Since this lizard eats both plants and meat, you need to offer it a balanced diet. Young dragons need more protein than older dragons. In fact, their diet should be about three-fourths insects and one-fourth vegetables. They should be fed at least twice a day. Adult dragons can eat more vegetables and fewer insects.

The insects you can feed a dragon include crickets, mealworms, wax worms, king worms, and earthworms. In addition, you should coat the insects with a calcium supplement for healthy bones. Bearded dragons enjoy vegetables such as spinach, carrots, and dark-leaf lettuces.

> Discuss

What text structure does this selection use? Circle the clue words that help you identify it.

As you read, record your answers to text structure questions on the Close Reading Worksheet on page 302. ✎➤

Purpose for Reading

Read along with your teacher. Each time, read for a different purpose.

First Read — Focus on skimming and scanning the selection.

Second Read — Focus on analyzing text structure.

Third Read — Focus on thinking critically about the selection.

In the Subzero Closet

Skim this page, then write one or two sentences that state its main idea. Record your answer on the **Skim and Scan Chart**.

Why does the writer call Antarctica "the last frontier" in paragraph 1?

1   No one actually knows who the first person to walk on Antarctic ice was, but when the Norwegian scientist Roald Amundsen returned from a trip there in 1911, he was the first person in recorded history to make it there and back home again. For Amundsen and the rest of the world, Antarctica was the last frontier.

2   Antarctica is a desert—a very, very cold desert. The average precipitation that falls there each year is less than in the Sahara. It is the coldest and windiest of the seven continents. The lowest temperature on the planet was recorded there, a frigid **–128.6 degrees** Fahrenheit. Wind speeds can exceed two hundred miles per hour.

3   Yet these extreme conditions haven't discouraged people from traveling to Antarctica. In fact, the number of tourists has increased to nearly fifty thousand people a year. Most travel between the months of November and March, when it's summer in Antarctica. Although it is too cold for most people to live there permanently, some scientists live there year-round in base camps, such as the American McMurdo Station and the Russian Vostok Station, where they study the ice, the environment, and wildlife.

4   Are you planning a trip to Antarctica and wondering what to wear? It will depend on when you are going and on the activities you'll be doing while you're there. When you're indoors, you can wear what you typically wear at home. It's dressing for the outdoors during winter that's the real challenge.

Best Dressed

5   As long as there have been winters, people have been obsessed with cold-weather protective clothing. No matter where they live, people have to be outdoors at least some of the time. Modern technological innovations, such as heated automobiles, minimize the exposure time for most people. However, many brave the cold for long periods by choice to go skiing, hiking, or hunting.

6   Since ancient times, people have used natural materials, such as animal hides, wool, cotton, down feathers, and silk, to keep warm in cold climates. Wool is a natural **insulator**; it does not allow body heat to escape easily. It also absorbs moisture, keeping it away from the body. British explorers of the nineteenth century often wore navy-issued wool uniforms on their expeditions. Some noticed that native people in the Arctic region wore animal skins and furs, instead. The polar expeditions that "went native" and dressed in skins and furs fared much better than the parties that stubbornly insisted on wearing wool. The latter quite often froze to death. In these extreme conditions, wool did not insulate the explorers well enough.

7   Options for cold-weather gear increased in the twentieth and twenty-first centuries with the development of synthetic materials, such as nylon, polyester, and spandex, to protect against extreme cold conditions. Clothes made from synthetic materials have become popular with scientists and explorers who work in the most extreme conditions on the planet.

8   Whether the material is natural or synthetic, it has to keep the heat that the body generates from escaping into the environment and to allow sweat to evaporate from the body. These two factors, **thermal insulation** and **moisture permeation**, are key in deciding which clothing to wear in extreme conditions.

Scan this page for subheads and boldface words. Circle them. What do they tell you about the information being conveyed in this section of the text? Record your answer on the **Skim and Scan Chart**.

How does the comparison in paragraphs 6 and 7 help you understand the larger point that cold-weather clothing has evolved over time?

Why would a scientist need to add or remove layers of clothing when working outside in Antarctica?

How is the information in this chart arranged? Why is this the best structure for this purpose?

Layer Up

9   If you plan to be active in extreme cold conditions, you must layer your clothes to help with thermal insulation and moisture permeation. This way, if you become too warm, you can remove a layer, and if you get too cold, you can add a layer. All of the layers together will make up your cold-weather clothing system.

Base Core Layer

The layers next to your skin should be made of fabric that is comfortable, soft, and able to wick, or draw, perspiration away from your body so you stay dry.

Middle Insulation Layers

Shirts, sweaters, and pants should be made of materials designed for cold weather, such as polar fleece, wool, or a synthetic fabric. This layer releases sweat and insulates the wearer.

Outer Layer

Jacket and pants must be made of windproof and waterproof material. The jacket should have a hood. Both jacket and pants should have cords or adjustable cuffs to prevent warm air from getting out and snow from getting in.

Hands

Two or three pairs of gloves or mittens are needed: a thin, insulating layer closest to your skin and a windproof outer layer. In fact, mittens are warmer than gloves, but thin gloves at the base layer are good if you need to do detail work with your hands.

Head

A pullover hat that covers your head, ears, lower face, and neck, called a balaclava, is ideal, but a hat with earflaps may suffice. Goggles and sunglasses or a face mask will protect your face from the wind and your eyes from the glare of sunlight off the snow.

Feet

Two pairs of socks, again layering thin, insulating socks with a thick, warm pair. Boots should have thick soles and should be insulated and waterproof.

Modern Clothing

10   The insulation value of an article of clothing depends on the material's thickness and its ability to trap air. Duck or goose down has traditionally been used as an insulator; however, down's ability to insulate drops when it is wet. Microfiber material made from a blend of polyesters has an insulating quality similar to down but still performs well when wet.

11   Moisture permeation was mentioned earlier as a key factor in keeping warm. In order to be successful, cold weather clothing has to be good at wicking. This means the material draws water vapor away from the skin through the clothing layers before it condenses. If it doesn't pass through the base and middle layers, the water vapor could turn to liquid, then freeze and be trapped within the clothing. This is why the base layer should be made of a wicking fabric such as silk or a synthetic like certain polyesters.

12   Additionally, a successful cold-weather clothing system has to prevent water from getting inside the clothes. Although precipitation is uncommon in Antarctica and the temperatures don't get warm enough for snow to melt, chances are, you will be traveling by boat, where you might be splashed. So the outer layer should be made of nylon or expanded polytetrafluoroethylene (more commonly known as Gore-Tex®).

13   Be sure not to sacrifice mobility or flexibility when piling on the layers. You need to be able to move about freely to perform whatever activities you traveled to the end of the world to enjoy!

Scan the text to find these words: *microfiber*, *silk*, and *nylon*. Circle them. What can you learn by reading the sentence in which you found each word? Record your answer in the **Skim and Scan Chart**.

Why is keeping mobility and flexibility in mind important?

Skim the subhead and paragraphs on this page. What do they tell you about the information you'll read? Record your answer in the **Skim and Scan Chart.**

What is the text structure used to organize the selection as a whole? Why was it used?

Compare

How does the information about cold-weather clothing systems compare to how you choose your regular clothes?

Follow the Directions

14 Cold-weather clothing requires maintenance. You can get started on that maintenance before you even step out the door. Be aware of what you are wearing before you set out, and make sure you have the equipment, supplies, and time needed to care for each item of clothing when you return. You'd hate to have to sacrifice your next day of adventure or research because you didn't have the right soap to wash your base layers. You may even wish to have one or more extra sets of clothing, just in case.

15 Each item of clothing in your system may require different care. You can't just throw everything in the washing machine and be done with it. Some items need to be washed by hand; others can't be put in a dryer. It's crucial that you follow the manufacturer's instructions so nothing is ruined.

16 Take good care of your cold-weather protective clothing, and it will take care of you.

Vocabulary: Domain-Specific Vocabulary

Domain-specific vocabulary refers to words and phrases that are commonly used by people who work in a particular field of work or study. The words have specific meanings and are often included in work-related documents and conversations. For example, automobile mechanics use words such as *engine mount, carburetor, ratchet,* and *floor jack.* Domain-specific vocabulary also includes symbols used in these fields; for example, math symbols (+, −, =, π) may appear in technical texts.

Try It The table below lists some domain-specific words, phrases, and symbols from "In the Subzero Closet." Find context clues near the unfamiliar words, and use what you already know about the words to write a definition for each. Then, check your definition against a dictionary.

Word	Context Clues	Definition
−128.6 degrees, p. 152		
insulator, p. 153		
thermal insulation, p. 153		
moisture permeation, p. 153		

Discuss Think about something that you know a lot about. What domain-specific words relate to that topic? Write the words below and discuss them.

Respond to Text: Integrate Graphic and Written Technical Content

"Have a Ball!" combines graphic elements with text to explain technical concepts.

Try It Think about how the selection uses graphic elements to illustrate complicated, technical concepts in ways that complement the text.

 Discuss **How did the time line, diagrams, and illustrations in the selection help in your understanding of the content of the selection?**

On Your Own Write a paragraph about the integration of graphic and written content in "Have a Ball!" Describe how the graphic elements affected your reading experience and the ways in which they worked in combination with the text of the selection to present information. Give examples from the text and graphic elements to support your response. Use the guide on the next page to help you organize your response. Write your answer on a separate sheet of paper.

Checklist for a Good Response

A good paragraph

✔ provides a topic sentence that clearly states your main idea.

✔ describes the graphic elements used in the selection.

✔ discusses how the graphics work with the text to help convey information.

✔ includes supporting ideas that develop the main idea.

✔ includes a concluding statement that restates the analysis of the graphic elements and text used in the selection.

How Graphic and Written Technical Content Worked Together

1. **Topic Sentence** Include this information in your first sentence:

   In "Have a Ball!" I used the graphic elements to better understand the

   text about _____.

2. **Detail Sentences** Tell about the ways the text and graphic elements present information. Use this chart to organize your ideas.

Text Elements	Graphic Elements

3. **Concluding Sentence** Your concluding sentence should state your analysis of how the graphic elements and text in the selection worked together to present information.

   _____

   _____

On a separate sheet of paper, write your paragraph.

Read on Your Own

Read the selection independently three times, using the skills you have learned. Then answer the Comprehension Check questions.

First Read	Practice the first-read skills you learned in this lesson.
Second Read	Practice the second-read skills you learned in this lesson.
Third Read	Think critically about the selection.

Touch-tastic!

Skim and Scan Skim the title and first two paragraphs. Predict what this selection will be about.

1   Cell phones. Tablets. Interactive whiteboards. Your fingers are most likely getting a good workout these days, thanks to touch screen technology. Touch screens can be found in people's pockets, in kitchens with interactive refrigerator doors and oven consoles, and in classrooms.

2   It seems almost like magic. You tap your finger on a screen to launch a game or slide your fingers apart to zoom in on the part of a photo that you want to get a closer look at. In fact, it's not magic at all. It's technology, and it's being used in more places every day.

Analyze Text Structure Circle clue words on this page that help you determine the selection's text structure. The first has been done for you.

The Basics

3   Touch screen technology lets you access information with the touch of a finger. It does this by using sensors and a computer processor. The sensors report where on the screen your finger is located, and the processor turns that information into a direction, such as *Reset the game* or *Zoom in on the photo*. The directions don't literally read like that because they're written in computer code, but the message is the same.

4   The sensors can also detect multiple fingers and the movement of those fingers. For example, tap once, tap twice, pinch, zoom, press and hold. You probably already know the reaction you will get when you move your fingers in those ways on a touch screen. You're communicating with the device using a touch technology language.

5   Three main types of touch screen technology are currently being used in most products: resistive, capacitive, and infrared. Read on to find out how each technology works.

Resistive Technology

6   Resistive touch screens are pressure sensitive. They have multiple layers. The first layer is glass or plastic, coated with a film that conducts electrical currents. Underneath this conductive layer are small spacer dots that separate it from the next layer, the resistive layer. When you turn on the touch screen device, an electric current runs between the conductive layer and the resistive layer, creating an electrical field. Then, when your finger pushes the conductive layer into the resistive layer, it changes the electrical current. The controller receives information about where exactly you are touching the screen.

7   Since resistive touch screens work because of pressure applied to the screen, you can use your bare or gloved fingers, a stylus, or even a pen point to touch the screen.

8   The least expensive touch screen technology, resistive technology is used in many smartphones. However, resistive touch screens do not have long lives. They tend to scratch easily, and since they depend on pressure to work, they are likely to wear out faster than the other two types of screens.

Identify Steps in a Process Draw boxes around the steps in the process of translating touch into a command using resistive technology. The first step has been boxed for you.

Integrate Visual Information Think about the ways the text supports what the graphic shows and how the graphic makes the text easier to understand.

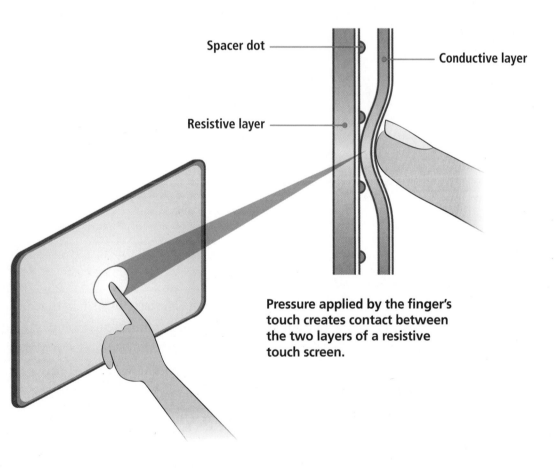

Spacer dot

Conductive layer

Resistive layer

Pressure applied by the finger's touch creates contact between the two layers of a resistive touch screen.

Capacitive Technology

Skim and Scan Scan the text to find the words *capacitive, electrodes,* and *infrared.* Think about what they mean.

Critical Thinking Think about why capacitive technology is best used for indoor products.

9   Capacitive touch screens depend on the small electrical charges that all human bodies carry. Inside layers of glass and metallic material, **electrodes** transmit a small current from the corners of the screen. When you touch the screen, your finger draws off a small part of this current, which creates a voltage drop. Sensors detect that change. The controller calculates the location of the change and relays the location to the device's central processor.

10   Because capacitive technology requires input from the electrical charge of your body, you must use your bare fingers to touch this type of screen. A gloved finger or a stylus will not work. For the same reason, it works best with products used indoors where atmospheric conditions are stable.

11   Capacitive technology is not as widely used as resistive technology, but it is still relatively popular in touch screen devices.

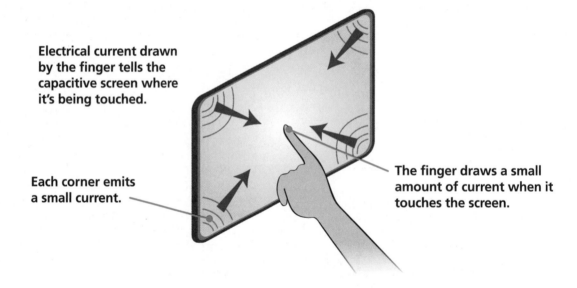

Electrical current drawn by the finger tells the capacitive screen where it's being touched.

Each corner emits a small current.

The finger draws a small amount of current when it touches the screen.

Infrared Technology

12   Infrared touch screens work using wavelengths of light that are invisible to the human eye. Devices using infrared technology create a grid of vertical and horizontal beams just above the screen. When you touch the screen, sensors detect the point where the beams are being interrupted.

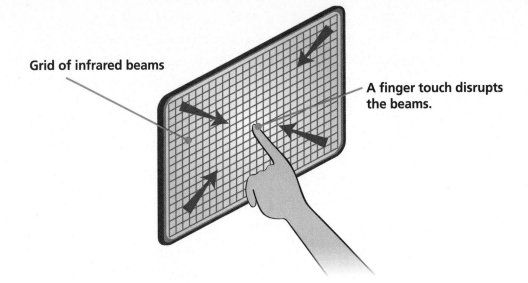

Grid of infrared beams

A finger touch disrupts the beams.

13   Like resistive touch screens, infrared touch screens can be operated using a bare or gloved finger, a stylus, or a pen point.

14   This type of technology is expensive, and problems often arise because of accidental activation due to the screen's sensitivity. These touch screens are most commonly used in large displays intended for outdoor use, such as automated teller machines.

The Touch Screen Brain

15   Whether a touch's location is detected by an interruption in the **charge** on the screen or a broken infrared beam, that information isn't worth much on its own. The location first has to be sent by the controller to the central processor—the brain of the device. The device interprets the touch in this way.

1. The touch screen turns your touch into electrical signals, which it sends to the device's processor.

2. The processor uses software to analyze the size, shape, and location of the touch.

3. Gesture software in the processor figures out what type of touch was made: scroll, pinch, or tap.

Identify Steps in a Process Draw a box around the text that tells you what must happen before the processor sends information to the applications you are using.

Critical Thinking Consider why a processor would need to send information to an application you are using.

4. The processor sends that information as instructions to the application you are using, telling it, for example, to enlarge a picture, print a file, or play a song. The processor also sends information to the screen, telling it how to appear as the result of your touch. For example, it might show the picture getting bigger, the printer being queued, or song information and album art.

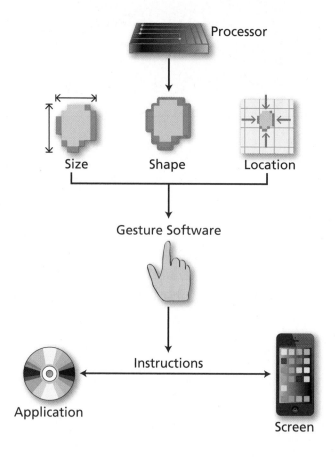

16   Today, you can use touch screen technology to call your grandmother or to play a game on your tablet. But scientists and engineers are constantly working on new ways to develop it even further. In the future, you may be able to touch your phone to change the color of your sneakers. Or you might touch a screen on your refrigerator to add your favorite flavor to the milk inside. The possibilities seem endless, so . . . what would you design a touch screen to do?

Critical Thinking Think about why the writer chose to focus on the three main technologies instead of all touch screen technologies.

✔ Comprehension Check

1. What are the steps in the process of your communicating with a touch screen and your tablet's application receiving the information?

   _____

   _____

   _____

2. How did the graphic on page 162 help you visualize that capacitive touch screens broadcast currents, as described in the text?

   _____

   _____

   _____

3. What was the selection's overall text structure? What other text structure was used within the selection?

   _____

   _____

   _____

4. If you wanted to review the information on how the central processor works, which section would you scan?

   _____

5. Why might resistive touch screens wear out faster than capacitive screens?

_____

_____

_____

6. Why might people who travel to or work in the Antarctic avoid using smartphones or other devices with capacitive screens?

_____

_____

_____

7. Read this sentence from the selection.

   Inside layers of glass and metallic material, electrodes transmit a small current from the corners of the screen.

   Circle the words that help you understand the meaning of the word *electrodes*.

8. Read this sentence from the selection.

   Whether a touch's location is detected by an interruption in the charge on the screen or a broken infrared beam, that information isn't worth much on its own.

   Circle the correct definition of *charge* as it is used in this context.

   A. *n.* price or cost

   B. *n.* debt

   C. *n.* quantity of electricity

   D. *v.* to accuse

   E. *v.* to defer payment

Lesson 7

Persuasive Nonfiction

Persuasive nonfiction is writing that seeks to convince readers to agree with a particular point of view or to behave in a particular way. There are many types of persuasive texts—magazine and newspaper editorials, political speeches, and some online blogs feature this sort of opinion piece. Generally, persuasive nonfiction writers try to state their case in such strong, logical, and appealing ways that readers find them hard to resist. For persuasive nonfiction to be truly effective, it must include pertinent and well-researched facts and reasons. Another persuasive technique is the use of rhetoric—powerful, precise language that moves readers emotionally. Which form of persuasion do you think the speaker in this photo is using, intellectual or emotional? How can you tell?

Skills Focus

RFIDs in Our Future

Author's Point of View

Fact, Opinion, and Reasoned Judgment

Cashing in Our Chips

Compare and Contrast   **Analyze Arguments**

Practice the Skill

Author's Point of View

When you read persuasive nonfiction, you need to identify the author's point of view, or what he or she is trying to persuade you to think or do. An **author's point of view** is his or her opinion on a topic, as expressed in an argument or a set of claims made about the topic. Sometimes the point of view will be stated plainly: "I think Mayor Russell is a disaster." But other times you will have to work to determine the author's point of view. It can be revealed by the choice of facts (statistics or other provable data that make particularly strong points) that the author includes. You should also be aware of the facts an author chooses to leave out of an argument, as this also reveals point of view.

Try It Read this persuasive nonfiction text.

Full-Throttle Future

Looking at this country's attitude toward high-speed rail, you might think we're proud to be unlike all the other developed nations, happy to wobble along on ancient railways—living in a nineteenth-century world while everyone else rockets into the twenty-first.

This pride would be misplaced. The arguments against high-speed rail—trains that whiz along at 180 miles per hour or more—just don't hold water. High-speed trains can help relieve automobile congestion. Moreover, train stations can be closer together than airports, since they typically take up much less space than airports. Business moves at the speed of travel, so everyone would benefit.

There's another argument for high-speed rail. Magnetic levitation rail has been shown to cause less pollution than planes and autos. Promoting this type of high-speed rail would decrease pollution and would help us do our part in the war on climate change. And that's a war worth fighting.

> **Discuss** What is the author's point of view? Underline facts the author includes. Can you think of any facts the author has omitted—aspects of high-speed rail the writer does not bring up?

As you read, complete the Author's Point of View Chart on page 303.

Practice the Skill

Authors making persuasive arguments must include facts, opinions, and reasoned judgments to support their points of view. **Facts** are provable things—statistics, dates, or events that can be checked to see if they are true. **Opinions** are expressions of feeling, belief, and taste. Opinions cannot be proved true or untrue; they can simply be agreed with or disagreed with. The U.S. women's soccer team winning the gold medal in the 2012 Olympics is a fact. But saying that they are the best soccer team of all time is expressing an opinion.

A **reasoned judgment** is a logical conclusion that is supported by facts and that appeals to the reader's common sense. A solid, reasoned judgment should always consider and address opposing arguments.

Try It Read this persuasive nonfiction text.

Menace in the Skies

While the use of unmanned aerial vehicles (UAVs) in war zones is becoming commonplace, not many people are aware that the use of UAVs, or "drones," in our domestic airspace is on the rise.

Startling new technological advances are outpacing everyone's wildest expectations. Drones blend into the background. They can be as small as a hummingbird and can slip into a house unnoticed. Drones' tiny cameras can see and record everything they encounter in high definition. Even the most law-abiding citizen with nothing to hide should be aware that nothing he or she does will be truly private in the future. This should make everyone nervous.

Discuss **What type of evidence is the author using here? Underline one fact and circle one opinion. Is there a reasoned judgment? Box it.**

As you read, record your answers to questions about fact, opinion, and reasoned judgment on the Close Reading Worksheet on page 304.

RFIDs in Our Future

by Karl Blossom

What is the author's point of view on RFID chips? Write your answer in the center box on the Author's Point of View Chart.

What facts does the author use in paragraph 3 to support his argument?

What other applications can you think of for RFIDs?

1   Imagine that you walk into a new classroom—you don't know anybody there. You don't know what these students do for fun, what music or movies they like—not a thing. But you want to figure out who to talk to, so you beam your handheld computer at each student, and tiny microchips in their name tags, or even under their skin, beam back everything you need to know: likes and dislikes, hobbies—you name it.

2   We gravitate naturally and easily to people who enjoy the same things we do or who do interesting things we'd like to learn more about. Armed with the information you would have in the scenario just described, you would be able to identify these people with similar interests right away. By the end of the day, you may even have a new friend or two—all due to the magic of a chip no bigger than a grain of rice.

3   While we aren't quite to that point yet, we are getting closer. With radio-frequency identification (RFID), we already have the capacity to plant tiny microchips in or on just about anything. These chips carry information of all kinds. A chip under your skin might tell a doctor how to locate your medical records or what allergies you have. Chips in cars already allow drivers to whisk through toll plazas without stopping— the chip shares account information with a computer in the toll booth. These chips are saving valuable time for commuters and travelers. U.S. passports are even chipped now, facilitating your comings and goings through airports at home and abroad.

4   The beauty of these microchips is not just in the data they contain. They are also very easy to use. Because the chips are so tiny, they can be placed virtually anywhere. One kind of RFID is so small it doesn't even need batteries. The information on this type of chip is accessed by a data reader or scanner. That device provides the energy to briefly activate the RFID. Then, once activated, the RFID shows the information contained in it to the reader.

5   So what could be wrong with such a fantastic device? Well, to some people, there are plenty of things wrong with RFIDs. For one, some will say this new technology could prove intrusive. Imagine having a pretzel company that knows exactly how many pretzels you've bought and when—as well as knowing when you're out of them. What if food companies used edible RFIDs to track your eating habits? While sharing this sort of information might be useful for some, to others it's downright creepy. The same thing applies to the use of RFIDs to track people. A parent might be delighted to know the exact location of a child. But that child might not be so happy about his or her every movement being tracked.

6   When does helpfulness become intrusion? At what point do we draw the line between efficiency and invasion? Clearly, as technology evolves, there must be more and better-crafted legislation to protect us from any abuses of RFID technology. Having the ability to see through walls, for instance, would have many advantages, but while Superman never did so, X-ray vision could easily be abused. Some would make that same argument about RFIDs, and those are the people we must convince that the benefits far outweigh any risks.

Why does the author present an opposing view of RFIDs on this page? Underline the words that provide this view. Write your answer in the upper left box on the **Author's Point of View Chart**.

What opinions does the author give in paragraph 5?

RFIDs at toll booths allow drivers to pay without stopping.

When Mary Shelley created the Frankenstein monster, she was voicing the fears of her era and her culture about technological innovation.

What information has the author chosen to omit when addressing the opposing argument given in paragraph 7? Write your answer in the upper right box on the **Author's Point of View Chart**.

How does the author use facts to deal with the argument against new technology?

Which view about how technology was feared in the past seems most ridiculous to you? Why?

7   Americans expect that their right to privacy be honored, and rightly so. Commercial companies would benefit greatly from knowing every detail of their customers' lives. Law enforcement agencies could benefit greatly from having every citizen chipped. But as those who argue against RFIDs will point out, democracy is not about efficiency—it's about individual rights. It's true that those rights can be eroded in all kinds of ways. However, it is also true that with careful planning, individual rights can be protected while still allowing everyone to benefit from the wonderful technological advances of our age—such as RFIDs.

8   There are always people opposed to anything new. Throughout history, there have always been naysayers to new technologies. Socrates, for example, found the idea of writing to be a threat to the human soul. He thought students wouldn't need to memorize information and would lose the ability to remember anything. Also, he maintained that they would read whatever they laid their hands on, including frivolous stories that would ruin their minds.

9   When trains were introduced in the 1800s, many people feared collisions and explosions. These fears were not always unfounded. However, the same cannot be said for fears that railroads were a "device of the devil," or that rail travel—simply sitting on a moving train—could produce a concussion.

10   Also in the 1800s, Mary Shelley wrote *Frankenstein, or the Modern Prometheus*, a novel involving a deceased human body reanimated by a scientist. The story of this sad and tragic monster is a metaphor for the frightening possibilities of technology. And technological fears are not confined to the far-distant past. A century ago—or less—people were afraid electricity would leak out of wires and outlets and cause harm to the general public.

11   Plenty of technology fears linger today. Some fear that once we perfect artificial intelligence, robots will turn on us and take over the world. Social media from Facebook to e-mail to Twitter and Tumblr have been pointed to as innovations that will destroy our culture and ruin young minds. The tendency of normal adults to use LOL or OMG in daily conversation is cited by fanatical lovers of formal language as a sign that our culture is evaporating. And of course the Internet itself has been held up as the tool of humankind's ultimate undoing.

12   These trembling critics of technology need to relax and focus on the positive changes that can be gained from careful acceptance of technology. Because, let's face it, these changes are inevitable. Yes, as with most new technologies, there is an apparent Jekyll and Hyde aspect to RFIDs. They have downsides, just as planes, trains, and automobiles do, but can we do without any of those innovations?

13   The standard way to control the negative possibilities of a new technology is to introduce legislation and regulation. Firm rules could protect American citizens from any truly invasive use of RFIDs. Opt-out technology could also be devised so people could choose to opt out, to not have RFIDs in their lives. This would undercut the potential upsides of RFIDs, but that would be the price those people would pay for turning their backs on technological advances.

14   As in all things, balance is the key. Certainly there will always be places for consumers to shop that don't use RFIDs and never will. Shoppers can vote with their pocketbooks on these and other matters. If an RFID chip lights up a sign on the dashboard of the car that reminds you your gas tank is running low, it is still up to you, the consumer, to respond or not to this information. Most people would agree that these reminders, whether about running low on shampoo or toilet paper or any of a thousand commodities we use every day, would be useful. A trip to the store could be beautifully efficient.

What claims does the author make to appease those who fear that RFIDs would invade our privacy too much? Underline those claims and write your answer in the lower left box on the **Author's Point of View Chart**.

Do people really use LOL and OMG in speech and conversation, or are those abbreviations used only in writing? Cite evidence from your own experience to support your answer.

What information about an employer's use of RFIDs is the author leaving out? Record your answer in the lower right box on the **Author's Point of View Chart**.

In the bottom box of the **Author's Point of View Chart**, write whether the author convinced you of his point of view or not, and explain why.

Judge

What was the most convincing part of this author's argument? What was the least effective aspect of it? Why?

15   Without a doubt, life with RFIDs would be smoother for everyone—frustration would be reduced; time management would be maximized. The time spent making decisions and finding a good friend or the missing item in the pantry could all be reduced. But it is not simply convenience to the individual that we should consider when it comes to RFIDs.

16   RFIDs would also mean huge benefits to corporations and big retail chains. What can be accomplished using RFIDs would enable them to employ far fewer workers to track inventory and do their accounting, thereby becoming more efficient and profitable. Further, RFIDs will be good for the environment, and as climate change becomes a bigger factor in our lives, we will no longer be able to keep our heads buried in the sand. More efficient ordering and shipping will cut down on fuel consumption for hauling and trucking. Being able to store goods only as long as necessary will cut down on waste. That sounds like a win-win for the companies and the environment.

17   In the end, our best defense against the downsides of RFIDs is to educate ourselves to their possible uses and learn where to draw the line with thoughtful legislation. As with all new technology, we want to enjoy the benefits and minimize the dangers. In the case of RFIDs, those benefits are getting brighter and stronger every day.

RFID chips can help retail stores operate more efficiently.

Vocabulary: Figurative Language: Allusion

Allusions are references to well-known characters or situations that have come to represent an idea. Allusions can be made to myths or figures from religion, literature, adages, or folktales; to novels, plays, and television shows; and to sports. For an allusion to be effective, most readers must be familiar with the reference. The phrase *sour grapes* is an allusion to Aesop's fable in which a fox, unable to reach a bunch of grapes, decides they must be sour. Most people relate to the tendency to minimize the value of something they cannot have, just as the fox does with the grapes. In arguments, allusions help the writer make a point.

Try It Read this sentence from "RFIDs in Our Future."

> Having the ability to see through walls, for instance, would have many advantages, but while Superman never did so, X-ray vision could easily be abused.

What do the words *Superman* and *X-ray vision* allude to?

> **Discuss** **Brainstorm some commonly used allusions. How could allusions be used to help convince someone of a point of view?**

The following sentences from "RFIDs in Our Future" contain allusions. Identify the allusion and then explain its meaning.

1. **Yes, as with most new technologies, there is an apparent Jekyll and Hyde aspect to RFIDs. p. 173**

   _____

   _____

   _____

2. **Further, RFIDs will be good for the environment, and as climate change becomes a bigger factor in our lives, we will no longer be able to keep our heads buried in the sand. p. 174**

   _____

   _____

   _____

Practice the Skill

Comparing and contrasting can help you better understand the relationship between two texts on the same topic. It can also clarify the differences between two ideas in a single text. When you **compare and contrast** two things, you see how they are the same, how they are different, and how they relate to each other.

When comparing two persuasive texts, examine how each author emphasizes different evidence and presents different interpretations of facts. By reading two persuasive texts that present different points of view, you can better understand the topic and form your own opinion based on the evidence that each author gives.

Try It Read these persuasive essays.

Copper vs. Fiber-Optic Cable

After the invention of the telephone, copper wire became the accepted medium for transmitting telephone calls. However, copper wire has a tendency to corrode, particularly when exposed to salt water. Fiber-optic cables, which are made of glass wire, do not corrode. Moreover, one tiny strand of fiber has the capacity to carry far more data—necessary in today's high-tech world—than a strand of copper. Fiber-optic cable is the perfect way to transmit texts, telephone calls, videos, and images. Copper fails in comparison.

Copper: America's Metal

In many ways, copper is the backbone of America. Copper was present at the founding of our country—Paul Revere was a coppersmith as well as a silversmith. As our great modern cities developed, copper was in the walls of every skyscraper. Copper is there today, keeping electricity running smoothly through our homes, schools, and workplaces. Copper is a versatile metal; its use in conducting electricity is unrivaled. While glass wire is fragile, copper is strong. While glass is brittle, copper flexes. Copper is here to stay.

> Discuss | The first essay is unemotional; the second presents facts designed to appeal to emotion. Underline the parts of the second essay that appeal to emotion. Circle the part of the second essay in which the author is presenting facts.

As you read, complete the Venn Diagram on page 305.

Practice the Skill

Second Read Analyze Arguments

As you **analyze arguments** in persuasive essays, be aware that authors will use many techniques to persuade you. To analyze their arguments, you must be aware of what sorts of appeals are being made.

Some methods of persuasion are straightforward—for example, a **reasoned judgment** spells out why you should believe something, while **facts** from trustworthy sources are used to persuade you. But certain persuasive techniques are less obvious and often signal weak arguments.

- **Loaded language** is strong vocabulary used to trigger an emotional response.

- **Exaggeration** is the overstatement of facts beyond what seems reasonable or true.

- **Bandwagon appeals** are arguments that encourage the reader to join a supposed majority in one single point of view.

- **Snob appeal** suggests that a certain way of thinking is more sophisticated or intelligent.

- **Humor** uses sarcasm or gentle joking to disarm readers and make an unsound idea easier to swallow.

As you read a persuasive text, note what the author is trying to get you to think and how he or she is going about it. Ask yourself: *Is he citing facts? Is she using language meant to cause an emotional reaction? Do the facts and ideas presented square with common sense and things you know to be true from actual experience? Does the writer thoughtfully address counterarguments or merely dismiss them as unfounded or "silly"?*

Try It Reread the persuasive essays on the previous page.

> **Discuss** What sort of subtle—or not so subtle—appeals are being made? Draw a box around examples of loaded language in the paragraphs.

As you read, record your answers to questions about analyzing arguments on the Close Reading Worksheet on page 306.

Purpose for Reading

Read along with your teacher. Each time, read for a different purpose.

First Read — Focus on comparing and contrasting texts.

Second Read — Focus on analyzing the author's argument.

Third Read — Focus on evaluating the text critically.

Cashing in Our Chips

by Nicola Gonzalez

What does this text so far share with "RFIDs in Our Future"? Write your answers on the **Venn Diagram**.

What persuasive techniques has the author used so far? Circle these examples and list the technique each uses.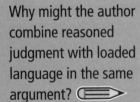

Why might the author combine reasoned judgment with loaded language in the same argument?

1   The five words you should be most afraid of when they come from a corporation are: "This will make life easier." The one fact you can depend on once you've heard that phrase is that whatever is being discussed will most certainly make *their* lives easier. And it will do so at your expense.

2   On some occasions and in some areas, the level of exploitation involved is almost invisible—you innocently enter your e-mail address on an online form when you make a purchase and then are forever subjected to newsletters from Radio Hut or Office Heaven. But what happens when this information sharing is out of your control? What happens when it's no longer your choice to disclose vital information? Information not just about how to contact you, but where you live, what you like to do, how you spend your money, what you view on the internet, and what your taste in clothing and entertainment is?

3   Much of this information is generally considered private, or at least privileged—particularly medical, economic, and legal information. And yet with the advent of a technology called RFID—short for radio-frequency identification—all this information and more can be jammed into a tiny space. In fact, there are already RFID in U.S. passports. Although encryption measures are in place, in theory, anyone carrying a passport with an RFID is broadcasting information that could be read when his or her passport is opened. Potentially, a stranger could learn your name, nationality, age, and birthplace, and even look at your passport photo.

Duplicating any part of this book is prohibited by law. © 2014 Triumph Learning, LLC

178   Lesson 7 • Persuasive Nonfiction

4   This is the pace of technology, working against us. The government inserts RFID chips in new passports, yet no one has figured out how to guarantee that the RFIDs cannot be hacked. One of the beauties of passport RFID chips is they require no power at all—they're **dormant** until switched on and made **active** by a chip reader. And while it's true in most situations a data thief won't know you're carrying your passport, in an international airport or certain other places, they certainly will suspect it. For a techie who knows how to set it up, a potato chip tube of the right dimensions hooked to a regular laptop can potentially be turned into an RFID reader that can hack any RFID that's around.

5   The main purpose of RFIDs, at least initially, was to serve as a solution to the inventory problems all companies experience. *How much do we have of what?* This was the constant headache of inventory managers, trying to keep the flow of product smooth from manufacturer to warehouse to shop floor to consumer. The chips work beautifully for this. Flip on a chip reader and pass it down a hall, and the boxes or shipping containers magically reveal their contents.

What is the author's argument? What is the author's argument in "RFIDs in Our Future"? Write your answers on the **Venn Diagram**.

Underline the sentence in paragraph 4 that the author uses for emotional effect. What emotion is the author trying to stimulate in the reader?

The U.S. government uses RFID chips to enhance speed, efficiency, and security for travelers.

RFIDs help companies track their inventory.

What information does this author choose to include that the author of "RFIDs in Our Future" did not? Write your answers on the **Venn Diagram**.

How does the author use humor to address a difficult subject? Underline the sentence that uses this technique.

6   And there's the rub. In the not-so-distant future, suppose you buy a sweater. You walk out of the store with your purchase. The chip in that sweater can be scanned from a satellite to determine its location, and thus the wearer's location. Of course the sweater might wind up on someone else's back, but the principle is clear—the manufacturer knows what you like. All your purchases are similarly tagged. Now merchants or corporations know where you live, what you like, what you spend your money on, and where you spend it.

7   As if monitoring this level of private information weren't invasive enough, there's a far darker side to this. Consider that such chips could be planted with no more effort than a slight injection in a human being. They're already being implanted in animals—some **municipalities** actually require their use for pets. Citizens in the surrounding **communities** have no choice but to comply with the requirement. Then lost animals can be identified, tracked, and returned to their owners. This is one thing when it's your dog, Snuffy— it's another when it's you.

8   The right to pursue one's life free of **surveillance** is so basic that we rarely consider the alternative. For example, we have laws against **phone tapping**. It isn't easy for many of us to envision a world in which we are not free to come and go without someone watching us. We believe in a world where we are free to roam to our heart's content or keep where we go and what we do our own business.

9   It is wrong to play hooky from work. However, even people who would never dream of skipping work would balk if employers could track their every move. This expectation of privacy is no different than our expectation to have control over our medical, financial, and legal histories.

10   Consider that all this information can be a key factor in getting a job, a bank loan, or even entering into a relationship. Once this data is available to the highest bidder or anyone with basic hacking abilities, society will change irrevocably. Fear and distrust will undermine the simplest relationships. Some people claim that careful consumers can simply avoid being subjected to RFIDs, but because RFID chips are so small and virtually undetectable, they can be anywhere and everywhere. Any object, any gift, or any casual exchange could result in the planting of what is essentially a tracking device.

11   Corporations, the government, anyone with an interest—or sufficient money—will be able to follow your every move. With your tastes and purchases tracked and analyzed, you will exist digitally, as a virtual consumer. As you stroll along the sidewalk, billboards will display the products you most desire, for sale at the price point you are most comfortable with, in the style that suits your eye color.

12   For most companies, this sort of tracking represents not a horror, but an ideal. Corporations sing this tune about RFIDs whenever the issue arises, saying they will be better able to service your needs. This will make things easier. And it certainly will—for them.

13   Yes, your shopping might become easier, faster, more efficient—but what exactly is this kind of thing worth? RFIDs promise convenience, a life of ease in which all of the customer service industry seems set to serve you. But the real master will never be you. You are the consumer. The master is the corporation, forever pressuring you to buy this or that, playing on the desires and dislikes it knows from your private information. You are presented with advertising choices that a devious software program has come up with to make every offer you receive as close to a sure sale as possible. Freedom of choice will be a thing of the past.

The author of "RFIDs in Our Future" claims that concerned consumers could "opt out" of RFID technology. How does this author counter that argument? Write your answer on the **Venn Diagram**.

On this page, the author makes the use of RFIDs seem even more threatening. Is the evidence convincing? Is it from a reliable source or just the author's opinion? What loaded word does she use in paragraph 12?

Circle an example of loaded language and exaggeration in paragraph 13.

What contrasting outlooks for RFIDs are presented in these two selections? Write your answers on the **Venn Diagram.**

Circle examples of loaded language used in paragraphs 14 and 15.

Judge

The author of "Cashing in Our Chips" has chosen to present her argument using very few facts. She cites no studies or research and includes no quotations. Appealing to people's fear can be a powerful persuasive technique. Did you find the author's argument convincing? Why or why not? If not, how could she have been more convincing?

14   There is no compelling argument for RFIDs. Other methods can allow the benefit of inventory control that corporations claim to seek, and people can be given good jobs to implement those methods. RFID's only true use is tracking citizens and unveiling this information for whoever wants it badly enough. From the moment the chip reveals its contents, you are a consumer to be tracked and sold to.

15   As individuals with our right to privacy at stake, we must remain vigilant against the subtle assault of this new technology. Because it is not only privacy that is being threatened, it is the very nature of free society that is at stake. A world of distrust, eyes tracking us from the darkness—that's not America.

Vocabulary: Use Word Relationships to Understand Words

When you encounter a difficult word while reading, you might understand it better by seeing how it relates to other words close by. Common word relationships include

- synonyms: two words that have similar meanings (*fast* and *quick*)

- antonyms: two words that have opposite meanings (*dark* and *light*)

- part to whole: one word is part of another (*soldier* and *army*)

- item and category: one word is a subset of another (*train* and *transportation*)

Try It Read this sentence from "Cashing in Our Chips."

> One of the beauties of passport RFID chips is they require no power at all—they're **dormant** until switched on and made **active** by a chip reader.

Discuss **Even if you don't know what** *dormant* **means, you can understand that it is the opposite, or an antonym, of** *active.*

Read these sentences. Then tell what relationship the words have.

1. They're already being implanted in animals—some **municipalities** actually require their use for pets. Citizens in the surrounding **communities** have no choice but to comply with the requirement.

   p. 180: _____

   _____

2. The right to pursue one's life free of **surveillance** is so basic that we rarely consider the alternative. For example, we have laws against **phone tapping**.

   p. 180: _____

   _____

Respond to Text: Analyze Structure of a Persuasive Text

The second selection, "Cashing in Our Chips," starts off by playing on readers' suspicions about corporate motives rather than stating an argument outright. Yet this is clearly part of the author's persuasive approach. How does this work?

Examining the structure of an argument is like looking under the hood of a car. Every part of the argument plays a role, much like the parts of a car's engine do. Here, the author uses a humorous tone from time to time to lighten the mood, while at the same time encouraging readers to be skeptical of corporations. When she examines the downside of RFID chips, their advantages are viewed in a negative light to keep her message consistent. The author does use reasoned judgment and supports some of her arguments with facts, but the overall argument depends largely on a negative tone that doesn't give support or hard evidence.

Try It Think about the structure of the argument in "RFIDs in Our Future." What are its parts? How do these parts contribute to the whole? Does the conclusion pull things together in a convincing way?

> Discuss **Was there something in "RFIDs in Our Future" that you thought worked particularly well? In what ways did the parts of the argument in that selection work together to make it effective?**

On Your Own Write a paragraph that examines the structure of "RFIDs in Our Future." Use the chart on the next page to help you plan your response. Then write your paragraph on a separate sheet of paper.

Checklist for a Good Response

A good paragraph

✔ clearly states the overall nature of the argument.

✔ explains the parts that make up the argument.

✔ demonstrates how these parts work together to support the argument.

✔ shows your understanding of the selection.

✔ includes a topic sentence, supporting ideas, and a concluding statement.

My Analysis of the Argument

1. **Topic Sentence** Include this information in your first sentence:

    The author of "RFIDs in Our Future" opens his argument with _____

    _____.

2. **Detail Sentences** Your paragraph should provide details that analyze the arguments. Use this chart to organize your ideas.

	Analysis
How does the author make his opening claim?	
How does the author support this claim?	
Does the author address counterarguments? What are they?	
How does the author wind up his argument?	

3. **Conclusion** End your paragraph with a concluding statement that sums up your analysis of the author's argument.

    _____

    _____

On a separate sheet of paper, write your paragraph.

Read on Your Own

Read the selections independently three times, using the skills you have learned. Then answer the Comprehension Check questions.

(**First Read**) Practice the first-read skills you learned in this lesson.

(**Second Read**) Practice the second-read skills you learned in this lesson.

(**Third Read**) Think critically about the selections.

GMOs vs. You

by Erica Teasdale

Analyze Arguments
Underline loaded language used in "GMOs vs. You" that might give rise to an unfounded fear of GMOs. The first two have been done for you.

Author's Point of View
What is the author's point of view on the issue of genetically modified foods? How do you know?

1   The phrase *GMO foods* is one of those catch phrases that appears everywhere in the news. But it never seems to be fully explained. This is not surprising, as the industry that produces such genetically modified organisms also sponsors much of the media. The truth about GMO foods is that no one at present truly understands how eating them will affect us. This would likely be true about any new product, but in the case of GMOs, it's doubly true. The science of altering the genetic makeup of fruits, vegetables, and animals is new. It has not been in existence long enough for sufficient long-term study to be conducted. And what we don't know could very easily be harming us right now.

2   There is one essential thing the public needs to know about genetically modified foods: The motivation behind this technology is almost solely economic. Scientists the world over tinker tirelessly with the genetic makeup of foods. They alter them so they are easier and quicker to grow. They alter them so they hold up better when being shipped vast distances and last longer on store shelves. This alteration is accomplished by introducing new DNA into an organism. The process creates new features nature clearly did not intend.

A Matter of Taste

3   Where is flavor in any of this? Where is nutritional value? What about support for local farmers and ranchers? A huge agricultural company can produce an apple that looks shiny but has no flavor or a piece of fruit that can sit on a shelf for weeks without changing in any way. But in doing so, they are satisfying an industrial need, not a human one.

4   The concerns of the consumer are presumed by industry to be merely a matter of price. Last time I checked, "consumers" are human beings. They are deeply interested in how satisfying and healthy the experience of eating an apple is. If an apple tastes like mush, most consumers don't care how cheap it was to produce. Nor do they care how easy it was to ship and store. They know they've been duped—and they won't be fooled again.

Analyze Arguments
Put a box around the sentence on this page that contains a clear exaggeration where the author is asserting an opinion.

To Label or Not to Label

5   People want to avoid being fooled again. Therefore, shouldn't people have a right to know whether or not something is a GMO? Currently, the federal government does not seem to think so. In states and communities all across the country, people are petitioning for the right to have this information clearly stated on the label. We can't make rational, informed decisions about buying genetically modified food if it hasn't been properly labeled.

Critical Thinking Has the author convinced you her point of view is correct? What details swayed you one way or another?

6   Just as a product's ingredients were once privileged information and are now public, so a food's origin should no longer be a mystery. If a tomato is the product of cloning in a laboratory, the producers of that tomato should have to affix a label that tells us so. We, the consumers, can do the rest. We can weigh the taste (or lack thereof), the health threats, and the environmental costs against whatever advantages there may be. We can decide whether we want to spend our money on that tomato or on one that was grown organically.

Consumers are increasingly concerned with what goes into their bodies.

Fact, Opinion, and Reasoned Judgment Is the author's reasoning in paragraph 10 effective support for her argument? How?

Critical Thinking After reading "GMOs vs. You," are you more or less likely to eat GMO foods? Why or why not?

7   Naturally, it could be argued that organic foods are already labeled. Therefore, people who don't want food that comes from a lab should simply buy organic or shop exclusively at farmers' markets. Why don't they raise their own food?

8   Choices that don't work for ordinary working people are not choices at all. The consumer with an average income cannot afford to live an entirely "organic" lifestyle. Some would argue that the increased costs of organic products aren't worth it. In any event, the argument about whether organic food is or is not good for you is one matter. It does not affect the basic human right to know whether or not the DNA in your beef has been genetically engineered into some sort of **Frankenfood**.

A Ray of Hope

9   When new technologies emerge, it is **imperative** for society to make rational, collective decisions about how those technologies can affect human health and well-being. It is equally **necessary** that we have a full and frank discussion of what we do and don't regard as healthy.

10   It has been said that sunlight is the cure for what ails us. In the context of GMOs, information is sunlight. Society has already decided that knowing what is in a product—its ingredients—is vital data for making a thoughtful purchase. Knowing what that product is—natural or unnatural, grown in a field or engineered in a lab—must be at least as crucial. Truthfully, labels are our sunlight. It is high time to shine that light on what we are eating.

Understanding GMOs

by Gustav Heller

1   For the past decade the media has treated Americans to a parade of frightening claims concerning GMOs, or genetically modified organisms. Those claims, though, are largely unsubstantiated. A careful examination of the facts reveals that GMOs may be one of the most important scientific innovations of our times. We are living in an era of global climate change. The threat of drought and other ecological disasters is a constant concern. Therefore, anything that can be done to improve the quantity and quality of the food we produce must be regarded as a vital survival tool.

> **Compare and Contrast**
> How does the nature of the argument in "Understanding GMOs" differ from that in "GMOs vs. You"? What evidence can you point to in the text for your conclusion?

GMOs Are Healthy

2   It may be true that a broad range of long-term studies have yet to be completed. However, the World Health Organization (WHO) has stated that no negative health effects have been shown to result from the consumption of genetically altered foods. In addition, the Environmental Protection Agency (EPA) and the Food and Drug Administration (FDA) examine every plant improved through biotechnology.

3   But unsupported notions of GMOs as a health threat are only part of the equation. There are other concerns as well. The truth is, these modifications can lead to more robust foods, and the foods are also easier to preserve. Because of this, a global industry has grown up. It has become economical to send crops and animals raised in one part of the world to another part of the world. This situation introduces a whole separate issue about the costs of shipping. These questions are best settled by an examination of scientific fact.

GMOs: Costs vs Benefits

4   One standard argument against GMOs is the environmental cost of sending agricultural products across the globe. This practice is made increasingly possible by the shipping-friendly characteristics genetic improvements provide, such as longer shelf life. While there is no denying the increase in fossil fuel usage such an industry promotes, GMOs have advantages that offset this problem.

Fact, Opinion, And Reasoned Judgment
How does the author use facts to deal with a possible counterargument on this page?

Critical Thinking Does the author raise issues an average reader would care about?

5   According to a paper from International Food Technologists cited at Nutriwatch.org, "Herbicide tolerance allows crops to be grown with less or no tillage, thereby conserving soil, fuel, and water." Another report, from the Council for Agricultural Science and Technology, found that biotech crops have significantly decreased soil erosion and preserved millions of tons of topsoil. They also steeply reduce herbicide runoff and greenhouse gas emissions.

6   These ecological benefits significantly make up for whatever carbon footprint the global food industry creates. But there is also the economic factor. Cheaper food makes feeding a hungry world more efficient. Biotechnology means lower corn and soybean prices—between 6 and 10 percent lower, according to an Iowa State University study. And that cheaper food is also healthier. According to the United States Department of Agriculture (USDA), biotech crops like rice are rich in beta-carotene. This is critical in helping with the vitamin A deficiencies common in the developing world.

In Summary

7   Our future, more than ever, is in the hands of science. We need to make every drop of fresh water count. We need to develop a global food economy that can sustain nations the planet over. And we need healthy food that appeals to many tastes. Genetically modifying what we eat isn't unnatural. The truth is, it might well be one of the best innovations humanity has ever been blessed with.

A future with GMOs may not just be good for us—it could be essential.

✓ Comprehension Check

1. What persuasive techniques are used in "Understanding GMOs"?

    _____

2. Read this excerpt from "GMOs vs. You."

    When new technologies emerge, it is imperative for society to make rational . . . decisions about how those technologies can affect human health. . . . It is equally necessary that we have a full . . . discussion of what we do and don't regard as healthy.

    How does the relationship of the word *imperative* to *necessary* help you determine the meaning of *imperative*?

    _____

    _____

3. Read this excerpt from "Understanding GMOs."

    [A]nything that can be done to improve the quantity and quality of the food we produce must be regarded as a vital survival tool.

    What does this sentence reveal about the author's point of view?

    _____

    _____

4. Compare the arguments of "GMOs vs. You" and "Understanding GMOs." What is the same about them? What is different?

    _____

    _____

5. Identify one opinion, one fact, and one reasoned judgment the author uses in "Understanding GMOs."

_____

_____

_____

6. Read this sentence from "GMOs vs. You."

    It does not affect the basic human right to know whether or not the DNA in your beef has been genetically engineered into some sort of Frankenfood.

    What is the allusion in the word _Frankenfood_? What does it mean?

    _____

    _____

7. How do the two arguments compare in terms of the use of hard facts?

    _____

    _____

    _____

8. What evidence in "Understanding GMOs" supports the argument that GMOs would be helpful to a population recovering from famine?

    _____

    _____

    _____

Lesson 8
Literary Nonfiction

Literary nonfiction (also called creative or narrative nonfiction) is a genre of writing that includes biographies, food writing, journalism, memoirs, personal essays, and travel writing. For a text to be considered literary nonfiction, it must be both true and written with attention to literary style and technique. The writer must not only communicate information but also present it in narrative form so it includes literary elements such as plot and character development, dialogue, and setting description. Therefore, literary nonfiction is as entertaining as it is informative and often appeals to a broad audience. If you saw this photograph with a magazine article, what would you hope to learn from the article?

Skills Focus

Animal Instincts

Summarize   **Evaluate Evidence and Claims**

Talking the Talk

Central Idea and Supporting Details

Analyze Development of Central Ideas in a Text

Practice the Skill

First Read **Summarize**

Summarizing is an important strategy you can use to help you monitor your comprehension of a text. To **summarize** is to tell only the most important ideas from a text in your own words. The purpose is not to retell a text or copy an author's style but to give an organized account of the most important information. Summaries should not include your own experiences or opinions.

Think of how you'd tell a friend about the plot of a movie you saw. You wouldn't tell every single thing that happens from the beginning to the end. You'd concentrate on the most important elements and scenes rather than on minor plot details that are not essential to the film. Good readers use several strategies to summarize, such as separating important from unimportant information, determining the main idea, and making inferences.

Try It Read the paragraph below.

In California, in 1976, the rains came rarely. The earth dried and cracked like the surface of the moon. Crops wilted and died. It was so hot and there was so little rain that water conservation measures were put in place. With water-use restrictions, people couldn't keep their swimming pools filled. The drought was bad news for farmers and swimmers alike. But one group of people thrived in the drought—skateboarders. Although people had been putting roller-skate wheels on boards since the 1950s, skateboarding became a real sport in the 1970s. Skateboarders discovered that they could perform all sorts of incredible new tricks in empty concrete pools. They began to compete with one another to master the most exciting and challenging tricks. That year, skateboarders truly demonstrated the expression "one person's famine; another person's feast."

> **Discuss** **What information is important enough to include in a summary of this text? What should you leave out? Draw a box around the main idea. Double underline the key details.**

As you read, complete the Summary Chart on page 307.

Practice the Skill

Second Read Evaluate Evidence and Claims

When you read, it's important to read critically—especially in the case of literary nonfiction, a genre that is fact based but employs literary devices to tell a story. As with any nonfiction text, literary nonfiction should be read with an eye toward identifying the **claims**, or statements the author makes, and evaluating whether they are valid, or reliable, based on evidence in the text and previous knowledge. **Evidence** is the facts an author provides to support any claims made.

When assessing the soundness of claims or the reliability of information, you should ask yourself the following questions: *Are the author's claims logical and believable? Are the claims based on facts and other appropriate evidence, such as expert opinions? Does the author leave out information that might weaken or disprove his or her claims? Does the author depend on opinions or emotional appeals to support claims?*

Try It Read the paragraph below.

> You've likely heard the expression "gone the way of the dodo." But perhaps you don't really know what it means. The dodo was a species of flightless bird that lived on the island of Mauritius off the coast of Africa. Scientists believe that the bird was not so much stupid, as its name might suggest, as it was secure and trusting. The dodo had no natural predators, so it flourished on its island home—that is, until hungry sailors landed on Mauritius. In the 1500s, Europeans began exploring the world by ship. Those who landed on Mauritius were starving and saw the large, friendly birds as easy meals. The sailors' dogs and pigs found the dodo's nests and gobbled their eggs by the dozen. This unique species that wasn't equipped for either fight *or* flight was completely wiped out by the year 1681.

> **Discuss** Evaluate the soundness of the claims the author is making. Circle the claims the author makes. Underline the textual evidence that supports these claims.

As you read, record your answers to questions about evaluating evidence and claims on the Close Reading Worksheet on page 308.

Animal Instincts

Underline important details in paragraph 1. Then, write a summary of the paragraph on the **Summary Chart**.

What evidence does the author use to support the idea that autism is not an uncommon condition in the United States?

The word *autism* comes from the Greek prefix *auto-*, which means "self." How is this an appropriate name for this condition?

1   Temple Grandin maintains that she has never had a friendship; she's never even wanted one. The fact that this includes friendships with animals comes as something of a surprise. You'd think Grandin, a renowned animal expert and someone whose life revolves around animals, would have formed a close friendship with a pet or two over the course of her lifetime, but there's been no special dog or cat, no beloved horse or rabbit. Grandin simply doesn't "connect" with others in that way. And although she's a brilliant scholar who's earned advanced degrees, written books, and given lectures all over the world, Grandin remains someone who has intense difficulty with physical contact. The **contradiction** between these two realities is the place where Temple Grandin lives.

2   Grandin was born in 1947 with autism, a condition that affects as many as 1.5 million Americans, according to autism-society.org. Although there are differences in the way the condition manifests, autism is broadly characterized by a number of symptoms: a feeling of being overwhelmed by sights, sounds, and physical sensations; an **inability** to relate socially; and a difficulty in expressing one's self verbally. Sensory experiences most people think of as ordinary can send an autistic person into a state of panic.

3   No one is sure what causes autism, but it seems to affect the part of the brain responsible for language and social relationships. People with autism process information in their brains differently than others do. This causes them to view and experience the world differently from most people, which can be very isolating.

4   This was Grandin's state of being for most of her childhood. Even as a toddler she showed signs of distress at sensory input. She shrieked at sudden noises, contact with a piece of material could make her skin feel like it was on fire, and she might lash out if someone tried to touch her. She wanted to make contact but was **incapable** of it; the sensations were just too overwhelming. She felt safe only under a bed or couch, wrapped up in blankets. At the time, doctors didn't understand autism because there wasn't much research on the condition. Doctors told her mother that Temple would never talk or live a normal life and suggested sending her to a hospital to live, but her mother flatly refused to consider it.

5   However, Grandin seemed to be growing more and more anxious. By the time she was a teen, she was having severe panic attacks. Finally, her mother, frustrated and confused, sent Temple to visit her aunt's cattle farm, thinking that a change of scenery would calm her down.

6   At first, Grandin's life on the farm was as horrible as life in the city had been: the noises there, though different, still terrified her. But in time, Grandin grew to love the cows; she felt a kinship with them. They, like her, hated loud noises and would jump and startle at unexpected sounds. As she spent more and more time around the cows, Grandin began to notice things about their behavior, specifically what made them anxious and what soothed them.

7   Grandin observed that when the cows had to be vaccinated or branded, they were herded into a "squeeze pen," a rectangular cagelike device with sides made of wood or metal that pressed against their sides. When Grandin realized that this pressure made the cattle calm down, she began to wonder whether it could help her relax as well. She convinced her aunt to let her crawl into the squeeze pen so that she could feel the sides press against her.

Underline important details in paragraph 4. Then, write a summary of the paragraph on the **Summary Chart**.

What evidence supports the claim that the young Grandin was unable to make contact with others?

Temple Grandin has contributed immensely to the world's understanding of autism.

Underline the events that led to Grandin's being sent to Hampshire Country School. Write a summary of these events on the **Summary Chart**.

What evidence supports the claim that Grandin did well at Hampshire Country School?

8   The sensation of the squeeze pen felt like a hug. The steady pressure of the walls against her sides shut out the noise in her brain like nothing else ever had. Grandin later wrote about this moment in the squeeze pen, "It was the first time I ever felt really comfortable in my own skin."

9   Grandin's mother worked hard to help her daughter adjust to the world around her. She hired tutors and specialists to help her fit into a mainstream class in school. But Temple did not fit in; she was teased mercilessly and called "tape recorder" because she endlessly repeated phrases. Grandin would become enraged and lash out—she bit a teacher in the leg and threw a book at a classmate, for which she was expelled. Grandin's mother then sent her to the Hampshire Country School, a boarding school for gifted children in middle and high school with special needs.

10   Grandin did well in her new environment. Her teachers understood her and cultivated her natural love of science. She was encouraged to take on new challenges, such as model rocketry. Perhaps most important was the fact that Grandin was allowed to work with horses. Grandin identified with the horses as she had with the cows at her aunt's farm. The horses were just as sensitive as she was— they, too, were spooked by loud noises and yet were instantly calmed by the pressure of her hand against their sides.

11   However, in spite of the support she received from the teachers at the school, Grandin's anxiety grew worse. Her mother decided that another summer at the cattle farm would be **beneficial** to her daughter.

12   At the farm, Grandin spent hours watching the cattle going through the squeeze pen. She remembered how calming the squeeze pen had been for her. Then, in an instant, Grandin hit on a solution to deal with her own anxiety. She built herself a plywood squeeze machine with an air compressor that allowed her to control the squeezing movement of its walls. Fifteen minutes in the squeeze machine, she found, could produce a state of calm in her that lasted for hours. In 1966, when Grandin set off for Franklin Pierce College, she took her squeeze machine with her. Administrators were horrified by the machine and ordered its removal from her dorm room—it did resemble some sort of medieval torture device. But Grandin challenged some students to try it, and those who did discovered that the machine did in fact have a relaxing effect.

13   In 1970, Grandin graduated with a bachelor's degree in **psychology** and began working toward her master's degree in animal science from Arizona State University. At the same time she started working for the cattle industry as a livestock editor, which is someone who writes about cows, horses, and other farm animals. This job gave her the opportunity to visit slaughterhouses.

14   Grandin quickly understood that the slaughterhouse environment was highly stressful for cows. She heard what the cattle heard—the clanging machinery, the workmen's shouts, the bellowing of the other cows. She saw what the cattle saw—glaring lighting, equipment dangling from the ceiling, uneven flooring—and understood their terror. After earning her master's degree, Grandin went on to pursue a doctorate in animal science. She began to consider redesigning the slaughterhouse so that the environment would be less stressful for the cattle.

15   Grandin's autism was no longer a deficit; it was a source of inspiration. Like many people with autism, Grandin thought in terms of imagery, not words. For Grandin, the word *hat* summoned up images of hats rather than the idea of "a thing people wear on their heads." She believed that animals thought in pictures, too. It was her belief that the cattle's panic could be minimized by reducing their exposure to fear-inducing stimuli. Using her ability to see the world in pictures, Grandin designed new slaughterhouse equipment.

16   Among her innovative designs was a chute that led cattle to slaughter along a curving passageway, since cows marching in a straight line would be able to see what was ahead and panic. She designed a dimly lit ramp to ease the cattle's transition from a lighted area to a darkened room, and she convinced management to repaint the walls soothing colors.

Underline the events leading up to Grandin building her own squeeze machine. Write a summary of these events on the **Summary Chart**.

How did Grandin's belief that cows experienced the world in ways similar to the way she did affect her slaughterhouse design?

Summarize "Animal Instincts." Write your summary on the **Summary Chart**.

In paragraph 18, circle evidence to support the claim that Grandin's life's work has been "as a friend to animals and people alike."

Analyze

What details support the idea that people with autism and animals share certain traits? Cite textual evidence to support your response.

17   Her autism not only inspired Grandin to redesign slaughterhouses, it helped her forge new relationships. Because Grandin experiences the world in unique ways, she is able to bridge gaps in a way that others might not be able to manage. For example, on the one hand, Grandin is celebrated by the beef industry. In 2010, she was awarded the National Cattlemen's Beef Association's Lifetime Achievement Award for her service to the industry. After all, her improvements to slaughterhouses benefitted not only the cows but also the farmers, who had fewer losses from animal injuries and more-efficient, less-stressful production lines. However, animal rights organizations have also honored Grandin for her work. In 2011, the American Humane Association granted Grandin their National Humanitarian Medal for outstanding service in protecting animals.

18   Grandin and many other people with autism are able to appreciate and value the way their brains process information differently than most others. For Grandin, seeing the world in images has allowed her to ease the lives of millions of animals and their caretakers. Moreover, thousands of children with autism and their families have been inspired and helped by Grandin's memoirs and websites, where she explains how her brain works and how she has found peace and success in an often overwhelming world.

19   Although Grandin claims not to have any friendships with people or animals, her life's work has been as a friend to animals and people alike. She has demonstrated the true meaning of friendship by helping those whom others might have ignored.

Vocabulary: Use Common Greek and Latin Affixes as Clues to Meaning

A **prefix** is a group of letters added to the beginning of a **base word**, the simplest form of a word that conveys its meaning. A **suffix** is a group of letters added to the end of a base word. Prefixes and suffixes are **affixes**, and when they are added to a base word, they create a new word with a new meaning. Many affixes are derived from Greek and Latin. Here are some common affixes and their meanings.

-able	Latin for *having the necessary skill or trait*
bene-	Latin for *good*
contra-	Latin for *against*
-ial	Latin affix that changes a noun into an adjective
in-	Latin for *not, opposite*
-ion	Latin affix that changes a verb into a noun
-logy	Greek for *study*
psych-	Greek for *mind*

Dividing an unfamiliar word into its base word and affixes can help you figure out its meaning.

Try It Read this sentence from "Animal Instincts."

Autism is broadly characterized by . . . an **inability** to relate socially.

Discuss **What is the prefix in *inability*? What does it mean?**

Find these words in the selection. Use the affixes above to define each word.

1. **contradiction**, p. 196 _____

2. **incapable**, p. 197 _____

3. **beneficial**, p. 198 _____

4. **psychology**, p. 199 _____

Practice the Skill

The **central idea** is what a text is mostly about. It is a statement that sums up the author's primary message, the idea that details in the text support. When you look for a central idea, ask yourself: *What is this selection mostly about?*

Supporting details are pieces of information—examples, reasons, facts, details, and other evidence—that tell more about the central idea. When you look for supporting details, ask yourself: *How does the author describe, illustrate, explain, support, or clarify the central idea?*

The central idea is often stated in the topic sentence of a paragraph or selection, but sometimes it must be inferred. In that case, you need to figure it out for yourself, using details from the text.

Try It Read the following paragraph.

From the air, Chuquicamata copper mine looks like a giant crater; the green, rocky hole contrasts with the red earth of the desert that spreads out around it. At two miles long and half a mile wide, it is one of the largest open-pit mines in the world. Chile's economy depends on its copper mines, so a town bearing the same name as the mine has sprung up in the desert near this mine. Like water in the desert, the mine is the lifeblood of the town. Everyone who lives in Chuquicamata depends on the copper that is pulled from the earth: the workers, their families, and the people who provide services for them—teachers, doctors, and other support staff. The mine is a vital Chilean resource, and all the people of Chuquicamata depend on it.

> Discuss Find the central idea and the details that support it. Circle the central idea and underline the supporting details. Remember, the central idea may not always be stated at the beginning of a text.

As you read, complete the Central Idea and Supporting Details Chart on page 309.

Practice the Skill

Literary nonfiction, like informational texts, contains central ideas and supporting details. Generally, a work of literary nonfiction will contain more than one central idea. These central ideas build on one another. In other words, effective literary nonfiction develops and supports central ideas that all work together. Thoughtful readers analyze or think about which central idea is being discussed or supported or built on as they work through a text. Then they think about how all the central ideas are connected throughout the text. As you read, keep in mind the way the central ideas develop over the course of the text and how they are connected.

Try It Read the following paragraphs.

Carrying a book bag that was almost as big as she was, six-year-old Ruby Bridges bravely marched up the steps of William Frantz Elementary School. Her mouth was set in a determined line. She looked neither up nor down nor side to side. Like all first-graders on their first day at a new school, Ruby Bridges was nervous, but unlike most children her age, she had reason to be.

The year was 1960, and Ruby Bridges was the first African American to attend an all-white school in Louisiana. She was accompanied by federal marshalls in order to enter the school safely. Mobs of angry white parents who didn't want their children to attend school with African American children lined the walkway to Ruby's new school. But Ruby didn't look at those angry faces; she placed one shiny black shoe in front of the other until she was through the front door.

> **Discuss** As you read, think about the central ideas in this piece and how the author develops them. Place a box around the central idea in each paragraph. How do they relate to each other? How are they connected?

As you read, record your answers to questions about analyzing the development of central ideas on the Close Reading Worksheet on page 310.

Talking the Talk

What is the central idea of paragraph 3? Underline the details that support this idea. Write your answer on the **Central Idea and Supporting Details Chart**.

What are the main ideas of paragraphs 1 and 2?

1   What would you call that amazing rain we had last week? A chunk-floater? A fence-lifter? A frog-strangler? A goose-drown'der? How about a trash-mover? They all mean the same thing—a torrential rain—but how you say it depends on which region of the country you come from. Different regional twists on the same language are called *dialect*.

2   American dialect refers to the speech patterns, idioms, expressions, and figurative language speakers use in different parts of the English-speaking United States. The way people really speak—the language you don't hear on the national news—is part of our national heritage and contributes to the rich cultural landscape that is the American experience.

3   You've probably heard people say that America is a great melting pot, a big stew of cultures, languages, and ideas all simmering and mixing together. For as long as humans have populated this land, there has been a great diversity of languages and cultures. The Native Americans who lived here at the time Europeans arrived spoke hundreds of different languages and dialects and celebrated hundreds of different cultures. When Europeans came and began settling, they brought their languages and cultures with them. With its vast land and resources and its democratic government, America, like no other country in the world, quickly became a land of immigrants from all over the world.

Salad or Melting Pot?

4   Given the vastness of the land and the diversity of the cultures (to say nothing of the soaring mountains, expansive lakes, and formidable rivers), the immigrants who came here spread out and were often cut off from other people. This created distinct pockets of culture and language. In time, almost all would speak English, but with influences from other languages and cultures. So instead of a huge melting pot where all the languages and cultures were eventually reduced into one, homogenous dialect, America was more of a giant salad, if you will. Each culture and dialect staying basically intact yet combined with others to create a delightful and healthy whole.

5   That was before modern technology. With the arrival of the industrial revolution, Americans began to move. They crossed those soaring mountains, expansive lakes, and formidable rivers to find jobs in a new world of bustling factories and industrial cities. These migrant people left their enclaves of culture and language, but they brought their dialects with them. You could imagine this time as a vigorous tossing of the salad. Cultures and dialects were mixing together and changing as a result. New dialects were formed from the mixing of old ones, and new words were created to describe people's new experiences. Expressions like "go through the mill" (slow and difficult process) came from the tough experiences of factory workers. "You woke up the wrong passenger" (you angered the wrong person) came with the advent of railroad travel in the 1800s.

6   However, too much technology—imagine a blender—can turn a delightful salad into a disgusting mush! And as travel around the United States became easier, the English that Americans spoke began to standardize. Devices like radio and then television threatened the diversity of American dialects. Nearly all the actors and actresses on radio and television spoke in one, standard dialect. In time, that dialect got beamed on waves to nearly every household in the United States. Naturally enough, people began to pick up that standard dialect, and American linguistic[1] diversity began to disappear.

[1]**linguistic** relating to language

> What is the central idea of paragraph 6? Underline details that support this idea. Record your answers on the **Central Idea and Supporting Details Chart**.

> What three central ideas does the author develop in the "Salad or Melting Pot" section? How do they relate to one another?

How to Speak American

7   Fortunately, a few people began to notice the vanishing dialects and took action. In 1889, the American Dialect Society (ADS) was founded with one of its major goals being to create a dialect dictionary. Each year from 1890 to 1930, members of ADS compiled and published lists of terms and expressions that they considered to demonstrate American dialect.

8   Then in 1947, Lewis Herman and Marguerite Shallett Herman published a book called *American Dialects* in order to teach regional accents to actors and writers who sought to sound authentic. An actor from New York or Hollywood could use their book if he or she wanted to speak like someone from rural Tennessee.

9   While the Hermans did not attempt to capture the individual dialect of each person they interviewed for their book, they did try to represent the speech of a region as a whole. The interview subjects—a majority of whom were born in nineteenth-century rural America— spoke in a way that reflected their particular concerns and issues. The Hermans may not have known it at the time, but they were helping to preserve fast-disappearing linguistic artifacts.

Individuals such as these men contributed to *American Dialects*.

10   The Hermans' book did serve to preserve some American dialects.
However, it was not a comprehensive dictionary of all the linguistic
variety in the United States. So in the late 1940s, Fred Cassidy, an
English professor at the University of Wisconsin–Madison, embarked
on a sixty year journey to create a dictionary of American dialects.
Cassidy may not have been the first traveler on the road to creating
such a dictionary, but he was the most persistent.

DARE to Be Different

11   A member of ADS, Cassidy knew of the lists of terms and
expressions ADS had been collecting for fifty years. He began testing
the lists in the Wisconsin area, using a questionnaire he had written
based on the ADS lists. He wanted to verify that they were accurate
representations of people's dialects. He presented his findings to
ADS, but still the dictionary project didn't get off the ground. Finally,
in 1962, Cassidy presented a paper at the ADS annual meeting. It
had a provocative title "The ADS Dictionary—How Soon?" The ADS
appointed Cassidy as the chief editor of the dictionary, and the project
took off.

12   Cassidy improved and expanded his questionnaire to 1,600
questions. He asked about everything from weather to school to
religion to money. Then he identified over one thousand communities
around the United States that he felt exemplified distinct cultures and
dialects. From 1965 to 1970, Cassidy recruited eighty fieldworkers to
travel to those communities and present the individuals who lived in
them with the questionnaire. Fieldworkers were to interview as many
elderly people as possible. Cassidy felt that the older a person was, the
more distinct his or her dialect would be. However, fieldworkers were
also instructed to interview young people. He wanted to record how
dialects were evolving and what new dialects were emerging.

13   For fifteen years, Cassidy and other editors compiled the
information from the fieldworkers. Then they added in information
from printed sources, such as newspapers, government documents,
and regional literature. Finally, in 1985, Harvard University Press
published the first volume (the introduction and letters A–C) of the
Dictionary of American Regional English (DARE). Its popularity took
off like wildfire. There were five reprintings in the first year alone. Fred
Cassidy lived to see Volumes II and III published (letters D–O) before
he passed away in October of 2000.

What is the section "DARE to Be Different" mostly about? What details does the author use to support the central idea? Record your answers on the **Central Idea and Supporting Details Chart.**

Why did *DARE* take so long to be published?

What central idea does the author develop in "Salad, Thanks!"? How does it relate to the overall central idea of the selection?

Judge

How does the author feel about Fred Cassidy? Do you agree or disagree with this point of view? Why?

Salad, Thanks!

14   *DARE* had lost its chief editor and greatest champion in the fight to document the dying dialects of the United States. Yet, the dictionary and dialects live on. In 2012, over seventy years after the journey began, the final volume of *DARE* was published.

15   Today, people from diverse backgrounds and for varied purposes rely on *DARE* for their work. Actors, authors, journalists, and playwrights consult *DARE* to make their work authentic and accurate. Doctors and psychologists use *DARE* to understand patients' folksy descriptions of their ailments. Or they use it to identify conditions that affect language-sensitive areas of the brain. Natural scientists use *DARE* when consulting locals about plants and animals they are studying. Even detectives known as forensic linguists use *DARE* to identify criminals by the dialect they speak.

16   However, *DARE*'s greatest contribution remains its preservation of American dialects. More than seventy years ago, Fred Cassidy saw the writing on the wall. He realized that America's salad culture of diverse dialects was in danger of becoming a melting pot of homogenous, media-dominated language. He, along with hundreds of fellow workers, recorded the American dialects. Whatever becomes of dialects in the United States, *DARE* will serve as both a record of and a source for this country's vitality and diversity.

Fred Cassidy spent thirty-eight years working on a comprehensive dictionary of American dialects.

Vocabulary: Figurative Language

Figurative language is the use of a word or phrase whose meaning departs from the literal meaning of the words. Writers use figurative language to make their writing more colorful and imaginative. There are many types of figurative language. A **simile** is an expression that uses the word *like* or *as* to compare one object or idea to another; for example, "I'm as busy as a bee." A **metaphor** is a direct comparison between two objects or ideas that doesn't use the word *like* or *as*; for example, "The cat's eyes were headlights in the night." An **idiom** is an expression whose meaning cannot be understood from its words alone; for example, "He cracks me up." **Personification** is giving human qualities or attributes to animals or objects; for example, "The wind tickled my nose." You can often determine the meaning of a figure of speech from the sentence context.

Try It Read this sentence from "Talking the Talk."

> You've probably heard people say that **America is a great melting pot**, a big stew of cultures, languages, and ideas all simmering and mixing together.

> Discuss **What kind of figurative language is the boldfaced phrase in the sentence? If you were unfamiliar with the expression, how could you figure it out? What does it mean?**
Read these examples of figurative language from the article. Identify the type of figurative language, and tell what the expression means.

1. a new world of **bustling factories**, p. 205 _____

_____

2. **Cassidy may not have been the first traveler on the road to creating such a dictionary,** but he was the most persistent. p. 207 _____

_____

3. but still the dictionary project didn't **get off the ground**. p. 207 _____

_____

Respond to Text: Assess an Argument for Soundness and Support Claim with Details

Both of the articles "Animal Instincts" and "Talking the Talk" describe people who have made important contributions to society. The authors of the articles use evidence and details to show how each person was significant and to describe the importance of the contributions. The validity of the evidence makes the arguments effective.

Try It Think about what you learned about assessing an argument and supporting a claim with details.

 Discuss **Assess the soundness of the claim in "Animal Instincts" by evaluating the details that support the claim. Base your answer on the textual evidence, including facts and details.**

On Your Own Write a paragraph in which you identify the main claim in "Animal Instincts." Cite the evidence that supports the claim. Decide whether you think the evidence is sufficient to support the claim. Use the chart on the next page to help you plan your response. Then write your paragraph on a separate sheet of paper.

Checklist for a Good Response

A good paragraph

✔ identifies the author's claim and the details that support it.

✔ explains the reasoning behind your answer.

✔ uses textual evidence as well as things you know.

✔ shows your understanding of Grandin's work.

✔ includes a topic sentence, supporting details, and a concluding statement.

My Assessment of the Argument

1. **Topic Sentence** Include this information in your first sentence:

   "Animal Instincts" makes the claim that Temple Grandin has significantly

   contributed to society by _____

   _____.

2. **Explain Your Answer** The sentences of your paragraph should provide
   details that show the evidence the author presents to support the claim.
   Use this chart to organize your ideas.

Claim	Supporting Details

3. **Concluding Sentence** Your final sentence should emphasize your
   assessment of the author's claims as sufficient or not.

   _____

   _____

On a separate sheet of paper, write your paragraph.

Read on Your Own

Read the selection independently three times, using the skills you have learned. Then answer the Comprehension Check questions.

First Read	Practice the first-read skills you learned in this lesson.
Second Read	Practice the second-read skills you learned in this lesson.
Third Read	Think critically about the selection.

Sign, Baby, Sign!

Central Idea and Supporting Details
What is the central idea of paragraphs 2 and 3? Circle the central idea. Underline the supporting details. One supporting detail has been underlined for you.

Summarize Think about the anecdote with Lily and Eli that begins the selection. What is it mainly about?

Critical Thinking
Why does Lily suddenly become energized in paragraph 2?

1   Lily sat slumped at the kitchen table, her elbow resting on a pile of unopened mail, her head resting in her hand. It had been another rocky night. From 1:15 to 3:15 she and her husband, Bill, had taken turns walking and rocking their nine-month-old son, Eli, up and down their hallway until he finally fell back to sleep. She knew the exact times because she could see their digital alarm clock by their bed at each lap down the hallway. Now Eli sat happily in his high-chair pushing banana puffs carefully around the tray with his forefinger. The sun streamed cheerily in through the window. Lily realized dimly that if he was playing with the puffs, then he was probably done eating them, but she was too tired to move just yet. Her head was like a thick fog. She tipped her face toward the window hoping the bright sunshine would clear the fog.

2   That's when she noticed Eli wasn't pushing his puffs anymore. <u>He was holding one fist in front of his face and opening and closing his tiny, chubby fingers.</u> Lily blinked slowly, willing her eyes to open again—there was something she wasn't seeing. Then she sat up and smiled broadly. "Milk, milk, milk," Eli signed over and over again. He wasn't just cleaning crumbs off his fingers, he was communicating. He was signing his first word! Lily shouted, "Milk!" Then she repeated the sign with both hands right in Eli's face, tickling his cheeks.

3   He giggled and said, "Mama!" Lily unhitched his tray and swept him up in a twirling embrace. They chanted the "milk-a, milk-a, milk-a" song as they danced to the refrigerator for a bottle of milk. The fog had lifted from her brain in one bright, glittering moment of communication.

Milk, Milk, Milk!

4   Like thousands of other American parents and caregivers, Lily and Bill have perfectly good hearing, yet they have chosen to teach their hearing child a modified version of American Sign Language (ASL). This language, created and used mainly by deaf people, has been shown to enhance communication in hearing people as well. Research suggests that babies who sign are more confident and less prone to frustration than other babies. Some people go so far as to suggest that signing babies could mature to be more intelligent and have better language-development skills than nonsigners. Regardless of these claims, it is clear that signing with an infant is a positive thing.

Evaluate Evidence and Claims <u>Double underline</u> the evidence from the story on page 212 that supports the author's claim that learning sign language can be exciting for parents and babies.

5   Like Bill and Lily, most parents start by choosing a sign that involves eating or drinking. These types of signs are entirely need based. This allows the baby to communicate his or her basic needs. Other examples of this type of sign involve diaper changing, identifying hot and cold, the need for help, and sleep. (Lily and Bill wish teaching Eli the sign for sleep would also teach him how to sleep better, but that's another story!)

6   Some signs are not as need based. They involve identifying aspects of the baby's world. For example, if the baby is fascinated by a ceiling fan in the bedroom or the antics of the family dog, that child is ready to learn the sign for *fan* and *dog*. Two other very popular choices are *Mommy* and *Daddy*. Learning these signs can be especially exciting to both parent and baby.

Making the Sign

7   Once parents and caregivers have determined the signs they want to teach their child, then they begin to use that sign repeatedly in context. For example, to teach the sign for *drink*, parents or caregivers would make the sign for *drink* (making a C with their hand and tipping it toward their mouth) each time the baby and parents drink anything. In this way, the baby starts to associate the sign with the action.

8   You might wonder: If a baby can learn to make the sign, why can't he or she learn to say the word? The reason is that most nine-month-old babies can't yet physically make the sounds. The muscles required for speech develop more slowly than the muscles in their hands. So babies at that age are equipped to communicate with hands before they can speak.

Summarize Draw a box around the ideas on this page that you would include in a summary.

Analyze Development of Central Ideas in a Text What is the overall central idea of this text? Place a box around the central ideas in each section. Think about how these relate to the overall central idea.

The Science of Baby Signing

9   Joseph Garcia is generally thought of as the "inventor" of baby signing. Although no one in his family was deaf, Garcia began studying ASL in 1975. Then he worked as an ASL interpreter in the late 1970s. This meant he would use ASL to translate English conversations to deaf people. Garcia began to observe something interesting in the hearing children of deaf parents. Because they were signing with their parents, they were able to communicate their needs and desires earlier than were the children of hearing parents.

10   Garcia began to research the use of ASL with hearing babies of hearing parents. He found that babies who had learned to sign at six to seven months of age were expressing themselves by their eighth or ninth month. This was considerably earlier than other babies. Garcia focused on creating a practical system for parents who wanted to teach their babies to sign. He published his first book on the subject, *Toddler Talk*, in 1994.

11   Since then, the field has expanded. Not only are Garcia's techniques used by parents and caregivers, they are used by speech language professionals to treat older children who are slow to develop verbal skills. In addition, many psychologists use signing with their patients who have trouble communicating verbally due to issues of anxiety and depression. Signing makes it easier for patient and **therapist** to communicate. Another possible benefit of signing is that it may help the patients to be more aware of the social gestures and nonverbal cues of others.

12   Like Lily, Bill, and Eli, most people are thrilled to discover a way to communicate with those who are most important to them. They find that using sign language has reduced frustration and increased communication. Now Lily and Bill can't wait for Eli's next sign!

This is the ASL sign for "I love you."

✓ Comprehension Check

1. What detail supports the idea that signing benefits hearing people other than babies?

_____

_____

2. Summarize Joseph Garcia's contributions to sign language.

_____

_____

_____

3. What evidence supports the claim that the use of sign language among hearing people has expanded?

_____

_____

_____

4. How does the author support the claim in paragraph 4 that babies who use sign language may be more intelligent? Is the evidence sufficient to support the claim?

_____

_____

_____

5. Summarize the section "Milk, Milk, Milk!" on page 213.

_____

_____

_____

6. What is the central idea of page 213? How does this idea relate to the overall central idea of the selection?

_____

_____

_____

7. Read this sentence from the selection.

   Signing makes it easier for patient and therapist to communicate.

   The affix -ist is Greek for "one who specializes in." What does the word _therapist_ mean?

_____

8. Read this sentence from the selection. What kind of figure of speech is this? What does it mean?

   Her head was like a thick fog.

_____

_____

Lesson 9
Historical Texts

Historical texts focus on real people and events of the past. Writers must conduct thorough research in order to convey this information correctly. They use a variety of sources, from encyclopedias and journal articles to letters written at the time, to gain a deep understanding of the topic and the era. Often, writers of historical texts include illustrations and photographs to help explain their ideas. This photo shows men in line to receive a free meal during the Great Depression, a period of worldwide economic hardship that lasted from 1929 to the start of World War II. What information would you expect to learn from the text?

Skills Focus

Who Was King Arthur?
Integrate Visual Information
Identify Steps in a Process

Child Monarchs
Draw and Support Inferences
Analyze Word Choice and Tone

Practice the Skill

Authors of historical texts often present their ideas through **visual information**, such as charts, maps, time lines, photos, and illustrations. Authors integrate visuals into their texts to communicate information and ideas that words alone may not express as well.

Try It Read this paragraph.

Many children dream of hunting for buried treasure, but few consider that they actually could do so someday. However, there are real-life treasure hunters working all over the world, trying to find lost loot. One of the main places treasure hunters search is the Gulf of Mexico, because it is the site of hundreds of shipwrecks. The weather patterns in the Gulf of Mexico are so extreme that, over the years, hundreds of ships have been sunk during storms. Finding where those ships sank is the work of historians and adventurers alike.

Shipwreck Locations in the Gulf of Mexico

Each triangle on the map represents a shipwreck location.

 Discuss How does the map support the main text? Circle the information that the map supports.

As you read, record your answers to questions about integrating visual information on the Close Reading Worksheet on page 311.

Practice the Skill

Second Read Identify Steps in a Process

A **process** is a planned series of steps that enable you to accomplish a task or goal. Whether running a government or making laws, people need efficient, clear processes to be sure things are conducted fairly and responsibly. For example, every four years, we follow the same process to elect a new president. When authors discuss history, they often relate the steps in these processes in order to explain how they work. In historical texts, these step-by-step explanations help you understand why people acted the way they did and why certain events happened.

Sometimes, authors put the steps in a numbered list so you can easily see their order. Other times, you must determine the order for yourself by looking for such clue words as *first*, *next*, and *then*. For example, an author describing how a U.S. president is elected might write: "First, the public votes for a presidential candidate. Then, based on each state's popular vote, a certain number of electors from the Electoral College are permitted to vote."

Try It Read this paragraph.

> Like explorers around the world, treasure hunters in the Gulf of Mexico follow a series of steps in order to locate sunken ships. First, they study shipping histories and records to understand what ships were traveling to what destinations and carrying what sorts of cargo. Then, the treasure hunters travel to the parts of the Gulf where the ships were most likely to have sunk. Often, they use robots to search for the wrecks, take pictures of them, and retrieve artifacts. Once items are recovered, treasure hunters usually turn them over to specialists for identification, cleaning, and restoration. Artifacts that are of great historical interest and in good condition may then be donated or sold to museums.

Discuss **What process is being discussed here? What are the steps in the process?**

As you read, complete the Steps in a Process Chart on page 312.

Purpose for Reading
Read along with your teacher. Each time, read for a different purpose.

First Read   Focus on integrating visual information.

Second Read   Focus on understanding the steps in a process.

Third Read   Focus on thinking critically about the selection.

❧ Who Was ❧
King Arthur?

Skim the time line. How does this visual help you predict what the selection will be about? ✏

Why did Geoffrey include Arthur in his historical book about Britain's rulers? ✏

1   According to legend, King Arthur once ruled Britain from his legendary court at Camelot. In his kingdom were damsels in distress and knights in shining armor. Stories present Arthur as a powerful and noble leader, a brave warrior, and the defender of Britain. Arthur is the fairy-tale image of the **medieval** king. These Arthurian stories have led many people to ask two major questions: *Where did the stories of King Arthur come from?* and *Was Arthur an actual person?*

2   Arthur has appeared in a number of different sources, including ancient Welsh legends and stories of Catholic saints. However, most people agree that the first complete account of his life appeared in a book by Geoffrey of Monmouth.[1] It was written in the twelfth century and called *History of the Kings of Britain.* In this book, Arthur is a warrior and a king who united the British tribes to defeat Saxon[2] invaders; he spent his life defending and expanding his British kingdom.

[1]**Monmouth** a Welsh town, close to the border with England
[2]**Saxons** tribes from present-day Germany

Arthur's supposed birth date

Arthur leads the Britons in defeating the Saxons.

King Arthur's Life and Legend

465   496

400 ——————————————————————— 700

501   542

Arthur is mentioned in a Welsh poem.

Death of Arthur

3   Clearly, in Geoffrey's book, Arthur was Britain's hero, and at the time the book was written, most people accepted these stories as true. Geoffrey's book was intended to be a historical work, not fiction, and Arthur's life and adventures were described alongside the lives of real-life rulers.

Arthur's Youth

4   According to Geoffrey, Arthur is the son of Uther Pendragon, a dishonest and unfaithful king. A wise man named Merlin takes Arthur away from his father and keeps him hidden from the world until he is grown. Eventually, King Pendragon dies. Arthur immediately replaces his father as king through the traditional medieval process. The **nobility** (wealthy landowners) from the surrounding areas gather and choose Dubricius, a church leader, to bless Arthur as their king. In a solemn ceremony surrounded by the nobility and other church leaders, Dubricius places the crown on Arthur's head.

5   Later stories describe a far more mythical process by which Arthur becomes king. According to these sources, after King Pendragon dies, his lords don't know who should succeed him, since they aren't aware of his hidden son. In these later legends, Merlin is not just a wise man but a magician. He makes a prophecy, or a magical prediction, that next to a lake there is a large stone with a sword stuck in it. The man who pulls the mysterious sword from the stone will be king. Many knights try over the years to remove the sword from the stone but fail. Meanwhile, Arthur grows to be a young man and returns to the court to serve his foster brother. When his brother's sword breaks, Arthur is sent to find another. Not knowing the prophecy, he pulls the sword from the stone and becomes king. Arthur keeps the magical sword, named Excalibur, for the rest of his life.

> According to Geoffrey of Monmouth, what are the steps by which Arthur becomes king? What are the steps, according to later stories? Record your answers in the **Steps in a Process Chart.**

> What role does Merlin play in the Arthurian legend?

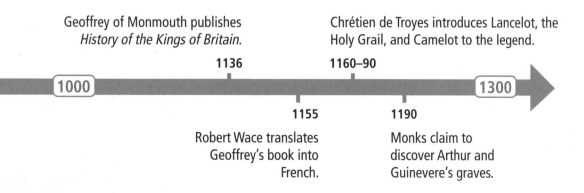

Geoffrey of Monmouth publishes *History of the Kings of Britain.*
1136

Chrétien de Troyes introduces Lancelot, the Holy Grail, and Camelot to the legend.
1160–90

1000 ———— 1300 ➤

1155
Robert Wace translates Geoffrey's book into French.

1190
Monks claim to discover Arthur and Guinevere's graves.

Examine the map on this page. How does the map relate to the text in paragraph 6? ✏️

Read paragraphs 7 and 8. What are the steps in the process of becoming a knight? <u>Underline</u> them. Record your answer in the **Steps in a Process Chart**.

King Arthur's Early Years

6   In 1155, Robert Wace completed a French translation of Geoffrey's *History of the Kings of Britain*. This version of the story introduces King Arthur's Round Table. Here Merlin designs an enormous round table that can sit 150 knights. King Arthur gathers men from all over Britain to join him in unifying and protecting the English people. Because the table sits so many, Arthur is able to bring many men into his service. Because the table is round, no one sits at its head. This means that King Arthur humbly shares the same rank as the men he gathers into his service. The Knights of the Round Table, as they become known, fight alongside King Arthur to unite Britain and protect it from invaders.

Becoming a Knight

7   Although King Arthur accepts many men who are already knights into his service, he also trains boys to become knights, a process that is long and challenging. At the time, English knights usually came from noble or wealthy families because it cost so much to buy all the weapons, armor, and horses. At the age of seven, boys who were eligible to be knights would become pages. These boys would go to live in the home of a lord, or wealthy landowner. The pages helped out as waiters, dressers, and general servants. They also studied religion, hunting, manners, and warfare. In addition, pages trained for battle, practicing with wooden swords and wooden horses.

This map shows the territory that the British controlled and the areas where other tribes invaded during the time of King Arthur's reign.

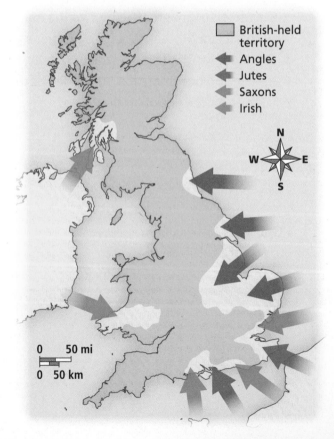

British-held territory

Angles

Jutes

Saxons

Irish

0   50 mi

0   50 km

8   When pages turned fourteen years old, they became **squires**. These young men took on more duties, such as assisting their lord in actual battles. They also learned how to speak well and dance and play music. After seven years of service as squires, these young men could finally become knights. This long process was difficult but necessary training in preparation for battles and adventures.

Why might poets have been the first to introduce the story of Lancelot and Guinevere?

The Holy Grail

9   In addition to the typical knightly activities of rescuing people and defending the land, the legends tell of Arthur and his knights also going on spiritual **quests**, or journeys, to find the Holy Grail. According to Christian tradition, the Holy Grail is the name of the cup that Jesus Christ drank from on the night before he died. Some people believed that an early follower of Jesus brought the cup to Britain and hid it to keep it safe. Chrétien de Troyes, a French poet, first introduced the Holy Grail stories to Arthurian legend. King Arthur and his knights are Christians, so the search for the Holy Grail has deep spiritual meaning to them. However, they never find it. Some people believe this failure gives the Arthur story a more real, human quality. After all, it is far more realistic for a king to have some failures and struggles than none at all.

King Arthur's Love

10   Perhaps Arthur's greatest life struggle is his marriage. Although Geoffrey's *History* does introduce Arthur's queen as Guinevere, there is little in his account about her. French poets, including Chrétien de Troyes, were the first to describe the sad story of King Arthur's lost love, relating how King Arthur meets a beautiful young woman while on one of his many adventures. He instantly falls in love with her and asks for her hand in marriage. From that moment on, King Arthur loves his queen faithfully, treating her with kindness and respect.

11   Then a handsome young knight named Lancelot joins King Arthur's Round Table. He is a great warrior and a faithful servant to King Arthur, who begins to look on the young knight as a trusted companion. This special friendship brings the young knight to the queen's attention. Guinevere and Lancelot fall in love. When Arthur discovers their love, Lancelot flees Britain for France with Arthur pursuing him.

Examine the photograph of Tintagel Castle. Why would people build the castle on this unlikely outcrop?

Why would historians focus on one part of King Arthur's life for their research?

Arthur's Death

12   Arthur remains in France, looking for Lancelot for some time. So Arthur's nephew, Mordred, takes over the throne. When Arthur returns to Britain, Mordred refuses to give up the throne. Arthur's knights fight Mordred and his supporters. During the war, most of Arthur's knights die. In sorrow and despair, Arthur returns to the lake near where he first pulled Excalibur from the stone. He flings his trusted weapon into the lake. Then he gets into a boat and sails away. Because King Arthur's death is never officially recorded, he is known as the "Once and Future King." Some people believed he would return to rule Britain once more.

Searching for the True King Arthur

13   Most of the Arthurian legends have changed over time. Historians have tried for years to find physical evidence to support the stories and prove that Arthur was real. Most scholars have focused on one part of Arthur's life and tried to identify the actual, physical location where Arthur may have been at that time. For example, there are many historians who try to verify that the ruin of Tintagel Castle is the place of Arthur's birth.

Arthur's Birthplace

14   Geoffrey of Monmouth was the first to report that Arthur was born at Tintagel Castle in far southwestern England. Today people visit the ruins and a small cave nearby known as Merlin's cave—the supposed site where Arthur was hidden as a boy. Evidence at the ruins shows that there was a castle, built as a solid defense against invaders, with a thriving community around it. But it is unlikely that this community would have existed at the time Arthur would have lived. However, Tintagel is a valuable national monument both for its contribution to the Arthurian legend and other aspects of historical interest.

Tintagel Castle today is a series of ruins on a rocky outcrop overlooking the sea.

Arthur's Castle

15   Although Arthur was supposedly born in Tintagel Castle, he reigned from Camelot—a castle, a city, and a legendary place of peace and justice. Historians consulting the many Arthurian documents have suggested a number of sites for the real Camelot. In fact, today there are thirteen possible places where Camelot could have been. The most popular spot is Cadbury Castle. Located in southwestern England, Cadbury Castle is actually a hill that was strengthened for defense over many years.

16   In 1965, a group of historians, who called themselves the Camelot Research Committee, began to uncover the castle by digging out this hill. They discovered that a fort and castle had been rebuilt there at about the time Arthur is believed to have lived. They even found a large feast hall. Could this be the possible location of the Round Table? Pieces of Mediterranean pottery found at Cadbury show that whoever lived there had enough money to import such items. He must have been a major king, which supports the theory that it might be Arthur. However, many historians argue that the name and location prove Cadbury Castle to have belonged to another king and not to Arthur.

Arthur's Final Resting Place

17   Glastonbury Tor[3] is a mysterious mound rising out of what was once marshland, suggesting that it may have once been an island. Legends say that Arthur went to Glastonbury to heal after being wounded in his battle with Mordred. He hurled Excalibur into the surrounding waters, then sailed to the island. Christian monks built a church on top of Glastonbury Tor, claiming to have found Arthur and Guinevere's graves there in 1190. Since then, the mound has drawn pilgrims from all over the world. Historians have studied the site and found strange ridges carved into the hill, suggesting it may have been an underground chamber or a maze of some sort. Arthurian enthusiasts believe the chamber once held Arthur's remains or even the Holy Grail. Today, people still continue to hike up Glastonbury Tor in search of healing or inspiration.

[3]**Tor** a high, rocky peak or hill

> Read the sidebar below. What are the steps in the process of a historic site becoming a Scheduled Ancient Monument? Record your answer in the **Steps in a Process Chart**.

> **Becoming a Scheduled Ancient Monument**
> Tintagel Castle, Cadbury Castle, and Glastonbury Tor are all protected as ancient monuments by the British government. The process by which a monument is "scheduled," or put on the list of historic sites, is complex and lengthy.
>
> First, the English Heritage Committee receives proposals for ancient monuments. Next, it conducts research to see if a proposed site fulfills all the criteria. (Criteria include the length of time a site was used and the rarity, value, condition, and fragility of the site.) Then, the committee advises the secretary of state for culture, media, and sport about the site. Finally, the secretary declares the site an ancient monument.

What might an illustration of King Arthur demonstrating chivalry show?

Arthur Becomes a Legend

18   Arthur has evolved from a great warrior praised in Welsh myths to a king in Geoffrey of Monmouth's history. Then French translators and poets focused on and developed different parts of Arthur's story. Some wrote about Arthur's political skill and his ability to unite and protect Britain, while others focused on his life of love and loss. Each writer took the stories that came before and added something new. Perhaps, as some historians believe, these writers researched and found actual truths about King Arthur. However, most scholars believe that the themes in the earlier stories appealed to the writers, who then wanted to contribute to the Arthurian legend themselves.

King Arthur Today

19   Those themes still appeal to audiences and artists today. Authors continue to write new works of historical nonfiction and fiction about Arthur and his knights, which still remain popular in film, on TV, and even in video games. Some of these stories continue to strengthen and support British national pride. However, the international appeal of the legends suggests universal values, such as **chivalry** and romantic ideals.

Interpret

The underlined phrases suggest events that have become part of the Arthurian legend. What are they?

20   Chivalry is the code that King Arthur's knights lived by. It includes being courteous, generous, valiant, and a capable warrior. Romantic ideals are not about love but rather about seeing the world as essentially good. King Arthur and his knights believed that good would eventually conquer evil, and justice would prevail. These romantic ideals still appeal to King Arthur enthusiasts today.

21   Even people who prefer reality to romantic ideals find themes in the Arthurian legend to which they can relate, such as love and betrayal, seeking and not finding, losing battles but living on. King Arthur has come to be part of a universal legend, appealing to people from all over the world, of all ages, and in all times.

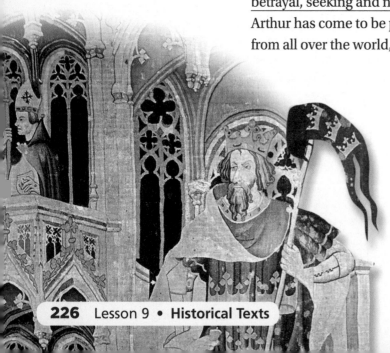

Vocabulary: Domain-Specific Vocabulary

Domain-specific vocabulary are words that are particular to a field of study. For example, in social studies texts, writers might use words like *civics* (the study of people's rights) and *economics* (the study of money systems). In historical texts, writers might use words like *anthropology* (the study of people and culture) and *monarchy* (a nation with one supreme ruler). Learning words that are specific to one area of study can help you better understand a text about that subject.

Try It Read this sentence from "Who Was King Arthur?"

> Arthur is the fairy-tale image of the **medieval** king.

Discuss What is the meaning of the word *medieval*? How is this word specific to the field of history?

Find the following domain-specific words in "Who Was King Arthur?" Then write their definitions by looking at the words, phrases, and sentences around them or by looking in a dictionary.

1. nobility, p. 221 _____

_____

2. squire, p. 223 _____

_____

3. quest, p. 223 _____

_____

4. chivalry, p. 226 _____

_____

Practice the Skill

To draw an **inference** means to figure out what an author is implying but does not state directly. Usually, authors do not explicitly state all the ideas they want to convey; sometimes, they merely suggest them. It's your job to "read between the lines" in order to get the complete picture.

To do this, you use the facts and details provided in the text and combine them with your own knowledge and experience. For example, a text can suggest what the famous General George S. Patton was like by describing the things he did and how he responded to others. You can then use that information to draw an inference about Patton's personality.

Remember, an inference is an educated guess, which means it must be supported with **evidence** from the text—facts, details, and quotations. Also, bear in mind that the inferences you draw will likely change as you read deeper into a text, gaining more information.

Try It Read this paragraph.

As far as we know, the Dresden Codex is the oldest book produced in the Americas that still survives today. It was created by the Maya of Central America in the eleventh or twelfth century. The Maya wrote with pictures and symbols. Scholars who have studied this book were amazed to learn that the Maya had developed an accurate calendar based on the movements of the planet Venus. In the Dresden Codex, astronomical events were recorded next to images from Mayan myths.

> **Discuss** Draw a box around facts and details in the paragraph. Based on these stated facts, what can you infer the author feels about the scientific interests and abilities of the Maya?

> As you read, complete the Inference Chart on page 313.

Practice the Skill

Second Read Analyze Word Choice and Tone

The **tone** of a text is the attitude an author takes toward the text's topic. An author uses language to convey tone as well as to give information. **Word choice** helps an author to convey and develop a tone. For example, an author might describe a French emperor as *puny* instead of *short*, if the tone he or she is aiming for is insulting or perhaps humorous. Or the author might use the phrase *small in stature* if the desired tone is more formal or respectful. An author also chooses words that will stir emotions in the mind of the reader. For example, describing the French Revolution as *bloody* conveys a different tone than describing it as *glorious*.

Words Used to Describe a Text's Tone		
angry	ironic	reflective
critical	negative	respectful
defensive	neutral	serious
humorous	positive	sincere

Try It Read this paragraph.

> When the astonished explorers entered the cave, they could hardly believe their eyes. The walls were covered with images that had been carved into the stone. Some of the pictures showed remarkable scenes of hunting. Others showed finely detailed maps of the stars. Could it be that Native Americans had created these pictures long ago? When the explorers set out that morning, they never expected to uncover something of such profound importance. What started out as a hike through the desert turned out to be a journey back in time.

Discuss ▸ **What is the tone of the paragraph? Underline the words and phrases that the author uses to help convey the tone.**

As you read, record your answers to questions about word choice and tone on the Close Reading Worksheet on page 314. ✏️➡️

Purpose for Reading
Read along with your teacher. Each time, read for a different purpose.

First Read   Focus on drawing and supporting inferences.

Second Read   Focus on analyzing the author's tone and word choices.

Third Read   Focus on thinking critically about the selection.

Child Monarchs

What did King Tut's subjects most likely think of him as a ruler? Draw a box around the fact in paragraph 4 that supports your answer. Write your responses on the **Inference Chart**.

What tone does the author convey in paragraph 4? Underline the words that convey the tone.

1   A monarchy is a system of government in which one person is the sole ruler until he or she dies or gives up the position. Usually, the monarch inherits the position from a parent. In traditional monarchies, the king or queen has absolute authority to rule the country. A group of advisors may help the monarch, but the king or queen alone makes major decisions, such as which laws go into effect and when to declare war.

2   This awesome power is challenging for one person to manage, and kings and queens often needed to have great wisdom in order to fulfill their duties to protect and care for their people. The challenge was much greater for children who inherited the throne and rose to power upon the early death of their parents. Because of their youth, many of these child monarchs were simply **figureheads**. They were respected as rulers, but they had no real decision-making power to lead their countries. That power fell mainly on their advisors, who were more often than not religious leaders. However, a number of notable child monarchs held on to their power and changed the course of history.

King Tut of Egypt

3   King Tutankhamen was an Egyptian **pharaoh** who ruled during the fourteenth century BCE. Popularly referred to as King Tut, Tutankhamen ascended to the throne at the age of nine or ten.

4   At first, young King Tut ruled under the direction of advisors. But during the course of his reign, he made some valuable changes that steered Egyptian society in a new direction. For one, he wisely reversed unpopular laws that had been put into effect by his father, Akhenaton, in an effort to control how people worshiped.

Draw a box around the last part of King Tut's and his father's names. What inference can you make about them? Record your answers on the **Inference Chart**.

5   In ancient Egypt, people worshiped many gods who were represented by powerful natural objects. Amun, sometimes spelled Amen, was the chief god, the god of the sun. In a move that angered many people, King Akhenaton decreed the minor god Aton to be more important than Amun and demanded that people worship Aton and no other gods. As part of his plan, Akhenaton declared that the city of Amarna be built for the sole purpose of sun worship that celebrated the deity Aton.

Underline words from paragraphs 7 and 8 that demonstrate the author's attitude toward the tomb raiders. What tone does the author convey by using these words?

6   When he succeeded his father, King Tut abandoned the city of Amarna and returned to Memphis, Egypt's original capital city. He restored Amun as the chief deity and allowed people to worship all of the gods. To show his commitment to the old religion, he changed his birth name from Tutankhaton to Tutankhamen.

7   Today, King Tut is probably the most famous of the pharaohs, but for thousands of years, little was known about him as a ruler. The pharaohs of Egypt were buried with valuable items, such as jewelry and sculptures, that the rulers wanted with them in the afterlife. However, many tombs were raided over the years by greedy robbers looking for gold and precious stones, and only some tombs remained intact.

8   Most of the tombs of the pharaohs of the period lie in a place called the Valley of Kings, near present-day Luxor. Archaeologists had searched the valley for years in hopes that some of its treasures remained undisturbed. In 1922, an archaeologist named Howard Carter discovered a tomb that had escaped the reckless tomb raiders' attention. It was buried near the tomb of Ramses VI, a later king, and it had remained mostly untouched for three thousand years. The entrance was blocked by a stone structure put up by workmen when Ramses's tomb was built. It contained a series of doors and four chambers. Imagine Carter's surprise when he saw "Tutankhamen" engraved on one of the doors. The tomb held a wealth of treasures, including the mummy of the child pharaoh.

Mary, Queen of Scots

9   While King Tut may be the best-known child ruler from ancient times, Mary Stuart is probably the best known of the Renaissance.[1] Popularly known as Mary, Queen of Scots, she had ruled two countries by the time she turned eighteen. Mary was the only surviving legitimate child of King James V of Scotland. King James V himself died just six days after Mary's birth. As the sole heir, Mary inherited the throne as an infant.

10   The infant queen was, of course, too young to make decisions for her country, Scotland, but she would influence history in an interesting way. In sixteenth-century Europe, King Henry VIII of England was eager to unite England and Scotland. So he proposed a future marriage between Mary and his son Edward. When the Scottish parliament[2] rejected the offer, Henry invaded Scotland and tried to force the marriage. During this time, referred to as the "Rough Wooing," Mary was shuffled around from castle to castle to keep her safe.

11   When she was five, Mary was taken to France. At the age of sixteen, she married Francis II, who ascended to the French throne a year later. At that time, Mary was considered the most beautiful queen in Europe. She was intelligent and well spoken. She had an oval face, shapely chin, and golden-red hair. She and her husband, Francis II, had been friends since they were children, and they were a happy couple.

12   Though Mary was Scottish by birth and already the ruler of Scotland, she ruled briefly as "queen consort" of France, too, until her husband died in 1560. After that, Mary returned to her homeland to resume her duties as queen of Scotland.

13   Mary had a strong connection to England as well as Scotland and France. Her grandmother was Margaret Tudor, who was the sister of Henry VIII. When Henry's daughter Elizabeth I ascended to the throne, many in Scotland believed that Mary's status as a Tudor gave her the right to rule England. The people who supported Queen Elizabeth plotted to convict Mary of **treason**. They convinced Elizabeth that Mary planned to have her killed. The queen had Mary imprisoned and eventually beheaded for her treasonous actions against the crown.

[1]**Renaissance** a period of vigorous artistic and cultural growth in Europe from the fourteenth through early seventeenth centuries
[2]**parliament** the group of people who make laws and govern a country

Mary, Queen of Scots

Queen Christina of Sweden

14   Fifty-seven years after Mary was beheaded in England, a young girl named Christina came to power in Sweden. Christina was the daughter of King Gustav II, a military hero. When he died in battle, the young princess inherited the throne at the age of six.

15   Being a child of privilege, she was raised by the most brilliant tutors in the country. After ascending to the throne, she studied subjects that were typically studied only by boys, such as history, politics, science, and math. She also studied literature and learned to speak several languages. Christina ruled Sweden with the help of advisors until her eighteenth birthday, when she became queen in her own right. By that time, she had ideas that were more visionary than those of previous rulers.

16   Christina was a unique woman of the times. She was witty, opinionated, and highly independent. Christina refused to marry, which upset many people. Because she never produced an heir to inherit the throne, her cousin Charles was next in line to rule Sweden after her death.

17   As it turned out, however, Christina did not rule up until her death. She chose to **abdicate** the throne to her cousin Charles. At that point in her life, she was at the height of her power, but she determinedly left her home country and went to Rome. Scholars still disagree about the reason for her abdication. Did she do so because she changed her religion from Protestant to Catholic and wanted to be closer to the seat of Catholicism in Rome? Or did she do it because she was tired of ruling and wanted to focus on bettering herself? While in Rome, she continued to study and gain knowledge, living out her days surrounded by musicians, artists, and scholars.

What can you infer about Christina from her studies described in paragraph 15? Write your answer on the **Inference Chart**.

Christina challenged tradition by doing things differently. Underline words and phrases that convey the author's feelings about Christina's rebelliousness.

Why did Christina most likely study subjects typically studied by boys?

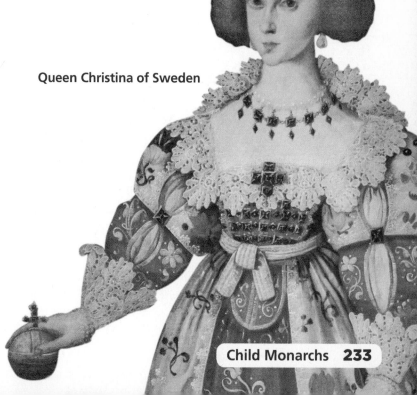

Queen Christina of Sweden

How effective a ruler was Puyi? What details support this inference? Write your answers on the **Inference Chart**.

What tone does the author convey when discussing the reign of Puyi? Underline the words and phrases that support your answer.

Analyze

Why do you think ruling families were willing to entrust power even to their youngest members?

The Shunzhi Emperor

Child Emperors of China

18   Child monarchs ruled in many parts of the eastern world, too. In 1643, five-year-old Fulin became the third emperor of China's Qing dynasty.[3] Eventually known as the Shunzhi Emperor, he inherited the throne after the death of his father. Because Fulin was so young, he ruled with the help of his uncle for the first few years of his reign. After his uncle died in 1650, however, the twelve-year-old Shunzhi became the ruling monarch.

19   The Shunzhi Emperor is remembered today as a remarkably open-minded leader. He was known for being tolerant and allowing people to worship as they saw fit. When he died at the age of twenty-four, his eight-year-old son, the Kangxi Emperor, ascended to the throne, ruling China for more than sixty years.

20   China had a child monarch in more recent times, too. Puyi inherited the throne from his uncle Guangxu in 1908, when Puyi was just three years old. His father, Prince Ch'un, never ruled because he was the second-born son in his family, and first sons were generally made emperor. Although he was Ch'un's first son, Puyi was actually given the throne because he was Guangxu's adopted son.

21   Puyi ruled during a very **tumultuous** time in Chinese history. Prince Ch'un was an important man in the Chinese government, but he misguided his son during his reign. It has been said that the dynasty lost its power to the Communists due to the mistakes of Prince Ch'un. Puyi lost the throne in 1912, but he lives in history as China's "last emperor." Puyi would ascend to the throne again in his life, but not as emperor of China. He fled Beijing in 1924. Between 1934 and 1945, Puyi was installed by the Japanese as emperor of Manchuria, a vast region of China that was controlled by Japan at the time. At the end of World War II, Puyi was captured by the Russians and returned to China, where he was tried as a war criminal. He was eventually released, and Puyi lived out his days as a common citizen, working as a gardener. He died in 1967.

22   Young rulers, whether they exercised real power or not, hold a fascinating place in history. While monarchies in which any ruler, adult or child, holds absolute power have become much more rare in the last century, they do still exist. And child monarchs, figureheads or not, are still possible in our modern world. Which ones will become important to history, only time can tell.

[3]**dynasty** a line of rulers from the same family

Vocabulary: Look up Definitions in Dictionaries and Glossaries

As you read a historical text, you may come across an unfamiliar word. Sometimes the word will be a specialized term that relates to a particular topic or subject. The word may be defined in a **glossary** that appears at the end of the text. Or you can use a **dictionary** to determine its meaning. Often, a dictionary entry gives more than one meaning for a word, but you can choose the right one if you understand the topic you are reading about and think about the context of the sentence.

Try It Read these sentences from the text.

> Because of their youth, many of these child monarchs were simply **figureheads**. They were respected as rulers, but they had no real decision-making power to lead their countries.

Discuss Use a dictionary to look up the meaning of the boldface word. Which meaning makes the most sense in this context? Why do you think it would be helpful to include this word in a glossary at the end of the text?

Use a dictionary to learn the meanings of each of the words below, and decide which definition makes the most sense in the context of the selection. Then create a glossary of these terms that would be helpful for readers of "Child Monarchs." Write the definition for each term in your own words.

1. pharaoh, p. 230 _____

2. treason, p. 232 _____

3. abdicate, p. 233 _____

4. tumultuous, p. 234 _____

Respond to Text: Compare and Contrast Text and Video

Historical information can be presented on video as well as in written texts. However, video conveys ideas differently. One obvious difference is that video uses moving images as opposed to still photographs. A video also usually includes sound effects, dialogue, and music. Sounds influence how the viewer interprets the material. For example, disturbing music might make a scene seem scarier than it would without any music.

Try It Read this excerpt from "Who Was King Arthur?"

Arthur remains in France looking for Lancelot for some time. So Arthur's nephew, Mordred, takes over the throne. When Arthur returns to Britain, Mordred refuses to give up the throne. Arthur's knights fight Mordred and his supporters. During the war, most of Arthur's knights die.

> Discuss **How do you imagine a video might present this information? What moving images might you see? What music might you hear?**

On Your Own Watch the video about the King Arthur legend that your teacher will show. Then write a paragraph that compares and contrasts information in the video and in "Who Was King Arthur?" Use the chart on the next page to organize your writing. Then write your paragraph on a separate sheet of paper.

Checklist for a Good Response

A good paragraph

✔ provides a topic sentence that conveys the main idea.

✔ describes at least two ways the information in the selection and the video are alike.

✔ describes at least two ways the information in the selection and the video are presented differently.

✔ uses details from the selection and the video to support the response.

My Comparison and Contrast of a Text with a Video

1. **Topic Sentence** Write a sentence that summarizes your main idea.

_____

_____

_____

2. **Detail Sentences** Complete the chart to compare how the selection and the video present information.

"Who Was King Arthur?"	Both	Video

3. **Concluding Sentence** Your concluding sentence should state the main comparison or contrast that you find between the two sources.

_____

_____

_____

On a separate sheet of paper, write your paragraph.

Read on Your Own

Read the selection independently three times, using the skills you have learned. Then answer the Comprehension Check questions.

First Read — Practice the first-read skills you learned in this lesson.

Second Read — Practice the second-read skills you learned in this lesson.

Third Read — Think critically about the selection.

The Search for Atlantis

Draw and Support Inferences Draw boxes around details in paragraph 3 that could support an inference that searching for Atlantis might be unsuccessful. The first one has been boxed for you.

Analyze Word Choice and Tone Underline the words in paragraph 2 that show Plato's attitude toward Atlantis. The first two have been underlined for you.

1   The lost city of Atlantis has fascinated people for centuries. Did it really exist, or is it simply a legend? The ancient Greek philosopher Plato described it in detail over two thousand years ago. According to Plato, Atlantis was a city the size of a continent that existed more than ten thousand years ago in the Atlantic Ocean.

2   In Plato's account, Atlantis was created and peopled by the Greek god of the sea, Poseidon. He fell in love with a mortal woman and created Atlantis for her and their children. Poseidon carved Atlantis from the mainland, flooding around it until it was an island. Then he and his descendants made it into a magnificent world. It was filled with lush vegetation and animals alike. Springs flowed with healing waters, and the earth held a wealth of gemstones and precious metals. Poseidon's descendants were highly intelligent and peace loving. They made brilliant achievements in the arts and sciences. They created buildings and temples as grand as any in the ancient world, adorning them with gold and silver. They forged roads and waterways, bridges and tunnels. Then Atlantis was swallowed by the sea.

3   The search for the fabled city began at the time of Plato's account and has continued to the present time. If Atlantis even came close to the magnificent place Plato described, it would contain a wealth of treasures and priceless insights into **antiquity**. However, if it was swallowed by the sea as Plato claimed, those treasures would be nearly impossible to find.

Duplicating any part of this book is prohibited by law. © 2014 Triumph Learning, LLC

238 Lesson 9 • Historical Texts

Finding the Impossible

4   Over the years, many different people have claimed to have found the city of Atlantis. They have identified locations for this legendary world on every continent on Earth. Because Plato claimed that the city was located off the Pillars of Hercules in the Atlantic Ocean, many of these explorers started their searches there.

5   The Pillars of Hercules are two rock cliffs that jut out from the water near the Strait of Gibraltar. The Strait of Gibraltar marks the western edge of the Mediterranean Sea. Beyond it lies the Atlantic Ocean. Searching for Atlantis near the Pillars of Hercules also made sense because in the past, some scholars believed there had been a strip of land connecting southern Spain and North Africa and extending far west to South America. They called this strip of land a "land bridge" and proposed that it could have actually been the site of Atlantis. Most scientists now agree that no such land bridge existed. Furthermore, no one has found physical evidence to support the theory that Atlantis existed in this area.

Integrate Visual Information On the map, (circle) the location of the Pillars of Hercules. Think about how the map reinforces information in paragraph 5.

Critical Thinking Think about why the land bridge theory is not reasonable.

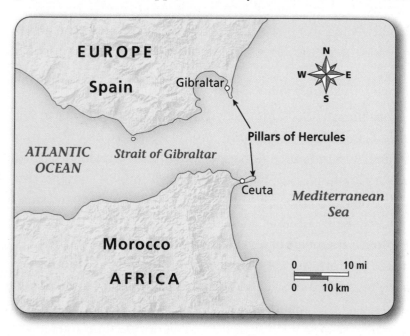

Searching Far and Wide

6   When concrete evidence of Atlantis wasn't found near the Strait of Gibraltar, explorers set their sights far and wide. Over the years, people have claimed the location of Atlantis in places as varied as the Caribbean Sea and Antarctica.

Analyze Word Choice and Tone Look at the heading on this page. Consider the tone that the author suggests by phrasing it as a question.

Analyze Word Choice and Tone Think about the tone conveyed by using the words *incredible*, *claimed*, and *skeptical* in paragraph 7.

Critical Thinking Some say, "What you look for is what you'll find." Think about how this expression applies to the search for Atlantis.

7   In the 1950s, pilots flying over the waters of the Caribbean reported seeing what looked like the walls of buildings in the shallow waters off Cuba. Then in 1967, the Edgar Cayce Foundation produced photos taken in the Bahamas. The photos showed underwater rectangular building foundations. The Edgar Cayce Foundation's founder had earlier made an incredible prediction: Atlantis would rise again in the 1960s. The photos, they claimed, were proof that Cayce was right. Archaeologists agree that these are building foundations made by ancient peoples. However, most are skeptical that the builders were the inhabitants of Atlantis. One major problem with any Caribbean site is that Plato would have had no way of knowing about such a civilization nearly two thousand years before Europeans reached the Americas.

8   In 1966, Professor Charles Hapgood first proposed that Antarctica could be Atlantis. Antarctica appears on ancient nautical maps. These maps existed long before James Cook discovered Antarctica in 1773. Critics say Antarctica is too cold to be Atlantis. Countering these criticisms, Hapgood claimed that the most recent ice age covered Antarctica with ice only after Atlantis disappeared. A few scholars accept Hapgood's theory. However, no physical evidence exists to support it.

Santorini, the Likeliest Location?

9   Since the late 1960s, researchers have gathered evidence to suggest that the Greek island of Santorini was Atlantis. Plato described Atlantis as a circular island with alternating rings of water and land. Geologists Floyd McCoy and Grant Heiken note that Santorini is comprised of circular ridges and that ancient paintings found on the island closely match Plato's descriptions. In the 1600s BCE, Santorini was inhabited by Minoans, members of a civilization rich with art and culture, centered in Crete. In 1640 BCE, a volcano erupted on Santorini, destroying the island. Scientists believe the eruption caused a tsunami that affected other islands, including Crete, and may have contributed to the collapse of Minoan civilization. This destruction could have led to the creation of the Atlantis myth.

10   However, these dates don't fit with those of Plato. They are off by about eight thousand years! Some historians argue that it is likely Plato meant nine hundred years before his time, not nine thousand. That would make the Santorini theory a perfect match. Another hole in the Santorini theory is that Plato described the size of Atlantis as larger than Libya and Asia *combined*. Santorini is a fraction of that size. Santorini theory supporters argue that Plato may have been exaggerating.

11   As with most theoretical locations for Atlantis, Santorini only works with modifications to Plato's descriptions; for example, by **hacking** thousands of years off the civilization's founding date and thousands of miles off the country's landmass. All potential sites have missing links and faulty reasoning that fail to support them. Yet scholars and scientists alike continue to search for the lost city.

Searching in Spain

12   Today, researchers use advanced technology to try locating Atlantis. Some, like Dr. Rainer Kuehne, have used satellite images. He has proposed a site in southern Spain, in the salt marshes[1] near the city of Cadíz, just west of the Strait of Gibraltar. The satellite images show two rectangular structures surrounded by rings. Plato's description of Atlantis included royal palaces and temples at the center of alternating rings of land and water. Kuehne believes the rectangles in the satellite images to be the foundations of temples to Poseidon.

13   In Plato's description, the island was five *stades* in diameter. This is equivalent to about 925 meters. The area Kuehne is studying is actually larger. He believes the discrepancy exists because modern-day interpretations of ancient measurements are off by 20 percent. When Plato's calculations are increased by this amount, the size of the site matches Plato's measurements exactly. He believes the reason the site is on the mainland and not in the ocean may be because of a poor translation of Plato's work. Therefore, Atlantis was not an island but a city on the mainland that was destroyed by a great flood.

14   Efforts to conduct an archaeological dig at the Cádiz site may be complicated. It lies within a national park. Before exploring any site, archaeologists must first get permission from the proper authorities. If the site is located on public lands, such as a national park, they must request a permit from the government. In their requests, archaeologists tell when and why they wish to explore the site. Government officials then review the permit application. If the permit is approved, archaeological teams can get to work.

[1] **salt marshes** low, coastal land, frequently flooded by salt water

> **Draw and Support Inferences** Draw boxes around details in paragraph 13 that support the inference that the quality of historical source material can have a significant impact on archaeological research.

> **Identify Steps in a Process** Think about the steps involved in getting permission for an archaeological dig. Number the steps.

Understanding the Allure

15   Many people continue to search for Atlantis. Most don't think they will find the **fantastical** riches that Plato described. But they hope to find enough evidence to prove that Atlantis was real. Others have abandoned their efforts. Some have come to the conclusion that the city Plato described existed only in his imagination. Alan F. Alford, a scholar of ancient religions and mythology, spent years studying Plato's description. He finally decided that the story of this city was simply a metaphor. Atlantis, he said, was a *symbol* for a lost paradise. It was a story that Plato told to show how devastating war can be. In the time just before the sea swallowed Atlantis, Poseidon's descendants had become greedy. They had begun to fight among themselves. In the myth of Atlantis, Plato shows that even the most wonderful place can be corrupted by greed and war. Perhaps Plato was warning his society that if they didn't stop their greedy and quarreling ways, they too would be struck by disaster.

16   Alford argues that Atlantis doesn't exist in a geographical sense. But it does exist very powerfully in the world's imagination. It is paradise on Earth. Perhaps we had better heed Plato's warnings against greed and quarreling. Otherwise we may be faced with serious environmental and political consequences of our own.

Critical Thinking
Think about who the author believes is blinded by greed and quarreling today. What consequences does the author refer to?

Many artists have imagined how Atlantis might look.

✅ Comprehension Check

1. Examine the map on page 239. What information does the map support in paragraph 5 on page 239?

   _____

   _____

2. Based on information in the selection, what can you infer about the Minoan civilization?

   _____

   _____

3. Read this sentence from the selection.

   As with most theoretical locations for Atlantis, Santorini only works with modifications to Plato's descriptions; for example, by hacking thousands of years off the civilization's founding date and thousands of miles off the country's landmass.

   Describe the tone conveyed by the word *hacking*.

   _____

   _____

4. What are the steps in the process for getting permission for an archaeological dig? Complete the process chart below.

   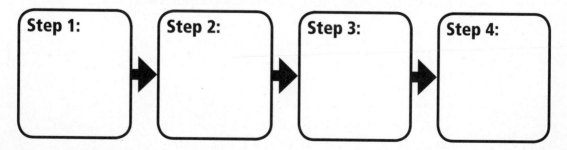

5. What main idea does the author convey about the search for Atlantis?

_____

_____

6. What consequences of greed and quarreling does the author cite?

_____

_____

7. Read this sentence from the selection.

> **If Atlantis even came close to the magnificent place Plato described, it would contain a wealth of treasures and priceless insights into antiquity.**

What does *antiquity* mean? Use it in a sentence.

_____

_____

8. Read these sentences from the selection.

> **Most don't think they will find the fantastical riches that Plato described. But they hope to find enough evidence to prove that Atlantis was real.**

Look up *fantastical* in a dictionary. Create a definition for the term that could be included in a glossary at the end of the selection.

_____

_____

Lesson 10

Primary and Secondary Sources

Primary sources are accounts of events written by people who were there at the time the events occurred. These sources include diaries, journals, letters, and speeches. **Secondary sources** are accounts written later, by people who were not present at the event. Authors of secondary sources often refer to and quote from primary sources in their writing. Secondary sources include encyclopedia articles, textbooks, and news reports. What would the primary-source account of this soldier about to fly on a combat mission include that a secondary source could not?

Skills Focus

A Bright Future: From the Journal of Willie Oliver

Cite Textual Evidence   **Primary Sources**

Art for America

Chronological Order   **Secondary Sources**

Practice the Skill

When you analyze a piece of writing, you form ideas about the text from the information that the author provides. First, look for key words and phrases that the author uses to convey his or her messages. Then, state those messages or ideas in your own words to better understand what you are reading.

Sometimes when you are writing or talking about a topic, you will have to show where your ideas come from. This is called **citing textual evidence**. For example, say you read a firsthand account of a hurricane, and your teacher asks what the author had to say. You could answer, "The storm was a terrible experience for the author." That's a broad statement, and you will probably be asked for details from the account to support it. You would need to cite places in the text where the author talks about a fallen tree crushing the family car and the hardships involved with living without power or hot water for five days.

Try It Read the following paragraph.

We leave for Guatemala today—the first of May. We will stay in the village for eight weeks, and none of us knows exactly what to expect. We've been trained for the work, sure. But most of us volunteers come from big cities in the Midwest, and none of us has been south of the border before. But we are going farther than that—into Central America, where we have been told we will live in small huts and spend our days building an orphanage. The experience will be life changing for everyone.

> Discuss   **What textual evidence would you cite to show that the experience will be life changing? Underline the details that support this claim.**

As you read, complete the Cite Textual Evidence Chart on page 315.

Practice the Skill

Second Read Primary Sources

    A **primary source** is a document that provides a firsthand account of an event. This means the author was present when the event took place, so the document provides a close-up, inside view of the event or topic. Legal documents and treaties can be primary documents. So are entries from travel journals, speeches, personal correspondence, autobiographies, memoirs, and sometimes blogs. Primary source texts contain the direct experiences, feelings, and reactions of a person who is living through and witnessing the subject of the text, which could be anything from a political campaign to a sports season to a war to a person's entire life.

    Primary-source documents are useful for providing a personal insight about an event or topic. Used alone, however, they might give too narrow a view of events for a thorough understanding, because they describe only one person's particular viewpoint.

Try It Read the following excerpt from the autobiography of a writer.

>   I never expected that the poem I wrote that day in the woods would someday become so famous. As I wrote, my only thoughts were to explain my feelings about the natural world. It was cold that day in the woods, but for some reason, I felt warm. I looked at everything I saw around me, and it seemed to breathe with life. It was that life that I wanted to convey—that life that existed in the natural world when no one else was looking.

> **Discuss** **What is the main kind of information you get from the text? Circle the details that tell you this is a primary source.**

> **As you read, record your answers to questions about analyzing primary sources on the Close Reading Worksheet on page 316.**

Purpose for Reading

Read along with your teacher. Each time, read for a different purpose.

First Read — Focus on citing textual evidence to support analysis.

Second Read — Focus on analyzing a primary source.

Third Read — Focus on evaluating the source critically.

A Bright Future:
From the
Journal of Willie Oliver

Underline the textual evidence that supports the idea that the WPA and the FAP were major undertakings.

Underline text that best supports the idea that art has been undervalued in American society. Record the evidence on the **Cite Textual Evidence Chart**.

What makes this text an example of a primary-source document?

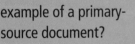

The following excerpts are from a fictitious journal written during the Great Depression of the 1930s, a time in U.S. history when many people were unemployed. President Franklin Delano Roosevelt, known as FDR, created a massive government program called the New Deal. As part of the New Deal, the government established agencies such as the Works Progress Administration (WPA). These agencies employed millions of unemployed people to repair and construct public buildings, roads, bridges, schools, libraries, electrical utilities, dams, and parks. In smaller projects, the WPA employed musicians, artists, writers, actors, and directors. One of those smaller projects, the Federal Art Project (FAP), which employed artists to beautify public spaces, operated from 1935 to 1943. FAP artists created more than 200,000 posters, murals, and paintings. This journal models the characteristics and text features common in authentic texts of this type.

1   Monday morning, April 10, 1939
7:10 on the bus to Canbury
I didn't need the rising sun, the chirping birds, or the milkman to wake me up this morning. I was up with hours to spare before catching the 7:05 bus. I can't believe it—I, Willie Oliver, got word from the FAP last week that I would be employed as an artist. *Employed* as an *artist*, and employed by the government, no less. Those words were unthinkable for anyone not long ago—let alone for a colored man struggling for years to find work doing anything. All those years

Duplicating any part of this book is prohibited by law. © 2014 Triumph Learning, LLC

248 Lesson 10 • **Primary and Secondary Sources**

Mural in the U.S. Post Office in Charlotte Amalie, St. Thomas, U.S. Virgin Islands.

doing hard labor since I came to New York . . . never a chance to draw or paint. And then the years of no work at all, when the Depression hit, and I couldn't even afford paint or pencils! Well, Willie, now's your chance.

2   This opportunity has been a long time coming. I'm glad that I kept at this journal all these years. It's a long ride to Canbury, so I'm going to look back over some old entries.

3   Sunday, March 22, 1936
This morning, I read about the controversy surrounding the Harlem Hospital murals. Apparently, Lawrence T. Dermody, the superintendent of Harlem Hospital, rejected four of the seven mural sketches because, he says, they portray too much of the Negro experience. He's worried that that experience may not be relevant twenty-five years from now, and he also thinks some of the subject matter of the murals (everyday life of coloreds) may offend some Negroes. I don't think I agree with Dermody, but I'd have to see the sketches to know for sure. People are protesting Dermody's decision. I'll ask around to see if anyone knows more about those sketches.

4   Thursday, March 26, 1936
I didn't get to see the sketches, but I hear they're of everyday people going about everyday life. My friend James said the protestors are planning on soliciting President Roosevelt's help. I know those murals will get approved now!

5   Sunday, December 19, 1937
Last week, James told me three of the Harlem Hospital murals are finished. So I went to see them today. They are called *Recreation in Harlem*, *Pursuit of Happiness*, and *Modern Surgery and Anesthesia*. They are pictures of my people—people I know from my neighborhood. I have seen these children laughing and playing, I have heard these women chatting in the street, and I have spoken with that old man on the porch. These people are holding on to their history, but they are also looking forward to a better future.

What textual evidence supports the idea that Oliver makes judgments carefully? Record the evidence on the **Cite Textual Evidence Chart**.

Why does Oliver say that the people in the mural are people he knows from his neighborhood?

Why does Oliver feel the need to visit Canbury? Record your analysis and the textual evidence that supports it on the **Cite Textual Evidence Chart**.

What is revealed in this primary source that might be left out in a present-day article on WPA murals? ✎▷

6 Friday, May 20, 1938

I just heard that the project at Harlem Hospital is not the only mural project for artists, that artists have been hired to create murals for hospitals all over New York. Now the FAP is hiring even more artists to create murals on schools and post offices and other buildings, all over the country. What an audience! More people will see these paintings than if they were hanging on the walls of museums.

7 Tuesday, June 14, 1938

I shined shoes today with James because his regular partner, Davis, was sick. Boy, did it feel good to be earning money again. James told me about a new mural at the Canbury Post Office. The government is commissioning artists. Canbury is a ways away from the city, but I want to see what the town is like. I want to meet the people who live there, and I want to learn about the things they do to get inspiration for sketching. This is my chance; I just know it. I have every intention of submitting some drawings for review. I guess I know where that shoe-shining money is going—bus fare to Canbury and art supplies!

Harlem Hospital was the site of several murals painted by FAP artists.

8   Wednesday, June 15, 1938

I wish I could say that I had a plan for the side of that post office from the first minute I set eyes on it, but the truth is that the more I stared at that wall, the more it loomed like a blank canvas before me. So I walked around Canbury and talked with folks who reminded me of the people I've known all my life. At the end of the day, though, I still had no solid ideas. I admit that I'm frustrated. I don't have enough money to travel out there every day, waiting for inspiration to strike me. I'll shine shoes with James in the morning tomorrow and then go back in the afternoon to try again.

9   Friday, June 17, 1938

I can't sleep. I'm too excited, and thoughts are whirling through my head like a tornado, so I'm going to write them down before I forget them. I can't get the image of Lohman Parks out of my head. He's an elderly gentleman I met in Canbury yesterday. He goes to the post office every day for his mail and any local news, and he's been doing that for fifty-five years. He watched me staring at that wall for a while, and then he sidled up and introduced himself, asked me what I was seeing in that wall, without a hint of sarcasm in his voice. When I explained that I wasn't seeing anything yet, but I hoped to see my very own mural there someday, he whistled and offered to walk me around town. He didn't tell me what to paint, just introduced me to the store clerks, the librarians, and the waitresses. Canbury isn't any better off than the rest of the country. Many of the businesses are closed, and some buildings have fallen into disrepair, yet there is something remarkable about Canbury that affected me. I plan to capture Canbury through its people, and Lohman Parks will be my first sketch!

10   Thursday, August 11, 1938

I submitted twenty sketches of the people of Canbury! What I keep hearing about is how many submissions were received and how long it will take the committee to review them all and select a winner. Still, I figure I have as good a shot as anyone of being awarded a commission. I wait on pins and needles. I need this job, but I also want it more than any other job I've ever tried for. Ah, be patient, Willie. It might be a long wait.

How does Lohman Parks help Oliver? Record your analysis and the textual evidence that supports it on the **Cite Textual Evidence Chart**.

How does Lohman Parks serve as a primary source for Oliver?

What can you infer Oliver did between June 17 and August 11? Draw a box around details that support your idea.

How does Oliver feel about the people of Canbury? Record your analysis and the evidence that supports it on the **Cite Textual Evidence Chart**.

How is Oliver's description of Darla different than her description of herself might be?

Interpret

How does the circling hawk image help explain how Oliver feels about the mural job?

11 Monday evening, April 10, 1939
On the bus back from Canbury
I reread some old journal entries on the ride here this morning. What a journey these past three years have been! I'm so grateful that the winding path led me here to be the muralist for the Canbury Post Office. What an honor!

12 Today was a whirlwind. I'm more exhausted than I've been in years, but ironically I'm also more energized than I think I've ever been in my life. Here's what happened: I got to Canbury earlier than my contact from the FAP, so I walked around the main streets to keep warm in the early spring morning. All the while I kept the post office in my sights. I felt like a hawk circling its prey, excitedly soaring above the world, fiercely keeping my goal in sight.

13 Finally, Richard Hawkins from the FAP got off his bus and waved me over. I gathered my supplies and hustled over to the post office, where he was waiting. The wall had already been prepped by some WPA workers, so it was officially time for me to begin my mural. Richard made sure I had everything I needed, and then he went into the post office to remind them of my presence, but I don't think they had forgotten. I'm sure Mr. Lohman Parks has been reminding them each day.

14 I only sketched a few figures on the wall today—Mr. Parks and Darla, that cheerful waitress from the diner I've been talking to at lunch all summer. It will take months before the mural's finished, but I can see it before me in my mind's eye. Like the people of Canbury, it's heartfelt and ordinary. The people of Canbury—like all Americans—are good people pressing on to a brighter future!

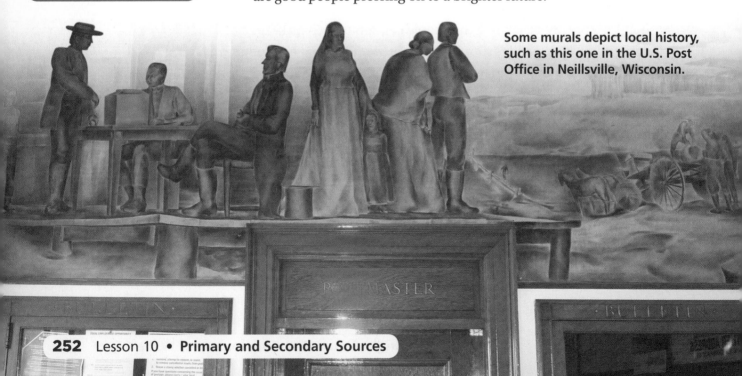

Some murals depict local history, such as this one in the U.S. Post Office in Neillsville, Wisconsin.

Vocabulary: Use Precise Language

To convey ideas effectively, authors must choose their words carefully. Using words that are too general can cause people to miss the intended message. Authors use adjectives and adverbs to make their writing more descriptive. An adjective is a word that describes a noun; for example, in the phrase *the red car*, the word *red* is an adjective used to describe *car*. An adverb is a word that is used to describe a verb. In the sentence *The red car quickly raced down the road*, the word *quickly* is an adverb that describes the verb *raced*. The more descriptive these words are, the clearer your understanding will be about what an author is describing. Authors use descriptive language to bring an event to life so that you can feel as if you are there.

Try It Read this sentence from "A Bright Future."

> All those years doing hard labor since I came to New York . . . never a chance to draw or paint.

Discuss ▸ **What adjective does the writer use in the sentence? What noun does it describe? Think of other adjectives you could use that would have the same effect. Does the meaning change a bit?**

Now, use precise adjectives and adverbs to describe the underlined words below. Your words must make sense in the context of the sentence.

1. People are <u>protesting</u> Dermody's decision. I'll ask around to see if anyone knows more about those <u>sketches</u>. p. 249

   _____

2. More <u>people</u> will see these <u>paintings</u> than if they were hanging on the walls of <u>museums</u>. p. 250

   _____

3. Finally, Richard Hawkins from the FAP got off his bus and <u>waved</u> me over. I gathered my <u>supplies</u> and hustled over to the post office, where he was waiting. p. 252

   _____

Practice the Skill

Chronological order is a method of organization in which actions or events are presented according to time of occurrence, going from first to last. Secondary sources usually use chronological order text structure because it is the simplest way to show how events affected one another. Texts presented in chronological order often include dates or spans of time, such as *three more years*, to mark the occurrence of events or the passage of time. In addition, signal words are used to denote sequence. The words *next, then, after, before, later, until,* and *following* are all used to show the time order of events.

Try It   Read the following paragraph.

Abraham Lincoln is considered by many to be one of America's most important presidents. He was elected in 1860, during a very difficult time for the nation. The country was divided over the issue of slavery. Within months following Lincoln's election, Southern states began seceding from the Union. These states formed the Confederate States of America in February 1861, even before Lincoln was inaugurated on March 4, 1861. Then, only a month later, on April 12, 1861, the War between the States began when Confederate forces fired on Fort Sumter in South Carolina, which was held by Union troops. The war went on for four years, until the South surrendered on April 9, 1865. Then, only days after the surrender, President Lincoln was shot on April 14, 1865. He passed away the following morning.

> **Discuss**   **What are the main events described in the paragraph? Underline the six main events that occur in the paragraph. Then circle dates and signal words that show chronological order.**

As you read, complete the Chronological Order Chart on page 317.

Practice the Skill

Second Read **Secondary Sources**

Secondary sources are just what they sound like; they provide secondhand information in an organized and accessible fashion. An encyclopedia article is a secondary source. Textbooks are secondary sources, and sometimes magazine articles can be as well. Secondary sources are written after the fact by people who were not present when the events being written about occurred. Secondary sources draw on primary sources for information and often include quoted material from primary sources. Primary-source documents provide firsthand information that secondary sources cannot. Secondary sources usually give a broader view of events than primary sources do because they can look at events from a wider perspective and they are written specifically to interpret and clearly present information to the reader.

Try It Read the following paragraph.

> Throughout the nation, thousands of people joined Martin Luther King Jr. by contributing to the civil rights movement. Artists fought for equal rights by producing plays, painting pictures, and writing stories about discrimination and injustice. People everywhere attended peaceful demonstrations such as the March on Washington. At the end of that march, King gave a speech that stirred millions of people around the United States. It is known today as his "I Have a Dream" speech. King dreamed of a nation in which all people were treated equally. He inspired both black and white people with his ideas, as shown in this quotation from that speech: "I have a dream that one day little black boys and girls will be holding hands with little white boys and girls."

> Discuss — **How do you know this selection is a secondary source? What primary source does the author draw on in this secondary source? Draw a box around the name of the primary source.**

As you read, record your answers to questions about analyzing secondary sources on the Close Reading Worksheet on page 318.

Purpose for Reading

Read along with your teacher. Each time, read for a different purpose.

First Read   Focus on chronological order.

Second Read   Focus on analyzing a secondary source.

Third Read   Focus on evaluating the source critically.

Art for America

by Marvin Bloom

Circle words in paragraphs 1 and 2 that signal time order. Describe and record two important events that occurred between 1929 and 1932 on the **Chronological Order Chart.**

What evidence tells you that this selection is a secondary source.

1   After the stock market crash of 1929, the U.S. economy was in turmoil. Banks had closed all over the country. Millions of people had lost their homes and jobs. Many people had lost hope. The 1932 election brought the hope that people were looking for.

2   When Franklin D. Roosevelt was running for president of the United States, he promised to implement a plan that would lift the country out of the Great Depression. "I pledge myself . . . to a new deal for the American people," he said in a speech at the Democratic National Convention in 1932. The American people listened, eager to put their faith in a man who assured them that America would not only survive but also thrive after he took office.

3   Roosevelt vowed that his New Deal would put Americans back to work, and he was true to his word. In 1933, Roosevelt took the oath of office. Within the first hundred days of his presidency, he started one of the most **aggressive** job-creation programs the country had ever seen. He issued a series of executive orders and was able to get Congress to pass every bill that he put before it. By 1935, he had established a government agency called the Works Progress Administration (WPA), which created jobs for nearly eight million people. Roosevelt's New Deal offered opportunities to people in states all over the nation and in many lines of work.

4   Through the WPA, Americans built roads, bridges, parks, schools, libraries, and hospitals all over the country. Roosevelt wanted the government to employ people to rebuild the economy. Then, as the economy improved, those people would find work with private companies.

Franklin D. Roosevelt

5   Roosevelt understood that rebuilding a nation involved more than just physical labor; it also involved the celebration of American spirit and culture. The WPA was an innovative work relief program. It did not provide work for just traditional workers; it hired artists, too. In fact, the WPA is best known today for its cultural arts projects. Never before had artists been offered work by the U.S. government on this scale or with the idea of documenting popular culture.

6   Roosevelt understood the **importance** of the arts to America. Under the umbrella of the WPA, the Federal Theatre Project employed actors, the Federal Music Project employed musicians, and the Federal Writers Project employed writers to write guides to all the states (except Hawaii), as well as many of the nation's major cities and attractions. More than six thousand artists worked in the Federal Art Project (FAP), which established one hundred community art centers. The artists of the FAP created paintings, sculptures, and murals.

7   The goal of the FAP was not just to employ artists. Roosevelt wanted to bring art to the American people. As he said, "Art is not a treasure in the past or an importation from another land, but part of the present life of all living and creating peoples." Ever since the Civil War, up until the Depression, industry and immigration had been booming, and the country was becoming urbanized. Artists had begun turning away from the classic European traditions and toward realism, studying the growing working- and middle-class cultures. This was a perfect setting for the New Deal arts initiatives.

What did Roosevelt do after taking office? Record the events on the **Chronological Order Chart**.

How does the primary-source quotation in paragraph 7 show that this is a secondary source?

How did Roosevelt encourage realism in art?

This mural in the Cohen Building in Washington, D.C., depicts aspects of the American workforce.

Circle the signal words that indicate the steps artists needed to follow to be employed by the FAP.

How does the perspective of the author of this text help identify it as a secondary source?

Why were so many artists' samples rejected?

8   So, through the WPA and the FAP, Roosevelt set his sights on supporting American artistic traditions. He employed artists from different backgrounds who represented the cultural diversity of the nation. He gave African Americans and other minority artists a chance to **succeed**. In fact, Roosevelt issued an executive order to ensure equal opportunities for all workers, including artists. Everyone had a **voice** in America's New Deal, and everyone came to the American experience with a unique point of view.

9   Roosevelt's vision, as implemented by the FAP, was for artists to represent the American experience—to show scenes from the lives of people who were living the American dream. To be considered for the FAP, artists had to follow a specific procedure. First, they had to show the government that they were unemployed and in need of assistance. Then, they had to submit samples of their work. The samples were carefully reviewed, and for a number of different reasons, many were rejected. The artists that were finally admitted into the program had to accept the projects they were assigned and remain true to the program's goals.

10   One goal of the FAP was to send a message to the American people. Most art created during the New Deal showcased the nation's history and emphasized its achievements in agriculture, industry, and science. Roosevelt knew that to rebuild the nation's strength after the Depression, he had to boost the spirits of the people. The struggles of the farmers and the poor conditions in the factories were not the subjects of FAP art. Instead, the artists painted scenes, for example, of early Texas boomtowns. They showed the smiling, happy faces of the people who struck oil; they depicted dances in country barns that brought young and old in the community together. The program was successful because Americans saw themselves in the images the artists created, they saw an America they could believe in, and they saw the land that they loved.

Murals were often painted on federal buildings, such as this mural on the U.S. Courthouse in Trenton, New Jersey.

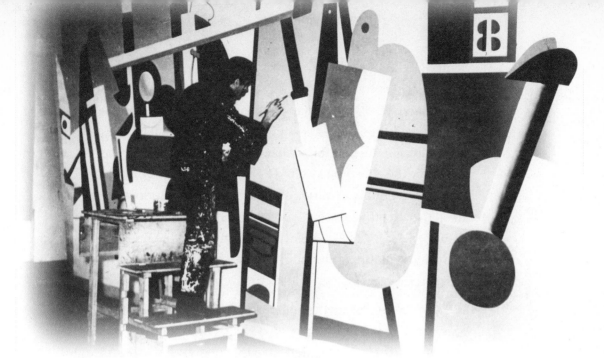

Arshile Gorky, an Armenian immigrant to the United States, was an FAP artist who became famous for his abstract images.

11   While many FAP artists created traditional paintings and sculptures, others created murals on and in public and private buildings in cities all over the country. Artists painted murals on the walls of libraries, schools, hospitals, courthouses, and post offices. Many of these murals celebrated American life and the American worker, while some illustrated stories of the nation's achievements. To tell the story of America's history in flight, an enormous mural was created on the side of a federal administration building. Together, the artists and the FAP spread the idea that Roosevelt's New Deal was working, that Americans could rebuild their own fortunes, and that the country would return to a position of strength. At the time, one artist said, "The project was terribly important. It changed my attitude toward being an artist."

Box the sentence in the text that comes from a primary source.

12   The idea for this nationwide art project was not unprecedented. The Mexican government only a decade earlier had funded its own muralists. In the 1920s, Mexican muralists had created enormous works of art on buildings all over Mexican cities. They had used their art to spread their political ideas to the Mexican people. Many people believed that program had succeeded because it had built national pride. Many of the New Deal artists in the United States went to Mexico to study the art of the Mexican muralists.

13   In a sense, the murals of the New Deal were produced with the same intent as the murals in Mexico. Roosevelt hoped that the art would make Americans feel patriotic and proud.

14   Although the program had its critics, many people felt the FAP was a great success. The program's supporters believed public art brought needed change to the country. It created "art for the millions," as the title of a book of essays by artists of the time styled it. And that was the goal of the program—to make art accessible to everyone, not simply the elite. Roosevelt's FAP made America a producer of art and a consumer of art, it took culture out of the galleries and put it out on the streets where everyone could see it, and it supported the creation of a body of American art. Still, by 1943, the program was over. Involvement in the war in Europe created jobs for Americans, ending the Depression and, along with it, the Depression-era jobs programs.

15   The work produced through the FAP displayed a wealth of ideas. Sadly, many of the works produced by this program have been lost. Of 2,500 murals that were created, at least a quarter have disappeared, having been lost, destroyed, or damaged over the years—some were simply painted over.

16   The legacy of the Federal Art Project lies not solely in the art itself, however. It lies in the development of art awareness in the American people and the jump start it gave to many artists' careers. Some of the best-known artists of the twentieth century got their start through the FAP. Jackson Pollock, for example, left the FAP during its **decline** in 1942 and later became a **leader** in the abstract art movement. More than anything else, though, the FAP helped put American art on the cultural map.

This is a city street scene.

Vocabulary: Connotation and Denotation

The **denotation** of a word is the definition you find in a dictionary. Words also have **connotations**, or emotional meanings, associated with them. Connotations can be positive, negative, or neutral. The words *compose*, *write*, and *scribble* all have a similar denotation: "to write something down." *Compose* has a positive connotation, *write* has a neutral connotation, and *scribble* has a negative connotation. Good writers choose words based on their emotional as well as their literal meanings. Careful word choice helps writers convey tone and get across their point of view.

Try It Read the following sentence from the selection.

> Jackson Pollock, for example, left the FAP during its **decline** [weakening, decay] in 1942 and later became a **leader** [top dog, boss] in the abstract art movement.

> Discuss

Look at the boldfaced words and the words beside them in brackets. Are the words in brackets more negative, positive, or neutral?

Read these sentences from the selection. Answer the questions that follow.

1. . . . he started one of the most <u>aggressive</u> [forceful, determined] job-creation programs the country had ever seen. p. 256

   Which word in brackets has a negative connotation? Which has a neutral connotation?

   _____

2. Roosevelt understood the <u>importance</u> [value, significance, meaning] of the arts to America. p. 257

   Which word in brackets has a neutral connotation? Which word has about the same connotation as *importance*?

   _____

Respond to Text: Analyze Primary and Secondary Sources

When writing a research paper about topics on academic subjects, you can cover the topic much more thoroughly if you use information from both primary and secondary sources. Using both allows you to fully understand and analyze a topic.

Try It Read this excerpt from a book about Marie Curie.

> Marie Curie did important scientific work throughout much of her life. She is perhaps most remembered for discovering the chemical element radium. In 1903, Curie, her husband Pierre Curie, and scientist Henri Becquerel received the Nobel Prize in Physics, and in 1911 she received a second Nobel Prize—this one in chemistry.

Discuss **What kind of primary-source information could be added to this paragraph to give readers more information about or insight into Marie Curie?**

On Your Own Write a paragraph that analyzes the two selections you just read. How is the primary-source journal different from the secondary-source selection? Analyze how "A Bright Future" contributes to your appreciation of the topic in ways that "Art for America" can't, and discuss how the breadth of "Art for America" helped put Oliver's journal account into historical context. Use the guide on the next page to organize your response. Then write your paragraph on a separate sheet of paper.

Checklist for a Good Response

A good paragraph

✔ provides a topic sentence that describes the two selections.

✔ analyzes the kind of information each source presents.

✔ analyzes how the information is presented in each selection.

✔ organizes the information in a logical way.

My Analysis of the Sources

1. **Topic Sentence** "A Bright Future" is a primary source and "Art for America"

   is a secondary source about _____.

2. **Detail Sentences** Use the chart to organize ideas for your detail sentences.

Element	Primary Source	Secondary Source
perspective		
what the source contributes to my experience		

   The breadth of "Art for America" helps put Oliver's journal account into

   historical context by _____

   _____

3. **Concluding Sentence** Your concluding sentence should restate and sum up
   the differences between the two selections with a fresh twist.

   _____

   _____

On a separate sheet of paper, write your paragraph.

Read on Your Own

Read the letter and article independently three times, using the skills you have learned. Then answer the Comprehension Check questions.

First Read Practice the first-read skills you learned in this lesson.

Second Read Practice the second-read skills you learned in this lesson.

Third Read Think critically about the ideas in the letter and the article.

Two Accounts of the Apollo 11 Moon Landing

Excerpt from a personal letter

July 20, 1969

Dear Ana,

Cite Textual Evidence <u>Underline</u> the parts of the text that demonstrate people's fascination with the moon landing. Two examples have been done for you.

Primary Sources Think about the primary-source information related to the moon landing this letter provides.

Critical Thinking Think about whether this letter is a reliable source to use for a research paper. Why or why not?

1   It's 9:00 a.m. here—which means I guess it's 6:00 p.m. in Sweden. See? I remembered that you're nine hours ahead of us, so you must be getting ready for dinner, and I just finished breakfast.

2   When I woke up this morning, the first thing I thought was that it was going to be an ordinary day—but then I remembered that <u>something is going to happen tonight that will make it extraordinary, if it happens—the very first moon landing!</u> I've been kind of sick of hearing about it, actually, even though I know it's a huge deal. Well, I guess I'll believe it when I see it—and if it does happen, you better believe I'll see it! My parents are having a party for everyone to watch together. <u>It's like the whole world is going to come to a standstill when that spaceship lands on the moon tonight.</u> I can't wait to see it, too, actually. I guess you're probably going to watch it there in Sweden. Are you? I think the whole world will be watching.

3   My parents invited all the neighbors, including a guy who used to work for NASA. He must be very excited, and I know my mom said everyone will want to ask him questions.

4   My parents are having this party because we have a big new color television. I know the Lannigans next door only have a small black and white set, but I suppose they won't be broadcasting in color from the moon—or will they? I don't know!

5   OK, it's 6:30 and I'm back. Things are so exciting now, finally, after nothing happening for the longest time. We were tuned to CBS with Walter Cronkite, and we'd been hearing the same things all day. Then, finally, around 4:30, the newscaster made the announcement, "The *Eagle* has landed." Did you know that the lunar module was called the *Eagle*? I've been learning a lot about the Apollo mission. Anyway, so the *Eagle* landed, but that was two hours ago! I'm going back downstairs to watch and wait some more.

6   Oh my gosh! Ana, did you see it? I can't believe how exciting it was. I know the constant news coverage was pretty tedious, but Neil Armstrong actually walked on the moon, and so did Buzz Aldrin. I felt sorry for Michael Collins, though—the astronaut who was **stuck** in the command module. How hard it must have been to be so close to the moon but not be able to touch it! But just think of it, Ana—we landed on the moon!

Your pen pal,
Maria

Cite Textual Evidence
Which part of the letter best expresses how exciting the moon landing was at the time? Double underline it.

Chronological Order
Think about how the letter writer organized her ideas and why she did so.

Critical Thinking Think about how this letter helps you understand the importance of the moon landing.

People all over the world gathered around television sets to watch the first moon landing.

Apollo 11 Moon Landing— Forty Years Later

Cite Textual Evidence
Underline the sentences from the text that best support the idea that Kennedy's speech was influential. The first one has been done for you.

Secondary Sources
Think about how you know this article is a secondary source.

Critical Thinking
Think about what the text implies about the relationship between the United States and the Soviet Union.

1   <u>In 1961, President John F. Kennedy gave a speech to Congress that changed the course of history.</u> In his speech, he explained that the Soviet Union was making achievements in science and technology, while the United States was falling behind. The president stressed the significance of making scientific advancements that would become necessary for human progress. To achieve that goal, he challenged Americans to put a man on the moon by the end of the 1960s.

2   In 1969, with the Apollo 11 mission, his challenge was met, although sadly, he did not live to see it. On July 20 of that year, American astronauts walked on the moon. At the time, the Apollo moon landing was the event of the century. It demonstrated America's ability to excel in science and engineering. It also opened up a world of opportunity for all humanity to explore outer space.

3   Americans accepted President Kennedy's challenge eagerly. In the years following his speech, scientists at NASA built a spaceship that would take astronauts to the moon and back. The spaceship consisted of two parts. It had a command module that would carry the astronauts into the moon's orbit. The second part was a lunar module with an engine that was capable of landing on and taking off from the moon's surface. The lunar module was equipped with legs that could support the vehicle on the moon's soil. It had a special storage compartment that held the scientific equipment the astronauts would need to conduct experiments. The lunar module also had a camera that would broadcast live coverage of the event.

4   People all over the world gathered in living rooms in front of their televisions on the night of July 20, 1969. It is estimated that 600 million people viewed the coverage. The programming continued for hours. People were spellbound.

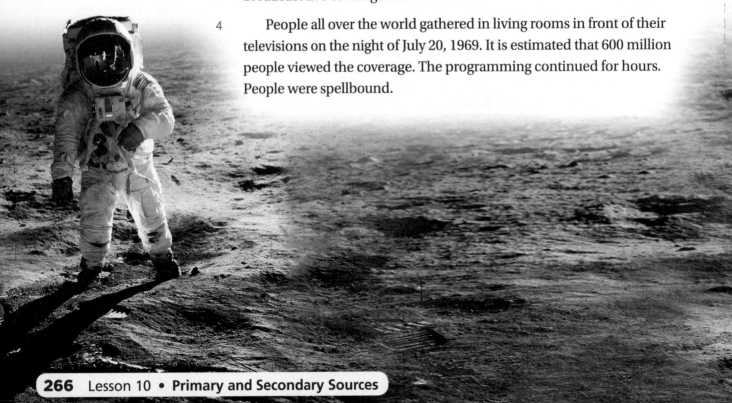

5   As millions watched, at approximately 1:46 p.m. Eastern Daylight Time, the lunar module (called the *Eagle*) separated from the command module and started its descent to the surface of the moon. It touched down on an area of the moon called the Sea of Tranquility. At 4:17, NASA astronaut Neil Armstrong radioed a message to Mission Control in Houston: "The *Eagle* has landed." Cheers broke out in the Mission Control room and around the world.

6   Americans watched in awe as Armstrong climbed down the ladder of the lunar module and stepped onto the surface of the moon. As he stepped onto the lunar soil, he uttered what has become one of the most famous phrases in history: "That's one small step for man, one giant leap for mankind."

7   While three astronauts went on the Apollo 11 mission, only two of them walked on the moon. Nineteen minutes after Armstrong took his first step, Buzz Aldrin climbed down and joined him on the moon's surface. Michael Collins remained in the command module. He was the CMP, or command module pilot, in charge of communications.

8   Armstrong and Aldrin stayed on the moon for two and a half hours. Each of them wore a special space suit that contained a portable life-support system that controlled oxygen, temperature, and pressure. The space suits enabled the astronauts to survive in the moon's atmosphere and its gravity, which is one-sixth that of Earth's.

Chronological Order
Circle words that help you identify the order of events.

Secondary Sources
Think about what this secondary source tells us about why Collins stayed in the command module that the primary source account cannot.

Secondary Sources
Draw a box around what can be cited as primary-source information.

Critical Thinking Some people consider the flag and plaques on the moon to be litter. Think about how the space program could be more responsible about littering.

9   While the astronauts were on the moon, they set up some scientific instruments that would continue to take measurements after they left. One experiment was to determine the distance between Earth and the moon. They set up another instrument used to measure moonquakes. They also collected samples of soil and rock, using scoops and tongs attached to extension handles. The two astronauts took photos of the landing site. They planted a U.S. flag on the moon and spoke with President Richard Nixon directly from the lunar surface.

10   Several hours later, the lunar module lifted off into outer space and traveled back to the command module. The astronauts said good-bye to the moon. Days later, the command module splashed down in the Pacific Ocean, and the astronauts were welcomed home as heroes and celebrities. They were formally honored by the president and celebrated throughout the world.

11   The American flag still flies on the moon today as a symbol of American achievement. A plaque remains there, too, left by the Apollo astronauts. It reads: "Here men from the planet Earth first set foot upon the moon July 1969, A.D. We came in peace for all mankind." Subsequent Apollo missions to the moon also left plaques behind. There are six altogether.

12   Five more manned missions to the moon ended in successful landings. Then the moon-landing program lost momentum and faded in significance. Attention shifted to other kinds of space exploration. After the Apollo 17 mission in 1972, no one has ever returned to the moon—not yet, that is. Scientists still dream of the opportunities that might exist for humans in space. They dream of someday colonizing the moon and perhaps traveling to other planets and other galaxies in the dark reaches of the universe. With the change during this century from government-funded to privately funded space programs, civilians might soon be traveling to the moon on commercial spacecraft.

✓ Comprehension Check

1. In what unique ways would each of these documents be useful for writing a research paper? What kind of insight do readers gain from each?

_____

_____

_____

2. What type of information is revealed in the letter that is not available in the article?

_____

_____

3. List three major events that led up to Armstrong walking on the moon as described in "Apollo 11 Moon Landing—Forty Years Later."

_____

_____

_____

4. What other kinds of primary-source materials would be useful for writing a research paper about the moon landing?

_____

_____

_____

5. Cite textual evidence in "Apollo 11 Moon Landing—Forty Years Later" that supports the idea that President Kennedy's speech affected scientific advancement in the United States.

_____

_____

6. People gathered in private homes, community centers, and other public spaces around the world to watch the moon landing. Why did people want to get together with a crowd to watch the event?

_____

_____

7. Read this sentence from the selection.

   People all over the world gathered in living rooms in front of their televisions on the night of July 20, 1969.

   How could the sentence be rewritten to include more precise language?

_____

_____

8. Read this sentence from the selection.

   I felt sorry for Michael Collins, though—the astronaut who was stuck in the command module.

   What is the connotation of *stuck*? Think of a word or phrase that would have a more neutral connotation to substitute for *stuck*, and then use it in a sentence.

_____

_____

Glossary

act a division of drama composed of one or more scenes, during which the time or place or characters on stage may change (Lesson 3)

affix a prefix or suffix that is added to a base word to create a new word (Lesson 8)

alliteration the repetition of initial consonant sounds in words (Lesson 4)

allusion a reference to well-known, real or literary characters or situations that have come to represent an idea; for example, "sour grapes" is an allusion to a fable by Aesop (Lesson 7)

analyze arguments to determine what sorts of appeals and techniques are being used by the author of a persuasive text, such as loaded language, exaggeration, bandwagon appeals, snob appeal, and humor (Lesson 7)

analyze interactions to determine the relationships between ideas or things (Lesson 5)

antonyms words that have opposite or nearly opposite meanings (Lessons 3, 7)

assonance the repetition of similar vowel sounds within words (Lesson 4)

author's point of view a writer's opinion on a topic, as expressed in an argument or a set of claims made about the topic (Lesson 7)

bandwagon appeal a persuasive technique that encourages the reader to join a supposed majority in a single point of view (Lesson 7)

base word the simplest form of a word that conveys its meaning (Lesson 8)

cause something that makes something else happen (Lesson 3)

cause and effect a relationship between words, events, or ideas in which one thing leads to another (Lesson 3)

central idea the most important concept an author wants to convey (Lessons 5, 8)

characters the people or animals that take part in a story or drama (Lesson 3)

chronological order a method of text organization in which actions or events are presented according to time of occurrence, going from first to last (Lesson 10)

cite textual evidence to identify details from the information an author provides to support an analysis of a text (Lessons 3, 10)

claim a statement an author makes in a nonfiction text (Lesson 8)

compare and contrast to identify how two things are the same, how they are different, and how they relate to each other (Lessons 2, 7)

connotation the positive, neutral, or negative emotional association that a word carries (Lessons 4, 10)

context clues hints within a sentence or paragraph that can help you understand the meaning of an unknown word. Context clues fall into several categories, such as example, explanation, description, antonym, and synonym. (Lessons 1, 2, 4)

denotation the dictionary definition of a word (Lessons 4, 10)

diagram an illustration that makes an idea, object, or process easier to understand, usually including text in the form of labels or ordered steps (Lesson 6)

dialogue tags information that tells you who is speaking in a drama (Lesson 3)

dictionary a reference source that contains an alphabetized list of words and their meanings, pronunciations, and parts of speech (Lessons 5, 9)

domain-specific vocabulary specialized words and phrases that are commonly used by people who work or study in a particular field (Lessons 5, 6, 9)

drama a story made up of acts and scenes that is performed by actors on a stage, primarily told through the characters' dialogue (Lesson 3)

dramatic structure the way a writer shapes what happens in a drama, usually by dividing it into acts, with one or more scenes in each act that move the plot along and indicate a change in place, time, or the characters on stage (Lesson 3)

draw inferences to figure out what an author implies but does not state directly, using clues from the text and your own knowledge (Lessons 1, 9)

effect something that happens as the result of a cause (Lesson 3)

evaluate evidence and claims to identify the statements an author makes and evaluate whether they are valid or reliable, based on evidence in the text and previous knowledge (Lesson 8)

evidence the facts an author provides to support his or her claims or opinions (Lessons 8, 9)

exaggeration the overstatement of facts beyond what is reasonable or strictly true; sometimes used as a persuasive technique (Lesson 7)

fables stories that teach a lesson, usually using animal characters that behave and talk like humans (Lesson 1)

facts data, details, statistics, dates, or accounts that can be proved true (Lessons 5, 7)

figurative language a descriptive word or phrase that means something other than its literal definition (Lessons 1, 7, 8)

first-person point of view a story perspective in which the narrator is a character who tells the story using the pronouns *I*, *me*, *us*, or *we* (Lessons 1, 2)

folktales timeless, placeless stories that can be reworked slightly to fit a specific culture's needs and that involve universal themes (Lesson 1)

glossary a collection of specialized terms and their meanings listed alphabetically at the end of an informational work (Lesson 9)

Greek and Latin roots basic word parts that have been borrowed from one or the other of these languages (Lesson 3)

historical fiction stories and novels set in a specific time period, with historical settings and characters that may be fictional or real (Lesson 2)

historical text a form of informational writing that focuses on real people and events of the past (Lesson 9)

humor the use of sarcasm or coaxing joking as a persuasive technique; its lightness can make an unsound idea easier to swallow (Lesson 7)

idiom an expression whose meaning can't be understood from the words alone, such as "She cracks me up." (Lesson 8)

illustration visual that shows how something looks or how a thing is done (Lesson 6)

literary nonfiction a genre of nonfiction writing in which literary techniques are used to convey factual information in an interesting way; may include biography, food writing, journalism, memoir, personal essay, and travel writing (Lesson 8)

loaded language strong, emotionally charged language used to frighten, anger, or flatter the reader of a persuasive text (Lesson 7)

metaphor a form of figurative language that compares two unlike things without using the word *like* or *as* (Lessons 1, 8)

multiple-meaning words words and phrases that have more than one meaning (Lesson 6)

myths legendary stories involving the heroes or gods of a particular culture (Lesson 1)

narrative poem a poem that tells a story and has a plot, setting, and characters (Lesson 4)

narrative point of view the perspective from which a story is told, usually first person or third person (Lessons 1, 2)

opinion an expression of feeling, belief, or taste that cannot be proved true or untrue (Lesson 7)

paraphrase to use your own words to restate a text (Lesson 4)

personification a form of figurative language that assigns human attributes and characteristics to nonhuman things, often to aspects of the natural world (Lessons 1, 8)

persuasive nonfiction writing that seeks to convince readers of a particular point of view or to behave in a particular way (Lesson 7)

plot the series of events that make up a story, including the conflict characters face and the events through which they resolve the conflict (Lesson 3)

poetry literary writing that is separated into lines and often stanzas in which a poet uses descriptive language and sound devices, such as rhyme and rhythm, to create meaning and evoke emotion in the reader (Lesson 4)

point of view the viewpoint from which a story is told; the attitude, perspectives, and outlooks that different characters have in a story (Lesson 1)

precise language carefully selected adjectives and adverbs writers use to make their writing more descriptive and clear (Lesson 10)

prefix a group of letters added to the beginning of a base word that creates a new word (Lesson 8)

primary sources firsthand accounts of authors who were present at the time particular events happened; may include personal diaries, travel journals, letters, memoirs, and speeches (Lesson 10)

pronunciation guide a part of a dictionary entry that displays special symbols that are used to show how a word is pronounced (Lesson 5)

reasoned judgment a logical, well-expressed reason for adopting a particular view that is supported by facts and appeals to common sense (Lessons 5, 7)

redundancy the repetition of the same words or ideas when there is no need to do so (Lesson 2)

rhyme a poetic device involving the repetition of sounds at the ends of words in a line of poetry; the pattern of those sounds is the rhyme scheme (Lesson 4)

scan to read by moving your eyes quickly down a page, looking for specific information (Lesson 6)

scene a division of drama within an act that moves the plot along (Lesson 3)

scientific text a text that provides factual information about a topic related to science, found in a magazine, newspaper, book, or on a Web site (Lesson 5)

secondary sources texts that are written after an event occurs and often rely on information found in primary sources; may include encyclopedia articles, textbooks, and news reports (Lesson 10)

setting the time, place, and circumstances in which a story occurs (Lesson 3)

simile a form of figurative language that compares two unlike things using the word *like* or *as* (Lessons 1, 8)

skim to read a passage quickly to get an overview of the main ideas in the text (Lesson 6)

snob appeal a persuasive technique in which the author implies that a certain way of thinking is more sophisticated or intelligent than another (Lesson 7)

soliloquy a speech given by a character alone on stage in which the character directly addresses the audience and reveals his or her inner thoughts and feelings (Lesson 3)

sonnet a poem that is commonly fourteen lines long, often with an eight-line section that describes a situation or problem, followed by a six-line section that builds on it or adds a new thought (Lesson 4)

speculation an opinion or educated guess on an issue made without established facts that support it (Lesson 5)

stage directions the instructions in a drama that indicate how characters should speak, react, and move on stage; stage directions include setting and time period (Lesson 3)

steps in a process the order in which a series of things must be done; often an important feature of a technical or historical text (Lessons 6, 9)

suffix a group of letters added to the end of a base word that creates a new word (Lesson 8)

summarize to restate briefly the main ideas and most important details of a text in your own words (Lessons 1, 5, 8)

support inferences to find clues and evidence in a text to support your ideas about what an author means but does not directly state (Lessons 1, 9)

supporting details facts and information that support the central idea of a text (Lessons 5, 8)

synonyms words that have the same or nearly the same meaning (Lessons 1, 3, 7)

technical text a text that explains how things work or how to do things (Lesson 6)

text structure the way an author arranges ideas in a text to help readers more easily understand what they are reading, such as description and compare and contrast (Lesson 6)

textual evidence facts and details in a text that support the reader's analysis of it (Lessons 3, 10)

theme the central idea that an author wants to convey by telling a story, usually a general idea about life, society, or human nature; theme is usually not directly stated (Lesson 2)

thesaurus a book or list of words that includes their synonyms and antonyms (Lesson 1)

third-person-limited point of view the story perspective in which an outside narrator has access to the thoughts, feelings, and memories of just the main character (Lesson 2)

third-person-omniscient point of view the story perspective in which an outside narrator knows everything and has access to what every character says, does, thinks, and feels (Lesson 2)

third-person point of view the story perspective in which an outside narrator, who uses the pronouns *he*, *she*, and *they*, tells the story and describes the events (Lessons 1, 2)

time line a visual representation that clearly displays the order in which events occurred over time (Lesson 6)

tone the attitude an author takes toward a selection's topic (Lesson 9)

traditional literature stories such as folktales, myths, and fables that have been handed down from one generation to the next (Lesson 1)

visual information ideas presented in graphic form, such as charts, time lines, photos, and illustrations (Lessons 6, 9)

visualize to form a mental image inside your head (Lesson 4)

word choice the selection of words an author uses to convey and develop a work's tone (Lesson 9)

word relationships the manner in which a word relates to other words and sentences close by, including synonyms, antonyms, part to whole, cause and effect, item and category (Lesson 7)

wordiness using more words than necessary when speaking or writing or using more complicated words or phrases than called for (Lesson 2)

Acknowledgments

Photo Credits 193 Getty Images; 31, 48, 206, 217, 232, 249, 256–258, 260 Library of Congress; 265 NARA; 267 NASA; 126, 127 NOAA Photo Library; 198 Shutterstock; 59, 87, 91, 113, 120, 129, 139, 153, 155, 156, 167, 170, 171, 174, 179, 180, 182, 187, 188, 190, 197, 204, 205, 213, 214, 224, 226, 231, 242, 245 Thinkstock; 135 usa.gov; 5, 172, 233, 234, 250, 252, 259, 266 Wikimedia Commons.

Illustrations 9–12, 90 Brock Nicol; 43, 44, 46, 56 Calista Ward; 100 Christine Chang; 63–66, 71, 72, 75 France Brassard; 101 Fred Willingham; 25–28 Giorgio Bacchin; 110 Ian Escott; 97, 98 Jeremy Tugeau; 81–84 Jim Eldridge; 107–109 Jim Madsen; 102 Patrick Gnan; 47, 53, 117–119, 125, 133, 142–148, 154, 208 Pete Bull; 92 Shawna JC Tenney; 35–38 Stacy Budnick; 16–20 Stephan Daigle; 141, 161–164, 218, 222, 239 XNR Productions.

Name: _____

Draw and Support Inferences Chart

Inference	Supporting Details from Text
Page 8: I can infer that Fritz feels chopping firewood is	
Page 9: I can infer from Fritz's special care of the sheep that	
Page 10: I can infer from Fritz's mother's scolding that	

Name: _____

✏️ Close Reading Worksheet

Second Read: Point of View (green boxes)

Page 8: The point of view of the story is _____.

I can tell because _____.

Page 11: The mother's point of view about life is _____

_____.

The behavior and dialogue that reveal her point of view are _____

_____

_____.

Page 12: The effect the wolf attack has on Fritz's point of view about his future is

_____.

Third Read: Critical Thinking (blue boxes)

Page 9: A quality Fritz displays that is shared the world over and makes this a folktale

is _____

_____.

Page 10: The wool from other sheep is less nice than that of Fritz's sheep because

_____

_____

Page 12: Fritz is more successful with his chickens because _____

_____

Identify—Page 12: The lesson that this story teaches is _____

_____.

The Boy Who Dreamed Too Much

Name: _____

Summarizing Chart

Page 16: Identify details about the jackal's character, and write them in a summary.	
Page 17: Summarize what has happened in the story so far.	
Page 18: What is Kakudruma's one fear?	
Page 19: Summarize the important plot points on this page.	
My Summary	

Name: _____

✏️ Close Reading Worksheet

Second Read: Figurative Language (green boxes)

Page 16: An example of personification is _____

_____.

Page 18: This example of personification means that _____

_____

_____.

Page 19: The simile in paragraph 27 means _____

_____.

Page 20: The metaphor in paragraph 40 is _____.

It means _____.

Third Read: Critical Thinking (blue boxes)

Page 17: Kakudruma's plan could fail if _____

_____.

Page 20: The jackal's trick angered the other animals because _____

_____

_____.

Identify—Page 20: The things that identify this story as a fable are _____

_____.

Narrative Point of View Chart

Question	Evidence and Analysis
Page 34: From what point of view is the story being told?	
Page 35: Which line suggests the narrator sees what Feyvl does? Which suggests the narrator has access to Feyvl's thoughts?	**What Feyvl sees:** **What Feyvl thinks:**
Page 36: What does Zippora think about the new spice boxes? What does this information tell about the narrator?	
Page 38: What is revealed about the narrator toward the end of the story?	

The point of view in "The Collector" is _____.

Name: _____

✏️ Close Reading Worksheet

Second Read: Determine Theme (green boxes)

Page 36: Fevyl is becoming _____

_____ .

Page 37: Feyvl's character is becoming _____

_____ .

Page 38: The theme of the story is _____

_____

_____ .

Third Read: Critical Thinking (blue boxes)

Page 34: The clues that tell me the story is set in the past are _____

_____ .

Page 36: Many Eastern Europeans probably came to the United States because

_____

_____ .

Page 37: The spice box collection represents _____

_____ .

Page 38—Analyze: In the end, the Kluger Collection (did / did not) have value because

_____

_____ .

Name: _____

Venn Diagram

page 42:

Shelby's mother   Uncle Terry

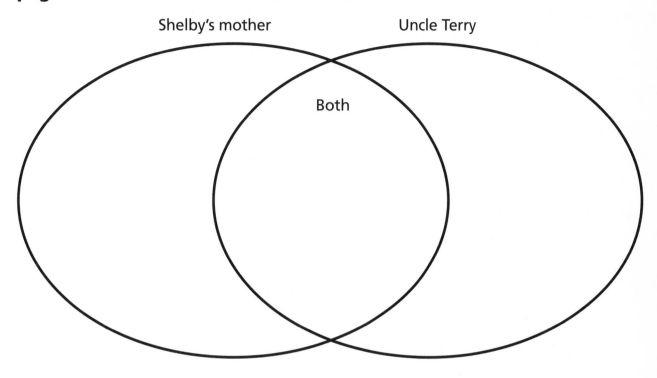

Both

page 47:

Shelby   Laura

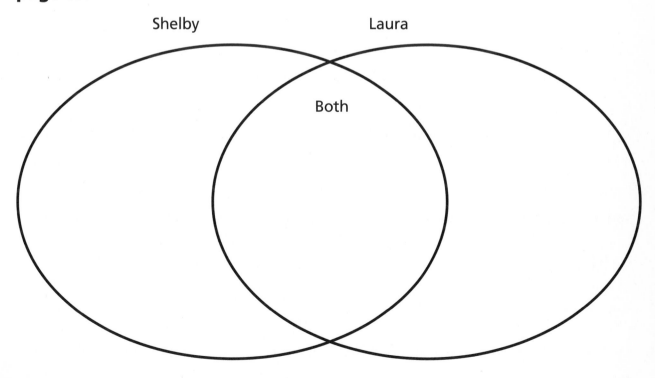

Both

Name: _____

✏️ Close Reading Worksheet

Second Read: Historical Fiction (green boxes)

Page 42: The aspects of setting that are crucial are _____

_____.

Page 44: The author uses the character of Shelby to _____

_____.

Page 48: The fact that this is a primary account tells you _____

_____

_____.

Third Read: Critical Thinking (blue boxes)

Page 43: The assumption Shelby makes is _____

_____.

Page 44: The author is _____

_____.

Page 46: Shelby resolves to do this because _____

_____.

Page 48—Connect: The backgrounds of Shelby and Laura are similar and important

because _____

_____.

The Summer Things Fell Apart . . .

Name: _____

Cause-and-Effect Chart

page	Cause	Effect
62		
63	Noise of the car engine	
64		Parents find a project to occupy Abby.
65		
66		

Name: _____

✏️ Close Reading Worksheet

Page 62: This scene is set in _____ in _____.

I can tell because _____.

Page 64: Thomas feels _____. Laura feels _____.

Page 66: I know this is a soliloquy because _____

_____

_____.

Third Read: Critical Thinking (blue boxes)

Page 63: The effect of Thomas Gooden's words is that _____

_____

_____.

Page 65: The costumes play a role because _____

_____

_____.

Interpret—Page 66: Abigail is excited by the soda fountain because _____

_____

_____

_____.

Name: _____

Cite Textual Evidence Chart

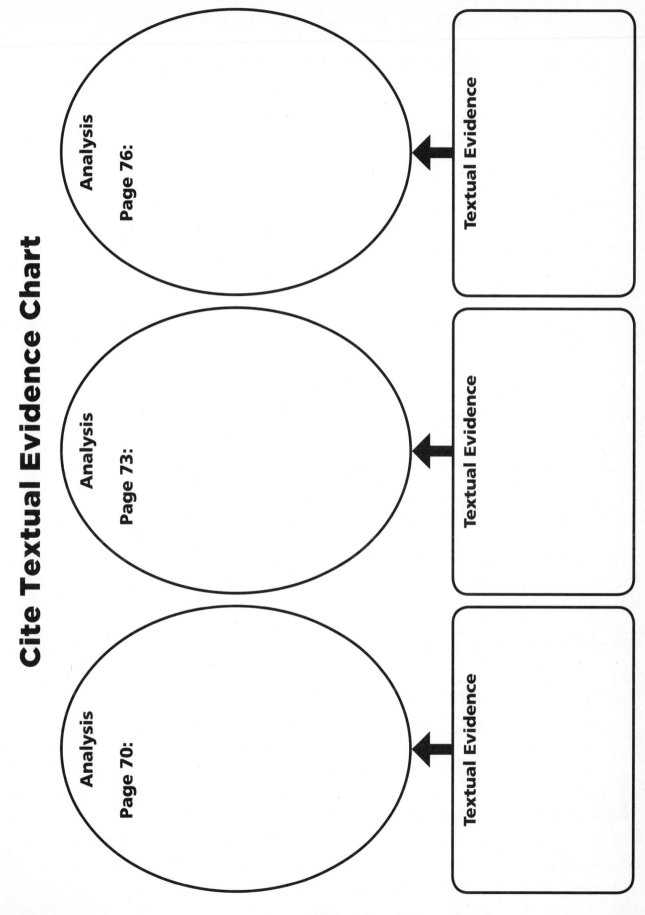

Analysis

Page 76:

Textual Evidence

Analysis

Page 73:

Textual Evidence

Analysis

Page 70:

Textual Evidence

Name: _____

✏️ Close Reading Worksheet

Page 70: What the setting reveals about Abigail's character is _____

_____.

Page 71: The conflict is _____

_____.

Page 73: The cave impacts Robbie and Abigail because _____

_____

_____.

Page 76: The setting reflects Abigail's character in the final scene because _____

_____

_____.

Page 72: Abigail knows Robbie is afraid because _____

_____.

Page 74: The descent into the caverns is a high point for Abigail because _____

_____.

Page 75: Laura's words support what I have learned about Abigail by _____

_____.

Judge—Page 76: Abigail's change (will / will not) be permanent because _____

_____.

Visualization Chart

The Lake Isle of Innisfree, p. 90

I wandered lonely as a cloud, p. 91

The Cat and the Moon, p. 92

Name: _____

✏️ Close Reading Worksheet

Second Read: Rhyme, Alliteration, and Assonance (green boxes)

Page 90: The rhymes in "The Lake Isle of Innisfree" _____

_____.

Page 91: The rhyming couplets in "I wandered lonely as a cloud" are located in

_____.

Third Read: Critical Thinking (blue boxes)

Page 90: The location of the speaker is _____

_____.

Page 91: The speakers' memories are similar because _____

_____

_____.

Page 92: Both the cat and the moon _____

_____

_____.

Judge—Page 92: Of these three poems, the one with the most powerful visual images

is _____

_____

_____

_____.

The Lake Isle of Innisfree . . .

Name: _____

Paraphrase Chart

	My Paraphrase
Page 96: The Ballad of King Arthur, stanza 1	
Page 97: The Ballad of King Arthur, lines 24–26	
Page 99: Annabel Lee, lines 21 and 22	
Page 100: Annabel Lee, lines 30–33	
Page 101: Shall I compare thee to a summer's day?, lines 13 and 14	
Page 102: The Oven Bird, lines 6–9	

Name: _____

✏️ Close Reading Worksheet

Second Read: Poetic Structure (green boxes)

Page 96: The dialogue in these verses_____

_____.

Page 97: This ballad would be easy to sing to music because _____

_____.

Page 101: This is a sonnet because it has _____

_____.

Third Read: Critical Thinking (blue boxes)

Page 98: The knights lose their temper because _____

_____.

Page 100: The effect of the final stanza is _____

_____.

Page 101: The speaker compares his beloved to a summer's day _____

_____

and _____.

Compare—Page 102: The poems' treatments of things are similar because _____

_____

and different because _____

_____.

The Ballad of King Arthur . . .

Name: _____

Central Idea and Details Chart

Central Idea	Supporting Details
Page 116:	
Page 117: Platypuses are among the oddest animals on the planet.	
Page 118:	
Page 119: Platypuses are unique animals.	
Page 120:	

Name: _____

✏️ Close Reading Worksheet

Second Read: Analyze Interactions (green boxes)

Page 116: At the time, scientists believed that _____

_____.

Page 118: Human settlement has affected the platypus by _____

_____

_____.

Page 119: The reproductive characteristics that might have confused scientists are _____

_____.

Third Read: Critical Thinking (blue boxes)

Page 117: Spotting a platypus in the wild is rare because _____

_____

_____.

Page 120: Australians might have adopted the platypus as an icon because _____

_____.

Analyze—Page 120: The discovery of the platypus changed the way scientists view the

animal world because _____

_____

_____

_____.

Name: _____

✏️ Close Reading Worksheet

First Read: Summarize (orange boxes)

Page 124: The main idea of the first page is that _____

_____

_____ .

Page 125: Hydrothermal vents are formed when _____

_____ .

Page 127: The symbiotic relationship between tubeworms and bacteria is _____

_____ .

Third Read: Critical Thinking (blue boxes)

Page 125: The physical property is _____, and its effects are _____

_____ .

Page 126: The two factors are likely _____

_____ .

Page 127: Some of the earliest life-forms may have been _____

_____ because _____

_____ .

Connect—Page 128: The discovery of deep-sea vents and life around them connects the

sciences in that _____

_____

_____ .

Name: _____

Facts, Reasoned Judgments, and Speculation Chart

	Fact	Judgment Based on Research	Speculation
Page 124			
Page 126			
Page 128			

Discovering Deep-Sea Vents

Name: _____

Process Chart

STEP 1	Ball manufacturers must first decide

↓

STEP 2	

↓

STEP 3	

↓

STEP 4	

↓

STEP 5	

↓

STEP 6	Before the last stitches are sewn,

↓

STEP 7	After the stitcher closes the final seam,

↓

STEP 8	

Name: _____

✏️ Close Reading Worksheet

Second Read: Integrate Visual Information (green boxes)

Page 145: The diagram shows that the cooling water _____

_____.

Page 146: The pattern in the diagram works with the text to show _____

_____.

Third Read: Critical Thinking (blue boxes)

Page 142: FIFA might introduce an official World Cup ball every four years because

_____

_____.

Page 143: Hand-sewn soccer balls are the most expensive because _____

_____.

Page 144: A heavy, wet leather ball could lead to injury because _____

_____.

Page 147: FIFA has international rules for soccer balls because _____

_____.

Analyze—Page 148: The ball could be called "the chameleon of soccer balls" because

_____

_____.

Name: _____

Skim and Scan Chart

Skim	Important Information
p. 152	Main idea:
p. 156	The subhead "Follow the Directions" tells me: Skimming the paragraphs tells me:

Scan	Important Information
p. 153	The subhead "Best Dressed" tells me: The boldface words *insulator*, *thermal insulation*, and *moisture permeation* tell me:
p. 155	microfiber, silk, nylon

Name: _____

✏️ Close Reading Worksheet

Second Read: Analyze Text Structure (green boxes)

Page 153: The comparison shows me that _____

_____.

Page 154: The information in the chart is arranged by _____ structure. It is the

best structure because _____.

Page 156: As a whole, the information in the selection is arranged by _____

structure. It is the best structure because _____

_____.

Third Read: Critical Thinking (blue boxes)

Page 152: The author calls Antarctica "the last frontier" because _____

_____.

Page 153: A scientist would have to add or remove layers because _____

_____.

Page 155: Mobility and flexibility are important because _____

_____.

Compare—Page 156: How I choose my clothing is (similar to / different from) the cold-

weather clothing system because _____

_____.

In the Subzero Closet

Author's Point of View Chart

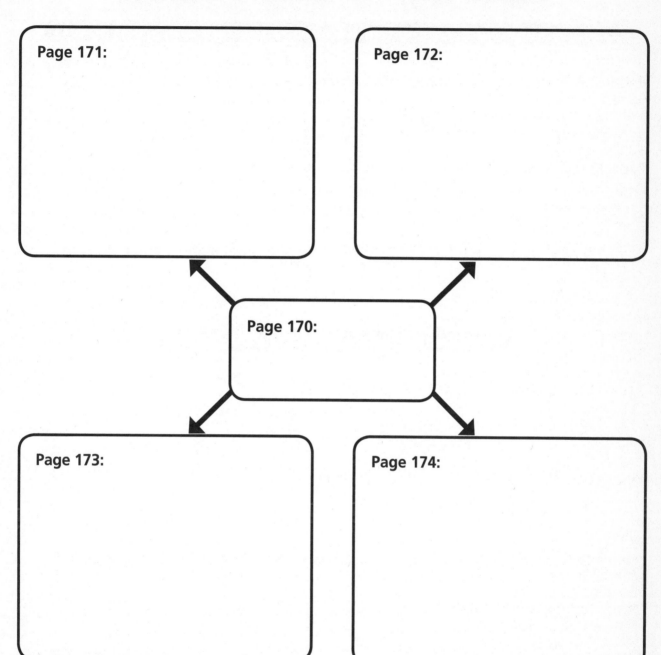

Page 171:

Page 172:

Page 170:

Page 173:

Page 174:

Page 174: The author's argument (is / is not) valid and reasonable because

Name: _____

✏️ Close Reading Worksheet

Second Read: Fact, Opinion, and Reasoned Judgment (green boxes)

Page 170: To support his argument, the author uses facts such as _____

_____.

Page 171: The opinions the author presents in paragraph 5 are _____

_____.

Page 172: The author uses facts to deal with the argument against technology by

_____.

Third Read: Critical Thinking (blue boxes)

Page 170: Other applications for RFIDs might be _____

_____.

Page 172: The historical fear of technology I found most ridiculous was _____

_____.

Page 173: People (do / do not) use abbreviations like LOL and OMG in speech and

conversation. I know because _____

_____.

Judge—Page 174: The most convincing part of this author's argument is _____

_____.

His least effective argument is _____

_____.

Name: _____

Venn Diagram

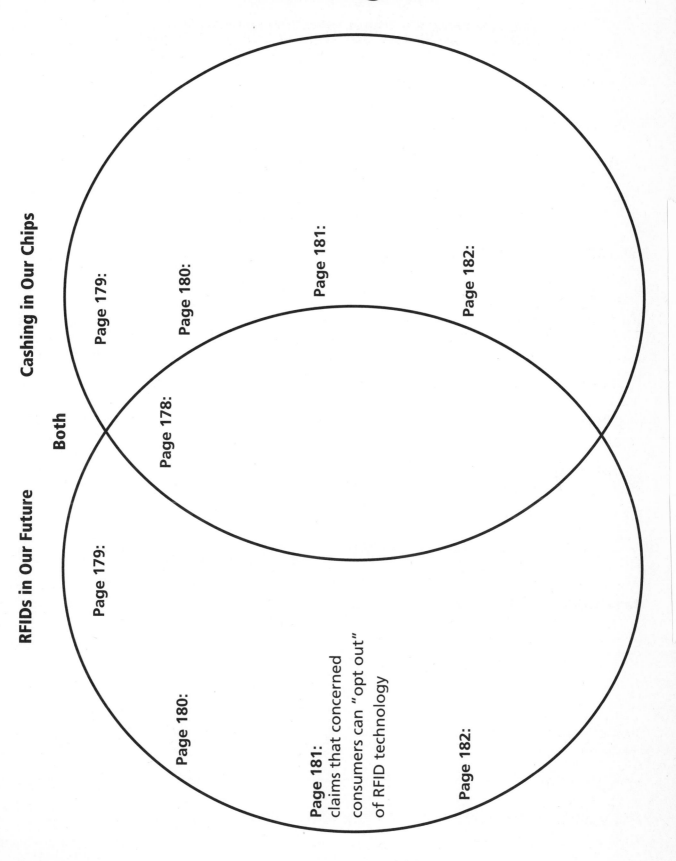

Cashing in Our Chips

Page 179:

Page 180:

Page 181:

Page 182:

Both

Page 178:

RFIDs in Our Future

Page 179:

Page 180:

Page 181:
claims that concerned consumers can "opt out" of RFID technology

Page 182:

Duplicating any part of this book is prohibited by law. © 2014 Triumph Learning, LLC

Name: _____

✏️ Close Reading Worksheet

Second Read: Analyze Arguments (green boxes)

Page 178: The author uses these persuasive techniques: _____

_____

_____

_____ .

Page 179: The emotion the author wants to stimulate is _____ .

Page 180: The author uses humor in the sentence _____

_____

_____ .

Page 181: The evidence is (from a reliable source / just the author's opinion) so it is

(convincing / not convincing) because _____

_____ . The loaded word is _____ .

Third Read: Critical Thinking (blue boxes)

Page 178: The author might mix reasoned judgment with loaded language to _____

_____

_____ .

Judge—Page 182: The author's argument (is / is not) convincing because _____

_____

_____ .

She could have made her argument more convincing by _____

_____

Cashing in Our Chips

Summary Chart

Page / Paragraph	Summary
Page 196, paragraph 1	
Page 197, paragraph 4	
Page 198, paragraph 9	
Page 199, paragraph 12	

My "Animal Instincts" summary:

Name: _____

✏️ Close Reading Worksheet

Second Read: Evaluate Evidence and Claims (green boxes)

Page 196: Evidence the author uses to support the idea that autism is not an

uncommon condition in the United States is _____

_____.

Page 197: Evidence that supports the claim that the young Grandin was unable to

make contact with others is _____

_____.

Page 198: Evidence that supports the claim that Grandin did well at Hampshire

Country School is _____

_____.

Third Read: Critical Thinking (blue boxes)

Page 196: The word *autism* is an appropriate name for the condition because

_____

_____.

Page 199: Grandin's belief affected her slaughterhouse design in that _____

_____.

Analyze—Page 200: Details that support the idea that people with autism and animals

share certain physiological traits are that _____

_____

_____.

Central Idea and Supporting Details Chart

Page / Paragraph	Central Idea	Supporting Details
Page 204, paragraph 3		
Page 205, paragraph 6		
Page 206, paragraph 7		
Page 207		

Name: _____

✏️ Close Reading Worksheet

Second Read: Analyze Development of Central Ideas (green boxes)

Page 204: The main ideas of the two paragraphs are that _____

_____ and _____.

Page 205: The first central idea, _____,

relates to the second central idea because _____

_____. The third central idea builds on these ideas because

_____.

Page 208: The central idea that the author develops in "Salad, Thanks!" is _____

_____.

This relates to the overall central idea because _____

_____.

Third Read: Critical Thinking (blue boxes)

Page 206: The Hermans mostly recorded rural dialects because _____

_____.

Page 207: It took so long to publish *DARE* because _____

_____.

Judge—Page 208: The author feels that Fred Cassidy is _____.

I (agree / disagree) with this point of view because _____

_____.

Name: _____

✏️ Close Reading Worksheet

First Read: Integrate Visual Information (orange boxes)

Page 220: The time line helps me predict that the article will be about _____

_____.

Page 222: The map relates to the text by supposedly showing _____

_____.

Page 224: From the photograph, I see that Tintagel Castle _____

_____.

Page 226: An illustration of a chivalrous King Arthur would show _____

_____.

Third Read: Critical Thinking (blue boxes)

Page 220: Geoffrey most likely included Arthur in his historical book because ____

_____.

Page 221: In the Arthurian legend, Merlin acts as _____

_____.

Page 223: Poets might have been the first to introduce this story because _____

_____.

Page 224: Historians would focus on one part of King Arthur's life _____

_____.

Interpret—Page 226: The events in Arthurian legend suggested by the text are

_____.

Steps in a Process Chart

Arthur Becomes King according to Geoffrey, p. 221

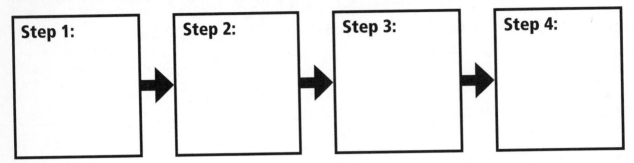

Arthur Becomes King according to Later Stories, p. 221

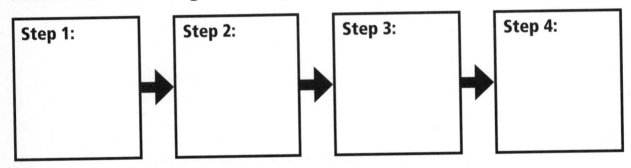

Becoming a Knight, pp. 222–223

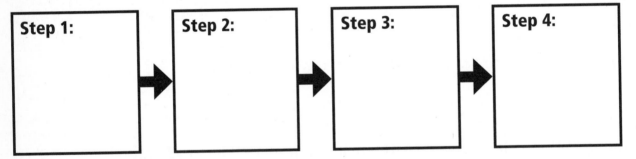

Becoming a Scheduled Ancient Monument, p. 225

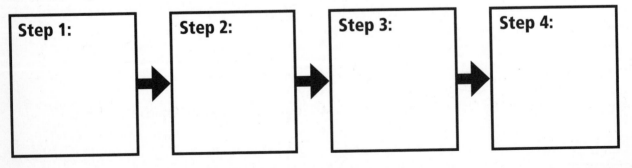

Who Was King Arthur?

Inference Chart

Facts	Inferences
p. 230: King Tut	The people's opinion of King Tut was
p. 231: 1. Tutankhamen 2. Akhenaton	
p. 232:	Mary Stuart could be described as
p. 233:	Christina of Sweden was
p. 234: 1. 2.	Puyi was a(n) ☐ effective ☐ ineffective ruler

Name: _____

✏️ Close Reading Worksheet

Page 230: The tone of paragraph 4 can best be described as _____

_____.

Page 231: The tone created by the word choices regarding the tomb raiders is

_____

_____.

Page 232: The tone conveyed in paragraph 13 is one of _____

_____.

Page 234: The words _____

convey a _____ tone when discussing the reign of Puyi.

Third Read: Critical Thinking (blue boxes)

Page 232: King Henry VIII most likely wanted to unite England and Scotland

because _____

_____.

Page 233: Christina most likely studied subjects typically studied by boys because

_____

_____.

Analyze—Page 234: Ruling families most likely entrusted power to young members

because _____

_____.

Name: _____

Cite Textual Evidence Chart

Analysis	Textual Support
p. 248 Art has been undervalued in American society.	
p. 249 Oliver makes judgments carefully.	
p. 250	
p. 251	
p. 252	

Name: _____

✏️ Close Reading Worksheet

Page 248: The journal entry is a primary-source document because _____

_____.

Page 250: Unlike an article on WPA murals, this primary source shows _____

_____.

Page 251: Lohman Parks acts as a primary source for Oliver because _____

_____

_____.

Page 252: Oliver's description of Darla is _____

_____

_____.

Third Read: Critical Thinking (blue boxes)

Page 249: Oliver most likely refers to the people in the murals as people he knows

from his own neighborhood because _____

_____.

Page 251: Between June 17 and August 11, Oliver _____

_____.

Interpret—Page 252: The hawk image explains how Oliver feels because_____

_____

_____.

Name: _____

Chronological Order Chart

Page 256, first event

↓

Page 256, second event

↓

Page 257 After Roosevelt took office, he

↓

Page 260 The FAP ended in _____ because

Duplicating any part of this book is prohibited by law. © 2014 Triumph Learning, LLC

Name: _____

✏️ Close Reading Worksheet

Page 256: Evidence that this document is a secondary source is _____

_____

_____ .

Page 257: The primary-source quotation from FDR shows this is a secondary source

because _____ .

Page 258: The author's perspective helps identify this text as a secondary source by

_____

_____ .

Page 260: The primary-source reference is to a _____ . It shows that this is

a secondary source because _____

_____ .

Third Read: Critical Thinking (blue boxes)

Page 257: FDR encouraged realism in art through _____

_____ .

Page 258: Many of the artists who submitted samples for murals were rejected

because _____

_____ .

Analyze—Page 260: The FAP was (effective / ineffective) because _____

_____ .